THE LIFE OF DEATH
The Bare Bones of Undertaking
A Memoir

Ralph R. Rossell

First published by Dog Ear Publishing
4011 Vincennes Rd
Indianapolis, IN 46268
www.dogearpublishing.net

ISBN: 978-1-4575-6049-1

This book is printed on acid-free paper.

Printed in the United States of America

To my wife, Elizabeth, whose faith in me never wavers, and to my children, Lisa Rossell Riccobono and Nicholas Rossell, both of whom I am very proud.

CONTENTS

"Show me the manner in which a nation or a community cares for its dead, I will measure exactly the sympathies of its people, their respect for the laws of the land, and their loyalty to high ideals."

—William Gladstone

INTRODUCTION

A young married couple and their son moved to the small sleepy village of Flushing, Michigan, in July of 1947. They moved to a spacious upstairs apartment in a large Victorian home that had been converted into a funeral home. The husband came to Flushing to work for his brother as an embalmer and funeral director. His brother and sister-in-law also lived above the funeral home, but in a separate apartment. That same month, a second son was born to the couple who had just moved to Flushing. That boy was me.

This is a collection of stories of my recollections of growing up in the funeral home and, upon my graduation from college, of carrying on the family business for more than forty-five years.

On Facebook, there is a group called "You know you grew up in Flushing if ... ". Anyone who had lived in Flushing was invited to relate their experiences. I started writing a few short stories about growing up in the funeral home and was surprised that I had a small following. A few people suggested, "Instead of writing on Facebook, why don't you write a book?" One person told me that if I did not write a book, he was going to take the material and publish it himself. When I announced to the group that I would give writing a book a try, I received an instant positive response. There were people wanting to place orders for the book before the first word was printed!

As this is my memoir, these are the stories as I remember them or as they have been told to me, though others may remember them differently. These stories are intended to give the reader a feel for what it was like for me to grow up, live in, and work in a small-town funeral home. In most cases, I have intentionally left out or changed names to protect the privacy of people involved. If you think you know the family I am talking about, don't be too sure. Many of these stories could be repeated about many families. Enjoy!

I.

GROWING UP in a
SMALL-TOWN FUNERAL HOME

A BRIEF HISTORY of ROSSELL FUNERAL HOME

*T*he first undertakers in Flushing were Stewart and Minard, who also owned a furniture store. Their business was located in downtown Flushing on the south side of the street. The records in my possession start in 1906 and show that in 1930, Herman Wheeler purchased the funeral business and moved it to his residence, which was the former Niles home. This is the present location of Rossell Funeral Home. Mr. Wheeler had an addition built to the back of the building and this included an apartment on the second floor. The kitchen of this apartment was featured in *Ladies Home Journal* magazine in 1936 because it had all the latest conveniences.

Herman Wheeler turned the business over to his son, Jerry Wheeler, who did not like being a funeral director and sold it to my uncle, Norman Rossell, in 1947. Norman kept the Wheeler Funeral Home name for a few years until the Rossell name was established in the community. My father, Ronald Rossell, Norman's younger brother by twenty years, came to Flushing to work for Norman. My father purchased the funeral home from his brother when his brother retired in 1962 and my brother and I bought out my father in 1978. In 1988, my wife and I purchased my brother's share and we have owned the business since.

BURIAL PRACTICES

The first funeral directors were called "undertakers" because they undertook the task of caring for the dead. Very often, they were the people who constructed the caskets or hired carpenters to do so; the funeral business was often connected with a furniture store.

When there was a death, the undertaker would go to the home of the deceased to embalm the remains and to dress and lay the person out on a cooling board. The cooling board was a wooden-framed cot with a canvas bed that folded up into a neat case that was easy to carry and store when not in use. It was called a cooling board because, before embalming was introduced, the deceased would have been dressed and then placed on a board that was on top of ice. Cooling boards were originally surrounded by flowers, not just for looks, but to mask the odors caused by decomposition of the body. After the advent of embalming, there was no longer a need for ice because the embalming process not only preserved the remains, but also killed inherent bacteria that continued to grow within the body. In fact, when the embalming process was introduced, the icemen were very upset because ice was no longer needed to delay decomposition and they were afraid it was going to run them out of that large portion of their business. It did.

The remains would lie "in state" on the cooling board in the parlor of the home, which was used for funerals, weddings, and other important occasions. After the period of visitation in the home, the undertaker would place the remains in a casket and proceed to the church for the funeral.

Many people did not have parlors or enough room to accommodate visitations, so furniture store owners and/or undertakers made places in or near their establishments to do the embalming and to provide places for visitation. Often, this was in the funeral director's own home, thus the advent of the "funeral home."

The last time Rossell Funeral Home took remains to a private home for viewing and visitation was for a prominent businessman in the community. The remains were embalmed and casketed in the funeral home and then taken to the family's home in the country. The house was a mid-sized ranch and the casket barely fit through the sliding glass doors that led into the man's bedroom. There was little room for people to pay their respects. The family had little time to themselves because people came at all hours of the day and evening. Floral arrangements arrived by the van load, and all the flowers had to be displayed wherever they would fit. Finally, on the morning of the day of the funeral, we brought the remains to the funeral home for the funeral service.

I heard a story of a family — not in Flushing — who had a private home visitation in which, when the family was alone, they undressed the remains and used a black marker to make lines that looked as if an autopsy had been performed. They took pictures of these marks and, after the funeral, sued the funeral director, claiming that the funeral director had performed an autopsy without the permission of the family. The family did not realize that the judge could order a disinterment.

Embalming

There are inherent bacteria in our bodies that continue to grow after death. Unless the process of decomposition is curtailed, the bacteria continue to grow and release a gas called putrescine. As this noxious gas is produced, bloating occurs and bodily fluids are pushed out of the orifices. You have no doubt seen and smelled this from animals that are dead alongside the road.

Embalming is a process whereby preservatives are injected into the body. These chemicals are injected into an artery and replace some, but not all, of the blood which is drained from a vein. The injected chemicals do two things: preserve the tissue and kill bacteria.

Embalming goes back to ancient times—think Egyptian mummies. The more modern process of embalming started in Europe, mainly for the purpose of preserving remains for dissection for medical studies. Embalming was introduced into this country during the Civil War because bodies put on ice could not travel long distances before starting to decompose. Embalming made it possible to transport deceased soldiers so they could be buried in their hometowns. The museum in Rossell Funeral Home displays a photograph of a soldier being embalmed near the battlefield.

Since embalming was usually done in the home of the deceased, the funeral director took his equipment and chemicals with him. The embalming process consisted of setting up a pole that supported a large glass container which held the embalming fluid. A rubber hose extended from the bottom of the container and was inserted into the incision leading to the artery. The container was arranged so that it could be raised or lowered; the higher the container, the higher the gravitational pressure. The blood was drained through a rubber hose, previously inserted into a vein, and was collected in heavy, square glass containers. The funeral director would take the blood with him and dispose of it later.

One time, after my uncle finished embalming in a deceased's home, he told his young assistant to take the containers holding the blood out, meaning to take them out to the car to be disposed of later. The assistant went outside, opened the containers, and splashed the blood in the front yard on the newly fallen snow. It was not a pleasant sight!

People often ask if embalming is necessary; some are concerned about body mutilation. If we did not embalm, however, the body would be far more mutilated from the decomposition process. Embalming allows the family of the deceased to have an extended viewing and visitation period. Also, if remains need to be transferred by common carrier, embalming is usually required.

Some religions prohibit embalming and the deceased is usually buried within twenty-four hours.

Autopsies

Many times, an autopsy is important—the obvious reason being to determine the cause of death. The morgues shown on TV are not the norm, however. The ones I have seen do not have five-foot computer screens on the wall or high-tech microscopes on benches, nor do women walk around in high heels and low-cut dresses. The remains are laid out on a stainless-steel gurney, where the clothes, if any, are usually cut off. The pathologist makes an incision around the back of the head and pulls the scalp up and over the face. Then a saw is used to remove the top of the skull to give access to the brain, which is removed. A large Y-cut is made with a scalpel on the torso, starting at each shoulder, meeting at the lower part of the sternum, and then continuing down to the pubic bone. All the organs are removed and inspected. All those not needed for further dissection, including the brain, are placed in a plastic bag. This bag is then put into the body cavity. After the autopsy is done, a few stitches are sewn to hold the skin flaps together. The funeral director then transports the remains to the funeral home.

Embalming autopsied remains can be a challenge. First, we reopen the torso in order to access all the ends of the arteries that have been cut. We inject these ends with embalming fluid and then tie them off with suture thread. We also do this procedure inside the skull. Next, we treat the internal organs with chemicals, place them in another bag, and put them back into the torso. After the embalming chemicals have been injected, we suture all the incisions, using very small sutures on the scalp so they are not visible when the body is lying in state. There was a pathologist at one Flint hospital who thought nothing of making an incision through the middle of each ear. When she did this, we had to use restorative wax and makeup to hide the incision.

Years ago, hospitals had to perform a specified number of autopsies per year to meet accreditation requirements. The hospital had to obtain permission from the families to do the autopsies; however, a medical examiner could order an autopsy without the permission of the family if foul play was suspected or if the death was the result of an accident. The hospital usually received permission from the family of the deceased by telling them that an autopsy was needed to determine the cause of death and, also, to further scientific research. The family was often told that only a minor incision would be made in order to inspect the organs. Toward the middle of the year, when the quota requirements were met, there were fewer autopsies. More often than not, the death certificate was filed with a cause of death before autopsy results were available.

In those cases where there was no real reason to do an autopsy other than for accreditation, the hospitals, often, would allow us to embalm the remains at the hospital before the autopsy. Since the remains were already preserved, this made it easier for the pathologist to perform the autopsy; it also made it easier for us to prepare the body for burial. When we received the call that an autopsy was going to be performed, we took all the equipment we needed and immediately, day or night, went to the hospital to do our work so the autopsy would not be delayed. We had several cases of our equipment ready to go at all times. Some of these items are now in the funeral home museum.

I have done embalming at the three major hospitals in Flint. Today, not as many autopsies are performed and, when they are, we do not go to the hospital to embalm beforehand.

Showing and Restoration

It wasn't until I was in high school that I found out I was red-green colorblind. I knew I had trouble with colors, but when I took a color test, I knew why. I have applied cosmetics to hundreds of deceased people, and rarely has anyone complained about my work; in fact, people compliment me. I did not really think about it that much, and I had never asked for help. There was a company that sold cosmetics to funeral directors, formulated especially for deceased people. The cosmetics came in a case, and on the back lid of the case was a numbered color chart explaining what colors should be used for different cases. I always went by that chart, wondering why nobody else did. Later, when I hired other funeral directors, they used different cosmetics than what I used and there was no chart. It was then that I realized they could see different shades that I could not see.

Funeral directors take great pride in their ability to make deceased people look as natural as possible for viewing in the casket. This is an important aspect of the funeral process, as it gives the family a better lasting picture of the deceased. Many times, families have told me they were glad they could remember their loved ones looking natural instead of how they had seen them in the hospital or morgue.

***

The following are examples of restorations I have dealt with.

A Flushing widow liked to take vacations in exotic locations and she was in a remote part of Brazil when she died. It was going to take some time to get her remains to a metro area where she could be put into a transfer casket and flown to the United States. It was important that she be embalmed as soon as possible to prevent her remains from decomposing on the journey through the jungle. I was told there was a doctor in the area who would attempt to embalm her although he had no formaldehyde. The only thing he could think to use was mercurochrome. He had an ample supply because he needed it when his patients had infections.

When the remains finally arrived and I opened the transfer casket, the woman was completely the color of mercurochrome—bright red. After the initial shock, I explained the situation to the family and assured them that I would do my best to cover the color. Except for a few balding spots on her scalp, she was presentable for viewing.

***

Most of the time, we do well creating a natural look. Sometimes we do too good of a job. In one case, for example, cancer had claimed a man's life. He had a huge tumor the size of a softball on his neck, near the side of his face. It was ugly and oozing. One of my funeral directors, who was just out of mortuary school, asked if she could remove the tumor and restore the facial structure so the man would look like he had prior to having the tumor. Sometimes, the disease is so bad that there is little we can do and I thought this was one of those times, but I told her she could give it a try. Many hours later, she completed the restoration work, then dressed the man and put him in his casket. It was amazing to see the work that she had done. You would not have known the man had ever had any disfigurement on his neck and face. When the family came in for the first visitation, they looked like they were going to faint. The young son shouted, "Where's Dad's tumor!?" They were so used to the tumor, it was natural to them. After about an hour, however, they came to me and said they were thankful they could remember him without the tumor.

***

A man died with his nose eaten away by cancer. There were just two holes where his nose had been, so I created a new nose for him. There are a lot of different kinds of noses, but I created a nose similar to the noses of the rest of the family. When they came for the viewing, they were shocked to see his nose back in place. One of the young grandchildren said, "Where did they get Gramp's nose?" The family thanked me for showing him the way they remembered him.

***

A young man had been speeding down Flushing Rd. and had lost control of his car, gone over the curb, up a bank, and careened into some trees, cutting the first two trees in half. His car flipped over, and he ended up under the radiator of his car, which emptied on his face.

He did not feel the pain of the hot water because he was already dead, but his face was burned, crushed, and cut up. This was a case in which we knew the casket would have to be closed. Even when we recommend a closed casket, however, we always do the best we can to restore the remains before we dress and casket them. In this case, I cannot remember how many stitches we used to sew up the man's face — probably hundreds. The skull had been crushed, so there was not much shape to his head. We did the best we could so he could be buried with dignity. When the family came in, the father wanted to see his son. We advised against doing so because it might have been more traumatic for him. I think he insisted we open the casket because he thought we had not done the restoration to the best of our ability. We did open it. The father leaned into the casket, looked long and hard at his son, and, with tears in his eyes, turned and said what a wonderful thing we had done. He thanked us profusely.

***

We can't satisfy everyone, though. An elderly woman of a prominent family in town died a peaceful death and looked like she was sleeping in her casket. The family came in — the woman's sister and two nieces. They approached the casket, looked briefly at the deceased, and then turned to me and said, "She does not look anything like herself." They asked if there was something that could be done. I knew I could not do anything to make the woman, whom I'd known for some time, look nicer than she already did, so I asked the women to step into the lounge and I would see what I could do. I closed the door, stepped back to my office, and poured myself a cup of coffee. About twenty minutes later, I opened the door, went to the lounge, and told the women I hoped that she looked better for them. They came back and exclaimed what a difference I had made and that they had known I could do better.

***

Another elderly woman, who was unmarried and lived in town, always sported a mustache and did nothing to remove her facial hair. By the time she died, she had almost a full beard. Because I thought this was a delicate subject, I asked the family if they wanted her facial hair removed. They said, "Yes. That would be nice." When the relatives came for the viewing, one of the grandnieces yelled out, "Where is Auntie's mustache?!" They were all aghast. When I had offered to remove the facial hair, they had thought I meant only the beard. Their aunt had been proud of her mustache, they told me, and it was a shame that it had been removed. I apologized, and spent the next hour recreating a mustache. Luckily, I knew the woman and knew what kind of mustache she'd had. The family was satisfied with my work.

**

While I was working in Detroit for the R.J. and J.R. Harris Funeral Home, we had what we called the Case of the Missing Body. The deceased woman's only survivors were nieces and nephews. She had prearranged her funeral and so had already picked out her casket, burial vault, and cemetery property. She even had brought in her burial clothing. Because the family members were all from out of town, they made the rest of the arrangements over the phone. They said they would arrive in time for the first viewing and visitation. When they arrived, they went into the room where their aunt was lying in state. After about half a minute, they came out in a state of shock. They told the director that the funeral home had the wrong body and that was not their aunt.

The director and the owner of the funeral home were very upset. They knew they had not mixed up bodies at the funeral home, so the funeral director in charge immediately called the hospital to explain the situation. The hospital had no idea what could have happened but was quite sure the correct remains had been released to the funeral home. Even the doctor who had pronounced the woman dead was contacted. The funeral home had made the removal from her deathbed.

After talking to just about everybody who had anything to do with the hospital, the family, who had been waiting in the lounge, came out and asked if they could look at the remains again. They went in, talked amongst themselves for a few minutes, then came out and said, yes, that was their aunt; they had not seen her in thirty years and that she never looked so nice.

***

A woman and her husband had left the bar and were riding their bikes across the bridge in downtown Flushing. While going down the sidewalk, the woman swerved, hit the curb, and was flung onto the street. Unfortunately, an eighteen-wheeler semitruck was crossing the bridge at the same time. All of the wheels went over her. The ambulance people had to shovel her remains off the pavement. The husband was in shock and really did not remember anything about the accident. When the family went to the hospital and wanted to see their mother, there was nothing to see but a pile of flesh and broken bones. The hospital told them that at the funeral home, they would be able to see her as they remembered her. In a case like this, we put what remains we have in a body bag and treat them with chemicals to slow the decomposition process. Then we seal the bag with a rubber sealant. When the family came in, they fully expected to see the woman as she had been before the accident. They told me over and over what the hospital person had told them. It was a sad day.

A similar situation occurred when a man, who was single, was taking aerial photographs from a helicopter in California when the helicopter crashed. At the moment of impact, the blade from the helicopter sliced the man's head in two. The man's sister was a receptionist at a local doctor's office in Flushing. The doctor, who at one time had studied to be a mortician, told the sister that she would definitely be able to view her brother because the funeral director could piece him back together. The funeral home in California we hired to make the removal and prepare the remains to be shipped back to Michigan told me the remains had been placed in a plastic bag, treated with chemicals, and sealed up. He said there was nothing recognizable and we should not open the sealed container. When the sister came in, she was shocked that she could not see her brother. She told me over and over what the doctor had told her. It was another sad day.

***

A man had died, and his family wanted the visitation and funeral to be as soon as possible; when they came in, they wanted the visitation to start that day. We had to hurry to make the removal and do the embalming, cosmetics, dressing, and casketing. Usually, I would do all of that, but because we were in a hurry, my dad came to help. After I finished embalming, my dad went to the office and got the clothing the family had brought in for me to put on the deceased. I hurried to dress the man, did the cosmetics, and my dad came in to help me put the man in the casket and the casket in the chapel. The family was due to arrive in about a half hour. My dad knew the family and wanted to greet them at the door when they arrived, so he went to put on the coat of his suit. He looked all over for it, saying he knew he'd had it on when he had come to the funeral home. What had happened was that when he had brought the deceased's clothing in to me, he had taken off his own coat, laid it down next to the deceased's clothing, and then gone back to the office. The family had not brought in a coat, only a shirt and tie; I had put my dad's coat on the deceased. We had fifteen minutes to take the man out of the casket, take off the coat, and put him back in the casket. The family never knew.

***

Many times, families bring in clothes that the deceased wore years before and expect them to still fit, even when it is evident that they will not. We ask families to sign a paper giving us permission to alter clothes, so, if we have to, we are able to cut the clothes to make them fit.

One time, a lady's husband was to be cremated. The family requested a visitation with viewing, so they purchased a casket and brought in clothing. The wife brought in a Harris Tweed coat with leather patches on the elbows that her husband had often been seen wearing. After the funeral, while people were leaving the funeral home, the widow approached me and said she wanted me to take off the tweed coat because she wanted her grandson to have it to wear. Luckily, I had not cut it up the back.

Sometimes, families bring in soiled and smelly clothes. Often, the underwear is so dirty that I end up throwing it out and putting on a set of new underwear from the supply I keep at the funeral home.

GROWING UP, PART I

I knew early on that my life was different from that of every other kid. In elementary school, it seemed as if everybody's dad worked in "the shop." I thought "the shop" was like what my father had in the basement of the funeral home—a room to fix and build things and to keep tools in—but I found out that "the shop" meant General Motors, also called Generous Motors because of the great wages and benefits. Some of my classmates referred to their fathers as engineers. I thought an engineer drove a locomotive and worked for the railroad company. It took a while, but I finally found out that General Motors was in the city of Flint, about ten miles away, and that the whole economy in the area was centered on building cars. "The shop" referred to the factory, and the engineers were the guys designing the cars.

When I was in elementary school, the teacher told us to draw a diagram of the home we lived in showing the layout of the rooms. I started to cry. The funeral home had a lot of rooms, and I did not know how to start.

My father was on duty twenty-four hours a day, seven days a week. I did not have a concept of having weekends and holidays off, not to mention evenings or nights. My father did not have the time to be a scout leader, coach a Little League baseball team, or do any of the other things that other fathers were able to do.

Our life was centered on "the call", meaning either a death call or an ambulance call. We would rush through dinners so we could finish before the phone would ring and my father would have to leave the table.

Laundry was done in an old wringer washer in the basement. On Saturdays, my mother would be at work in the corner of our large kitchen, ironing sheets on a Mogul, a large machine with a cloth cylinder that would do the actual ironing. The sheets were used in the ambulance and the embalming room.

Kids were always asking me if it was scary living in the funeral home, and they also wondered if ghosts lived there. I asked my father about this. He told me there were no ghosts and that dead people would never hurt me—I should be afraid of live ones!

EARLY ON

Again, my dad was always on duty, because in addition to the funeral parlor, we also had an ambulance service. Because someone was always in the funeral home, we took all the fire calls and police calls. When there was a fire, we pushed a button on the wall that sounded the siren. The fire chief would call to see where the fire was. When someone needed the police, we flipped a switch on the wall that turned on a red light on the telephone pole in front of city hall. When the officer drove by and saw the light, he would stop by to see who needed him.

Although she did not visit often, my uncle's elderly mother-in-law would occasionally stay with my aunt and uncle in their apartment. One night, she got up around one a.m. and had to use the restroom. She couldn't find the light switch, but the push-button felt familiar to her, as early light switches had often been buttons, so she pushed it. The next thing I remember, other than the fire whistle blowing throughout the town, is my uncle running down to the fire hall, yelling, "There must be a short in the system!"

It was uncanny how many times family dinners were disrupted by an ambulance or death call. More people died in their homes back then because there were not many nursing facilities available. Families took care of their own loved ones and did not have to depend on two incomes to survive, so there was usually a woman who cared for the elderly in the home. When someone died at home, the family would call the funeral home and expect us there right away. We would go to the home and bring the deceased to the funeral home. Sometimes the family would follow us back to the funeral home, day or night, make the arrangements, wait until the remains were embalmed, dressed, and put in the casket; once this was completed, the wake would begin. Normal visiting hours were from 8:00 a.m. to 10:00 p.m. Some families never left and stayed in the funeral home until the day of the funeral.

When my brother and I were young, we learned early on to be very quiet during funerals and visitations. A common phrase in our house was "Shh, be quiet!" Luckily, our large bedroom was on the third floor of the funeral home, so being quiet was not a huge problem for us.

My father would clean and set the chairs for the funeral early in the morning and then go outside, no matter the season or the weather, to wash the funeral cars. Much later, a heated garage was added on to the funeral home where the funeral cars could be washed. When my brother and I learned to drive, we took advantage of the power wash and the heated garage in order to earn some money. We had a clientele who would have their cars washed every Saturday. We went to a client's house, brought the client's car back to the funeral home, washed the outside, cleaned the inside—including the inside of all the windows—and then returned the car. We charged $1.00 for a regular wash and $1.25 if they wanted the white walls on the tires cleaned.

A death certificate always had to be signed by an attending physician, coroner, or medical examiner before we could obtain a burial permit. If a person died at home and we were able to contact the family doctor and he agreed to sign a death certificate, we could go ahead and bring the deceased to the funeral home. If the patient was not under a doctor's care or if the family doctor did not have enough information to determine the cause of death, however, we had to contact the coroner or medical examiner. A coroner can be anyone appointed to make a determination as to the cause of death, whereas a medical examiner is an actual doctor. Now, there are no more coroners in Michigan.

Dr. N.A.C. Andrews, a medical examiner, lived across the street from the funeral home. We would often call him so he could go with us to the place where a person had died, and he usually would make a determination of death there. If the death occurred at night, we would have to wait for the doctor to shave, bathe, and get dressed in his finest; he would not go out without a suit on, and he always carried his little black bag.

If we could not arrange to have Dr. Andrews come with us, we had to take the remains to Hurley Hospital to be examined by a medical examiner. Sometimes, an autopsy would be performed to determine the cause of death.

Day or night, if a deceased person was Catholic, we notified a Catholic priest who would administer last rites to the deceased. Sometimes, when we knew the deceased person was Catholic, we called the priest and then picked him up at the church rectory on our way to the deceased's house. Otherwise, we would have to wait at the residence until the priest arrived before taking the deceased to the funeral home.

Visitations

When funeral plans were made, it was fairly common for the visitation to last for several days. Air travel was not as available as it is today, train travel was slow, and some people simply had to drive from a long distance to get to the funeral home, meaning it sometimes took several days for everyone to arrive. Funeral homes did not charge for extra days. People always wore black and were very quiet in the funeral home.

When there was a Catholic Rosary service, all the women were required to wear black veils; we had small black plastic rain bonnets with the funeral home name printed on them that we passed out to women who forgot to bring veils. We also had a ready supply of rosary beads for people who forgot to bring their own.

When there was a Rosary service, usually conducted at the funeral home the evening before the funeral Mass, the priest never drove himself to the funeral home. Wherever he was, we picked him up and brought him to the funeral home and then took him back after the Rosary service.

On the day of a Catholic funeral, we also went to pick up the priest to come to the funeral home to say prayers before the casket was closed, and then we would hurriedly take him back to the church so he could be ready for the Mass when the procession arrived. This is still done today, but rarely. Later on, I said the prayers at the funeral home, but now the prayers are said when we arrive at the church.

Fainting!

It was almost a certainty that at least one of the mourners would faint at some time during the funeral process and it was always women who fainted. Fainting usually occurred when a woman entered the funeral home, approached the casket, was greeted by another mourner, just before, during, or just after the funeral, and often at the cemetery. The fainting would occur only when other people were present.

The funeral home had a ready supply of little glass capsules filled with ammonia and wrapped in cloth braids. When the capsule was squeezed, the glass would break and the ammonia would revive the person who had fainted. Most of these faintings were not fainting as the dictionary would describe but were shows of great mourning. We could always tell if a woman had really fainted by the way she reacted to the ammonia. If the woman had truly fainted, the ammonia would have little immediate effect, but if the woman had fainted for show, she would throw her head back and get away from the ammonia as soon as we put it under her nose.

Sometimes there would be a female mourner who would faint a lot—several times in a few hours! A funeral director in Detroit taught me a trade secret for how to discourage this kind of behavior: hold the ammonia up to the fainting person's nose, keep the capsule between your first two fingers and keep the thumb of the same hand pressed tightly under the person's chin so when the woman drew her head back, she could not escape the ammonia. It worked. If a woman started to faint over and over, we would only have to do that once and she would not faint any more, at least when we, who knew the trick, were around. It is seldom now that anybody faints at a funeral, so I still have two boxes of about fifty capsules each that have been stored away for many years.

Years ago, we could use the ammonia, hand out Band-Aids, or give aspirin to people. Now if we were to do that, the law would say we are making ourselves out to be medical personnel, which means we would be liable for any damages—in other words, for a bad reaction to whatever is administered. What we do now when someone requests something is to lay the item on a table and walk away so they can pick it up at their own risk.

Family Room

Many funeral homes had what was called a family room. Some still do. This was a room that was usually off to the side of the main part of the chapel so the family would have a ringside seat but be isolated from the rest of the mourners. When people came for a funeral, we would ask if they were family or friend, and if family, they would be escorted to the family room.

It was always amazing to me how many people who were not family said they *were* family, only because they wanted to be in the same room with the family. We often heard, "I am closer than family, so I should be able to sit with the family." We also heard, "I am a family member. I don't want to sit with the rest of the family." When we added a chapel on to the original funeral home, we did away with the family room so everyone could mourn together without being separated from each other.

Differentiating between family and "closer than family" can also be a problem in the parking lot when we line up cars for a funeral. We always try to have the immediate family's cars lined up in back of the funeral coach so they do not have to walk so far when we arrive at the cemetery, but, invariably, people want their cars up front because they are either distant relatives or are "closer than relatives."

One time, however, when I was lining up cars in the parking lot and a man drove in, I asked if he was family or friend and he told me he was family but that I should put him in the back of the line, as far away from the rest of the family as he could get. He also sat in the back of the chapel; he did not want to sit with the rest of them.

Air Conditioning

Before the comforts of air conditioning, buildings were not insulated well, if at all, and the funeral home could become very warm, especially if there was a large group of people. The funeral home had ceiling fans but would also hand out cardboard fans with sticks on them so people could fan themselves. These fans had a religious picture on one side and an ad for the funeral home on the other. The funeral home supplied these to all the local churches as well.

When the first air conditioners came out, my Uncle Norman had a large, heavy window unit installed in the lounge, which also had a fireplace that was nice in the winter. The room could be closed off by large oak sliding doors. This was one of, if not *the* first electric air conditioner in Flushing. That summer, the visitation attendance increased by an incredible amount, especially when it was hot and humid outside. People who hardly knew the deceased were coming to pay their respects; they walked in, looked at the deceased, and then headed for the air-conditioned lounge and stayed until closing.

As mentioned before, I shared a bedroom with my brother on the third floor. The room had once been part of the attic and had some insulation but was very hot in the summer. I would have gone down to sleep in the lounge at night when we were not busy with a funeral, but my uncle, as tight as he was, would only allow the air conditioner to be turned on when it was absolutely necessary, and certainly not for our family's comfort.

GROWING UP, PART II

Veterans of Foreign Wars (VFW)

The Veterans of Foreign Wars Post 5666 was a big influence in my life as well as on the Flushing community. After WWII, there were many active veterans in the organization, including my father. Their first meeting place was above a store on the north side of Main St. Later on, they built their own facility a few blocks away. I have memories of my father and his comrades every Memorial Day and Flag Day loading up flags on tall poles and slowly driving up Main St., placing flags in the holes that were already in the sidewalk. The street would be lined with flags on both sides. On Memorial Day, there was a large parade. The parade would stop at the tall flagpole in front of the community center, now Parish Hall, where a gun salute to fallen veterans was performed. Then the parade would proceed down the street and end at the Civil War monument in the old section of Flushing Cemetery. There, they would also have a gun salute. I remember how proud I was of my father and his compatriots of the VFW.

We spent a lot of time at the new VFW facility, but nonmembers were not allowed on the second floor. I know there was a slot machine up there, as well as a few poker tables.

For years, the community enjoyed the Friday-night fish fry that was a big fundraiser for the organization; families could either eat at the VFW Hall or get takeout.

As a service to the community, the VFW provided free wheelchairs, walkers, crutches, and hospital beds, as well as folding chairs that people could use for their own functions or parties. Because someone was always at the funeral home, we stored all of these things and kept a log about when they went out, who had them, and when they were returned. At first, the large, heavy hospital beds had been stored on the third floor of one of the downtown buildings on the south side of Main Street. It was a big job hauling them up and down the narrow stairs, however, so they were later kept in the garage behind the funeral home.

Since the funeral home also loaned out its folding chairs along with those belonging to the VFW, the chair-loaning business kept us busy every weekend; people would call and request a certain number of chairs and come pick them up. They were expected to return the chairs the following day so the chairs would be available for other people, but, often, we would have to call and ask where the chairs were, and when we did, we would be cursed for waking them up after an all-night party. Over the years, chairs started disappearing because people would keep one or two and we would not catch the deficiency when the chairs were returned. Recently, a friend told me she saw some of the funeral home chairs for sale at a consignment shop! She knew they were ours because "Rossell" was stamped on the back of each one.

It was my job to call people who had borrowed medical equipment to make sure it was still being used. Some people had just disappeared, others had stored the equipment away and forgotten to bring it back. One time, I called a man who had borrowed two walkers. He told me he still had them and that they worked beautifully for stands when he painted his kitchen cupboard doors. He returned them covered in splattered paint. They had been new when he had received them, and he didn't understand why I was upset.

Years later, the VFW and most funeral homes stopped loaning things because some organizations had been sued when people had been hurt using the equipment. For example, an organization was sued when a person, standing on a wooden folding chair to put up decorations, had fallen. Rossell Funeral Home continued to receive requests to borrow equipment, but we had to turn them down because of the liability. I don't remember anyone writing a letter of thanks to the VFW or to the funeral home for any of the borrowed items.

The Flint River

The one place all the neighborhood kids were forbidden to go was the Flint River, which flowed through town; not only because it was a dumping place for the sewage and chemicals from Flint, but also because the river was dangerous for swimming. My father always reminded me of the funerals for the children who had drowned there. In spite of the warnings, my friends and I spent a good amount of time there. Even though the village dump was downtown right next to the river, it was only when we were older that we realized how yucky our favorite exploring site really was. The following story is an illustration.

My friend Rod Huttenga and I raised tropical fish as a hobby. We both had our own aquariums in our homes. Mr. Tanner, a friend of my parents, had a fifty-gallon aquarium and many small aquariums. He raised tropical fish and sold them to a tropical fish store. He also gave Rod and me tropical fish, along with some good advice, including how we could get free fish food.

Deciding to take Mr. Tanner's advice, we went to the Flint River with our shovels and five-gallon buckets. We each dumped a shovelful of muck into our buckets, with a few inches of water on top. Then we put the buckets in dark places in our basements. The next morning, a ball the size of a softball, made up of tiny, squirming tubifex worms, had risen from the muck and was in the water. The worms were creepy, but the fish loved them.

It wasn't long before my mother discovered the bucket in the basement of the funeral home. Not only did the squiggly mass of worms creep her out, but the odor in the air was terrible. That ended my free fish food.

After learning how to get free fish food, I never put my bare foot into the river again.

My Childhood Church: The Baptists

I was raised in the Christian faith at the First Baptist Church of Flushing. Sunday for me started out with a pre-Sunday school rally. After the rally, all the kids split up and went to their assigned Sunday school classes. After Sunday school, we met up with our parents and went to the Sunday worship service. On Sunday evening, I went to youth group, and, after that, our family went to the evening worship service. On Wednesday evening, we went to the Wednesday prayer service.

The church had an average attendance on any given Sunday of around eighty. It was an independent church, which means it was not a member of any larger church conference; the church was run by a board of deacons, made up solely of men because women were not allowed to hold office.

Often, during the service, which I did not particularly pay much attention to, I would read the creed that was printed inside the front cover of the hymnal, which was in a little wooden pocket shelf attached to the back of every pew. I read the creed because it was the only reading material that was handy, except, of course, for the Bible. The creed was a page long, and other than pledging to adhere to the ordinances, disciplines, and doctrines of the ministry of the church, it forbade members to sell or drink alcohol as a beverage. The church had many prohibitions, including no dancing, no going to movies, and no use of tobacco. We were also taught that Sunday was the Sabbath, the day of rest, and we must keep it holy by not working.

Members brought their own Bible to church every Sunday, holding it so they would be ready to look up a particular chapter and verse that the pastor was going to preach about.

I had a good religious training, and I have maintained a faith in God, but I have separated myself from the Baptists. All while I was growing up, I just didn't understand the actions of the members. For instance, during Sunday-morning services, one of the deacons counted the people in attendance. After doing so, he would step outside, where, from our pew, I could see him having his "during the church service" cigarette. A lot of people in our church smoked, including my father.

Another case of members doing something the creed forbade them doing was drinking. There was one very active family whose son was a good friend of mine. One time, we were visiting my friend's grandfather's home. My friend and I went to the grandfather's basement to see what the adults were doing down there. They were all sitting around the grandfather's still, taking a little nip. At least, that is what they told us. I don't know why, but I knew what a still was; maybe we had studied about stills in history class when we were learning about prohibition. From the first time I saw one, I was curious as to how they worked. Apparently, this one worked very well, since everyone there was having a really good time!

I can say that my parents were, for the most part, nondrinkers; however, my mom kept a bottle of whiskey in the highest kitchen cupboard, and I saw her take a sip out of the bottle at least one time. She would serve the whiskey to Dr. Andrews when he and his wife came over to play bridge. Dr. Andrews would only drink Cutty Sark Scotch Whisky. Cutty Sark was more expensive than other whiskies, so my mother would buy a cheaper brand and keep the Cutty Sark bottle filled with that. The doctor never seemed to notice. One time, my mother got the bottle down and had me smell the whiskey. It smelled bad. She told me it was called rotgut because it was not good for you. I wondered, if it was so bad, why it was in our house and why the doctor was drinking it.

The extended Rossell families were always known as teetotalers (nondrinkers), but, clearly, some of them drank. After I graduated from college and was living alone in the apartment in the funeral home, one of the distant cousins of our family died and was in state at the funeral home. I told the family that during the visitation, if they wanted to, they could go upstairs and help themselves to some snacks I had in my apartment. There was pop in the refrigerator. While I had been in college, one of my friends had given me a half gallon of whiskey. I had not opened it and had stored it high in one of the kitchen cupboards. Several days after the funeral, I opened the cupboard and found the bottle still there—empty!

While attending the Baptist church, I was told that we should not dance because it could arouse sexual desires. When the school had a dance or prom, the church would organize a party in the basement of the church so kids would have an alternative to the school dance. I went to the dance instead. And, God forbid, should we date anyone from another faith.

Movies were forbidden because they could lead one astray. It was never explained why it was okay to watch movies on television at home and why it was fine to see the latest movie at the theater. Nobody hid the fact that they did both.

The minister of the Baptist church had been there a long time. The first time I ever heard about real strife in the church was when one of the deacons was caught having an affair with the minister's wife. (As kids, we were told they had been caught kissing.) The minister and his wife had two children, and the deacon, who also was married, had two children, one of whom was a friend of mine. There were two schools of thought about the affair in the church: half the congregation said the minister and his family had to go; the other half said the deacon and the minister's wife were sinners like everybody else and should be forgiven. The minister and his family left the church.

The Baptist church was big on revivals. In revival services, we were reminded what terrible sinners we were and that, if we did not publicly confess being a sinner and acknowledge that Jesus was the only one who could save us, we would surely burn in hell. There were many altar calls, in which people were invited to leave their pews, come up to the altar, confess that they were sinners, and ask for God to forgive them; thus, they would be saved. A lot of people were saved many times; I saw the same people go forward more than once.

Sometimes, at the revivals, people were saved just by raising their hands. The minister told everyone to bow their heads and close their eyes so no one would be looking around. He then said that if you wanted to confess that you were a sinner and wanted to be saved, all you had to do was raise your hand and he would see that and praise God for your decision. After everyone had bowed with their eyes closed, the minister would look around and say thank you to those who had raised their hands. He said, "Thank you!" quite a few times. I looked around at the same time, but I never saw as many hands as he did.

In our church, after people were saved, baptism followed. There was a tank the size of a large hot tub behind a curtain in back of the podium of the church. The person being baptized and the minister were garbed in white robes. They would step into the water, where the minister asked if the person had confessed being a sinner and accepted the Lord as their savior. He then dipped the person over backward into the water. I was about twelve years old when I was baptized.

There were maybe ten or fifteen kids in my Sunday school class. I knew most of them, but one Sunday, a new kid came in who was dressed differently than the rest of us. We sensed right away that he was not from our area. What happened during that class has stayed with me my whole life. The Sunday school teacher was describing heaven to us when the new boy raised his hand. At first the teacher ignored him, but, finally, the teacher asked if he had a question. The boy asked if there were going to be horses and wagons in heaven. The teacher looked at him, said, "Of course not!", then continued his teaching. We never saw that boy again.

During another Sunday school class, the teacher was telling us about the Sabbath and to keep it holy; this was the day of rest, and we were not to work on Sunday. I always wondered, if Sunday was the day of rest, why I had to get up and go to church all day. One kid raised his hand and asked if his dad was going to hell because he worked in the shop and had to work on Sunday. I was interested in the answer to this question, too, because my father worked on Sundays—"Death knows no holiday," after all. The Sunday school teacher told him that of course there were exceptions, because God understood that these big machines could not be shut down and cars were being built seven days a week.

I have always taught my children to be very wary of a person who says he is a good Christian. A Christian trying to be good is one thing, but having to tell someone you are a good Christian is unnecessary because your actions should demonstrate your faith.

First Job

My first job was at the Bejeck Pharmacy in downtown Flushing. I made sixty-five cents an hour. It was an old-fashioned drugstore: it included a soda fountain that served refreshments, light snacks, and ice cream, along with malted milk shakes.

Back then, many of the stores had hardwood floors. To help keep the dust down and to keep the floors from drying out, the store owners would mop oil on the floor. This was done on Saturday night after the store closed so the oil would soak into the floor until Monday, when the store reopened. My first day on the job was a Saturday. Upon closing, Mr. Bejeck showed me where the can of oil and mop were and told me to go ahead and oil the floor, then lock the door on my way out. Everybody left me to it. I thought the whole can of oil had to be used, so I went up and down the store, pouring oil out of the can. I then started at the front door and smoothed it all out with the mop until I got to the back door. I left the mop by the back door, locked up, and left. Monday morning, Mr. Bejeck was the first one in the back door. He did not look down; he stepped in, slid, and fell over backward. The oil was still standing on the floor. I was in school, so Mr. Bejeck had to call someone in to soak up the oil. A sign was put on the door, warning people to watch their step. Mr. Bejeck had to go home and change out of his oil-soaked clothes. He was not happy, but he acknowledged he had not told me to use only enough oil to moisten the floor. Thankfully, I was not fired!

Mr. Bejeck was very tight with his money and never allowed an employee to have a coke or a scoop of ice cream without paying. He had an assistant pharmacist, Ray Herholtz, who worked on alternating nights. Right at closing time when Ray was on duty, he would let the part-time workers make their own banana splits on the house. Did I mention real whipped cream?!

One of the employees of Bejeck Pharmacy was Mrs. B. She was a grandma type from the "old country" who was sweet and kind. Her job was mainly to work the register and help people find what they were looking for on the shelves. Once, a few of the regulars were sitting on the soda fountain stools when a young teenager came in the store. Apparently, the teenager was an athlete and needed a jock strap or supporter. Mrs. B waited on him. He politely told her that he needed an athletic supporter, and Mrs. B. took him over to the display. The boxes were clearly marked S, M, and L. Mrs. B, in all sincerity, asked him, "Short, medium, or long?" The boy turned red, then turned and walked out of the store. One of the men at the soda bar was spitting out his coffee because he was laughing so hard!

HOW I ENDED UP CARRYING ON the FAMILY BUSINESS

I was raised while living in the funeral home in one of the two apartments on the second floor. When I was young, Flushing was a close-knit community. There were a lot of homes and families in the downtown area, with kids in the neighborhood of the funeral home. There were backyards big enough to build forts, play baseball and foot-ball, and do all the things kids used to do outside. Nobody had locks on their doors. If you wanted to play with another kid, all you had to do was go to their house, open the door, and say, "Do you want to play?" Because the funeral home had a big backyard and an old car-riage barn (used as a garage), there was lots of room for kids to play, even though my uncle Norman had to shoo us away during a funeral.

I did not enjoy school. I daydreamed my way through all the lower grades. I spent my kindergarten year in the old Flushing School on the corner of Chamberlain and Hazelton Streets, which housed kindergarten through twelfth grade. Central Elementary School was built on Coutant St. in time for me to go to first grade there. I went back to the old high school for seventh grade, and then, because the community was growing and school attendance was also growing, they made space for some of the classes at the football fieldhouse, where I completed eighth grade. The old school was turned into the junior high school, and the new Flushing High School was built on Carpenter Rd. in time for me to go to ninth grade and complete high school there.

In my high school years, even though I went to dances and sporting events, I was involved in few extracurricular activities because I always had a job. I did, however, enjoy dating and cruising in my 1948 Pontiac Silver Streak, known as "Poncho". I worked at the local pharmacy, peddled the *Flint Journal*, helped my father at the funeral home, washed cars on the weekend, and worked in the produce departments of Big Value Foods and K-Mart Foods in Flint.

In high school, a student could take the general education classes or could sign up for the college-prep courses. My student advisor was a man named Web Whitmir. He contacted my parents and told them I would never make it in college and urged them not to have me sign up for college-prep classes. Thankfully, my parents told him I was to take college-prep courses. It wasn't until Facebook that I learned Mr. Whitmir discouraged almost all of my classmates from college prep, and there are many who still have bad feelings about him.

Upon graduating from Flushing High School, all of us thought we had it made because there were so many possibilities. Some got married and started families. The men had basically three choices: college, factory, or military. College was an incentive because, as long as you were going full-time, you could get a deferment from the military draft. It was 1965, and the Vietnam War was still raging. General Motors was a real incentive because the pay was good — you could go out and buy a home and a car — and there were full health benefits as well as a life insurance policy and a pension. If you were a production worker and a union member, you could retire after thirty years. If you were drafted, your military time counted toward the thirty years.

Even though I was on a college-prep course, my grades were average. After graduation, my parents offered to pay for me to go away to college, but I chose to enroll in the local Flint Community Junior College (now Mott Community Junior College). By doing so, I could live at home and keep my part-time jobs. There were a lot of men enrolled in the junior college, merely trying to avoid the draft. On my first day of algebra, the instructor, Ms. Tripp, said, "I know a lot of you do not care whether you learn algebra or not, but as long as you are in my class, you *are* going to learn algebra!" And we did. Another notable instructor was Robin Widgery. He was on loan from General Motors Institute to teach a public-speaking course. After taking his course, I never had a problem standing in front of a large audience to give a presentation.

After receiving my associate degree, I transferred to the University of Michigan–Flint, housed in one building, then located on the same campus as the junior college. I took medical-preparation courses and finished with a major in biology and a minor in Spanish. (It was in Spanish class where I met my best friend and wife of more than forty-five years.) I worked in produce at the grocery store; later on, I worked second shift at the Fisher Body plant of General Motors, where car bodies were made. In the summer, I worked in the Genesee County parks for the Genesee County Road Commission and took one evening course at the university. I also was a substitute teacher for Flint Community Schools. One of the best experiences I have ever had was teaching, for an extended period, a fifth-grade class at Jefferson Elementary School in the north end of Flint. I related well with the students, and I still remember some of their names. It would have been easy for me to change direction and become a school teacher.

My curriculum in college was geared toward pre-med because I had thought of going to dental school. My brother, who was two years older, had always wanted to be a funeral director and had gone to mortuary school after going to Flint Community Junior College for two years. After receiving my bachelor of arts degree from UM–Flint in 1970, I applied to only one dental school and I was not accepted. I continued working at Fisher Body, and, shortly thereafter, I was called up for the draft.

The government instituted a lottery system for the draft into the military. The reasoning behind this was so those who were not drafted could get on with their lives and not have to worry daily about being drafted and heading off to war. Because I had graduated from college, I had lost my draft deferment. My brother was married and working with my father at the funeral home, living in the apartment vacated by my aunt and uncle, and had no deferment. We were both called to military duty. When we were drafted, we had to go to Fort Wayne in Detroit for a draft physical to see if we were medically fit to be in the military.

Many of my classmates were on the same bus that went to Fort Wayne. The draft physical exam was very close to the one depicted in the movie *Alice's Restaurant*. I remember, right at the start, an enlisted man told us the procedure and that, toward the end, we would be having a urine test; even though I had to go right then, I held it in all during the exam process, only to find out that the man, who spoke in a southern drawl, had said a *hearing* test. After the long day of having our bodies poked, prodded, and looked at, we were done and either passed or received a medical deferment. I passed, at least for the moment. Just before we left to depart on the bus to go back home, an enlisted man came into the room and said the examiners had forgotten to ask if anybody had allergies. I stood up and said, "I do."

While working for the county road commission, I had been stung by a bee; later that summer, while clearing woods at my parents' cabin, I had been stung a second time and had gone into anaphylactic shock. I had been alone at the time. Luckily, I knew what was happening and ran to the cabin and used a razor blade to cut deep around the sting to avoid as much poison getting into my system as possible. I was in bad shape, probably in shock, because, although there was a phone, it never occurred to me to call anyone. I had never known what "cold sweat" meant until then. Even though I was sweating profusely, my skin felt like it had been in a refrigerator. Hives covered my body for several days. The only thing that gave me comfort was sitting in my car with the windows up (it was ninety degrees outside) during the day and lying in a cold bathtub with Epsom salts at night. After three days, I started feeling better. When I returned home, I visited Dr. Andrews.

He told me I had probably been in anaphylactic shock and that I was lucky to be alive. He said I should, of course, avoid bees, wear a medical alert bracelet, and carry an EpiPen with me (a syringe with epinephrine). The epinephrine keeps the air passages from swelling and suffocating you.

I told the enlisted man that I was allergic to bees and bullets—not the best thing to say! He shouted in my ear and told me not to be a smartass; then he asked if I could have a doctor write a letter about the allergy. After I said I could get a letter, I was given a medical deferment.

My brother passed, but instead of being drafted into the Army, he chose to enlist for three years in the Air Force.

Unlike my brother, I had never considered being a funeral director, but, because my father needed an assistant while my brother was away, my mother suggested that I apply to mortuary school, get my mortuary science license, and help my father until my brother came back from the military. I went to Wayne State College of Mortuary Science, the only mortuary school in Michigan, and talked to the administration. I had already had the proper undergraduate credits, and, because I had grown up and worked in the funeral home, the one year of formal apprenticeship training was waived; they admitted me. Nine months later, I graduated from mortuary science school, passed the state board exams, and began working for my father as a licensed funeral director. My parents had bought a new home of their own and told me I was welcome to continue living in the apartment above the funeral home. It was also during this time, I married the love of my life, Elizabeth Taylor (not the actress).

After my brother had been in the military for a few months, he told my father that he would not be returning to the funeral home to work. He said something about going into the Christian ministry when he finished his time in the military. I saw opportunity knocking at the door and stayed on, with the idea of eventually taking over the business. When my brother came back from the military three years later, however, he told my father that he wanted to once again work at the funeral home. When my father told me that my brother was coming back to work, I decided to stay on. My father retired in 1974 and sold the business to my brother and me in 1978. When we went to the local attorney, Howard Bueche, to finalize the sale, we were told that working in a family business is the hardest thing in the world to do. He was right!

THE JOBS I HAD WHILE in COLLEGE

I previously mentioned jobs I had while in college. These are stories about those jobs.

Big Value

My work in the produce department at Big Value Foods started in high school and continued on into college. This store had a metal cabinet where we kept work clothes. It was not uncommon to put on our shoes and find that our boss, Ed Gillan, had put a rotten potato in the toe of the shoe — or sometimes a bunch of grapes with a note that said, "Don't wine."

In order to unload watermelons, the truck driver that delivered them would back up to the rear door of the store, and then he would stand in the back of the truck and throw watermelons at the produce employees to catch and stack inside. The driver found it amusing to throw thoroughly rotten watermelons at us and watch them disintegrate as we caught them. I couldn't eat watermelon for years!

On an exceptionally busy night at the store, Ed "The Prankster" Gillan decided to make the store manager a ham sandwich. He took the sandwich to the front of the store, where the manager was scurrying around making sure everything was going right. I saw the manager thanking Ed profusely for thinking of him. The next thing I saw was the manager on the floor in front of the cash registers, pulling the rubber bands out of his throat that Ed had put in his sandwich. Ed came back and said, "I don't think that was the best thing to do." If Ed had not been a top-selling produce manager, he would have been fired on the spot.

I do not remember why, but, on one occasion, the night cleaning people could not come in. The store manager asked if I could stay and mop all the floors. I agreed and he locked me in the store. It was eerie being in the store alone all night, but I got the job done. Then I had a nap on the register counter until the first workers arrived.

Teaching

I was a substitute teacher for Flint Community Schools. I taught at various schools, but, in one school, a teacher had a serious operation and was out of the classroom for a few months. I was her substitute for a fifth-grade class at Jefferson Elementary School. That was when I learned about teachers' love for their students. It is a real joy to know you are contributing to a child's education. I still remember many of the students I taught there.

The majority of the students at Jefferson Elementary School were African American. One student I had was Harold, who had an attitude; he was not going to listen to a white teacher. When I told him to do something, he sat in his chair and mutely glared at me. I told him if he did not shape up, he would have to stay after school. He did not shape up.

One school rule was that after the bell rang at the end of the school day, the students got out of their seats, put their chairs on their desks, picked up any papers that were on the floor near their desks, and dropped the papers in the wastebasket on the way out the door. This made it easier for the janitor to sweep the floors. Because Harold and I were staying after school, I told the other students that they would not have to pick up the papers. After the students left, I told Harold that as soon as the papers were picked up and put in the basket, he could go home.

Harold just sat there, glaring at me, so I told him that as long as we were staying, we could do our spelling lessons. I started to spell words, starting with "Spelling, s-p-e-l-l-i-n-g. Spelling, s-p-e-l-l-i-n-g"—and then I changed the word. This continued for about twenty minutes, until Harold stood up, walked to the back of the room, and started kicking and shuffling papers to the front of the room. When he was done, I kept spelling and pointed to the basket. After a few minutes, he picked the papers up and put them in the basket. Then I told him he could go home.

This went on for about a week until Harold finally just got out of his seat and picked up the papers. When he was about to walk out the door that day, I told him he did not have to stay after school anymore.

Guess who won the class spelling bee? You're right! Harold, much to the amazement of the "A" students. Harold stood there, beaming from ear to ear.

Flushing County Park

My good friend Stace and I worked together during summer breaks from college at Flushing County Park. There were also several other students and some full-time workers. The whole crew worked hard but also had a lot of fun. Occasionally, we got into trouble.

The River

Flushing Park had old concrete fire grills for people to use. They were large cubes, maybe 4' x 4' x 4', and were solid concrete except for the middle, which held a grate to cook on. These fireplace grills were old and crumbling, and the park was getting ready to put in cast-iron grills that sat on posts and could swivel so the draft could be adjusted.

The park had a large pit out in the middle of the woods that garbage could be dumped into. When the hole was half filled, a bulldozer would come in and push dirt to cover the garbage and leave a hole for the next pile of garbage.

One morning, our boss, Jim, came out to the barn and told us he was going to be gone for the day and, while he was gone, he wanted us to take out all the old concrete burners. He told us to take the tractor, wrap chains around the burners, haul them down to the garbage dump, and drop them into the pit. There were maybe twenty of them. Jim said the bulldozer would be coming in later in the day to bury them. Then he left for the day.

When we started to haul the first cube of concrete toward the garbage dump, we thought it would be a whole lot more fun to drag them out behind pavilion #1 and push them over the cliff into the Flint River. And it was! We did take the precaution to yell like crazy, "Look out below!" Those chunks of concrete smashed their way through the trees and shrubs, and, when they hit the trail below, they shot out into the middle of the river. It was spectacular! They all settled to the bottom of the river, so no one would be the wiser. The bulldozer came and covered up the garbage and we headed back to the barn.

Later in the summer we were working in the park when we saw Jim coming out from behind pavilion #1, looking peculiar. His eyes were bulging out and he was red in the face. What we had not thought about previously was that, as summer progressed, the water level in the river dropped drastically; all those grills were sticking up out of the water. Jim came up to us and said, "What on earth were you thinking?"

I looked at Stace, Stace looked at me, and in unison we said, "FISH HABITAT!"

Jim had an expression that he used quite frequently, and he used it then: "You dumbass college kids!" Then he walked away. Even after all these years, if you walk behind pavilion #1, you can still see those chunks of concrete in the river. And fish are living there, too.

The Posts

Over the years, we found a lot of stuff people either lost or left behind in the park: baseball gloves, bats, softballs, tennis rackets, golf balls, and all kinds of other things. They were kept in a big lost-and-found box in the barn. Most of the stuff had been there for three or four years.

One morning, Jim came out to the barn and told Stace and me that he was going to be gone for the day. He showed us twelve one-gallon pails of brown paint that were lined up in the barn. He told us to take them down to the ball diamond and paint all the wooden posts that surrounded the area, and he said that if we got done early, we could kick back and enjoy the rest of the afternoon until quitting time.

We thought that was great! We figured we could whip that job out before noon and have the afternoon to play cards. We went down to the diamond, started to paint, and realized right away that there was no way we could finish that job before quitting time. That was when we noticed a whole bunch of kids playing down at the other end of the field. We went over there and told them we were going to have a contest to see who could paint the most posts and that we had prizes! You could not believe how the paint flew! Those posts were all painted before noon, and every kid got a prize from the lost-and-found bin. We went back up to the barn and played cards for the rest of the day.

Near the end of that day, we saw Jim drive into the park and go into his house at the entrance of the park. A little while later, he came out of the house looking a bit peculiar. Again, his eyes were bulging out, and his face was red. He told us that since he had gotten into the house, his phone had been ringing off the hook. Parents were calling to ask how their kids had gotten brown paint all over their clothing. I looked at Stace, Stace looked at Jim, and then Stace looked back at me and said, "We should have put up 'wet paint' signs!"

Once again, Jim used his frequent expression, "You dumbass college kids!", as he walked back to the house.

Silver Paint

The new fire grills we had installed had been in place for about a year and were starting to rust, so Jim came out to the barn and told Stace and me to take the silver Rust-Oleum paint that was in the barn and go around and paint all of the grills. He said he was going to be gone for most of the day. Stace and I decided that I would go down the south side of the park and he would go down the north side of the park and we would meet up at the end.

Well, when I got to the end, there was no Stace. I knew I wasn't painting any faster than he was; we were not having a contest and had not made any bets to see who would get to the end first. I decided I would keep painting until I caught up to him. When I got to the north playground, I saw what was taking him extra time. Stace had been looking at the large boulders that separated the parking lot from the playground and had decided they would be much more noticeable if they were painted silver, so he was painting them.

Just about the time I arrived, Jim came around the corner in his yellow county truck. He looked a little peculiar. His eyes were bulging out, and his face was red. He came up and said, "What on earth were you thinking?"

Stace looked at me. I shrugged my shoulders. Stace then looked at Jim and said, "Safety, Jim! Safety!"

Jim said, "You dumbass college kids!", and drove away.

The Factory

I worked second shift at Fisher Body, where car bodies were made for General Motors. I went to work at 3:00 p.m. and usually went home around 11:00 p.m. or midnight unless we worked overtime. The pay, benefit, and working environment were good, but it was very noisy. My ears rang for an hour after work. I am sure the tinnitus and hearing loss I have now are a direct result of the noise at Fisher. I worked on the line in torch solder, putting hot lead on the seams of welded joints and smoothing it out the best I could. Later, the solder would be sanded before being painted. I also hung doors. I think I hung about 120 doors a night.

On the way home after work I often stopped at Gregory's Coney Island for something to eat, then went home and slept for a few hours before going to school. Sometimes I was so tired, I would fall asleep in class. One time, my physiology professor, Dr. Golden, reportedly walked near me and was about to wake me up, to scold me, when the student next to me told him I had been working all night. Professor Golden walked on, saying, "He's a good student. We will let him sleep." I got an A in the class.

MORTUARY SCHOOL

There is only one school in Michigan to study mortuary science: Wayne State University School of Mortuary Science, in Detroit. A new building has been built since I attended, but when I went there, the mortuary science school was not on the main campus but was located in a very old building that looked like a converted warehouse with little thought to décor. In fact, there was no décor; it was just drab everywhere. It was cold in the winter and there was no air conditioning in the summer.

One incident I recall well happened during the Detroit garbage strike. One day, during a science lecture, it was ninety-eight degrees outside and the humidity was unbearable. The old factory-type windows that allowed the students to look out to see the alley were open, and what little breeze there was wafted in the odor of a huge pile of garbage.

While the science lecture was going on, we students watched a dog that was tied up to an old iron railing trying to grab a dead rat that someone had killed next to the garbage pile. The rat, bloated and already in advanced stages of decomposition, was barely out of his reach. The dog stretched on his leash to the point that we thought he would strangle himself, but he finally clawed the rat to himself. We watched as he gnawed his way through about two-thirds of the rat. Suddenly, a look of anguish appeared on the dog's face. He looked to the sky, jettisoned yellowish-greenish goo out of his mouth, laid on his side, and moaned. Several of the students left their seats and rushed to the restroom. Our oblivious professor, Dr. Pool, looked up, saying, "Some people just cannot take my lecture on what diseases can do to a body.", and then continued his lecture. The rest of us took shallow breaths, trying to keep our lunch down.

The garbage strike got so bad that some people took to gift wrapping their garbage, then driving downtown, parking next to the curb, and leaving their cars unlocked with the packages in the back seat. They would return to their cars in a half hour or so to see if someone had stolen the package. They would repeat this every few days, but parking in different locations each time. Of course, if they had left their car overnight, the car would have either be stripped of any removable parts or stolen altogether.

The students never wanted to be near the school at night because it was a dangerous place to be. The parking lot for the college was a meeting place for drug dealers and prostitutes. One time, a man drove down the street early in the morning and pushed a prostitute out of his car and onto the street. She lay there for a while before crawling to her knees, standing up, and staggering down the street.

There was a diner around the corner from the college called Seldon's, and down the street and in back of the college was Seldon's Bar. One night, someone threw a bomb outside of Seldon's Bar, blowing out the windows.

Before classes, some of my classmates and I would go to Seldon's Diner for coffee and donuts. The donuts and coffee were good, but I started to drink coffee opposite the handle because I did not want my lips touching where some of the patrons sipped their coffee. I could see the cups being washed in the back of the diner; they would merely be sloshed around in tepid soapy water and then put back on the rack.

Drunks would come into the diner at the same time every day, and a lot of them would order oatmeal and then dump a whole container of sugar on it. We also saw the same drunks down at the blood donor building selling their blood.

Down the street from the school was a factory that made English muffins. When it was hot outside, the windows would be open and I could see in. It looked so dirty in there that I would never buy that brand of muffin.

The dean of the college was a small, Walter Mitty-type of character named Dr. Pool. Behind his back, we referred to him as "Cess Pool".

Dr. Pool taught some classes, as did his assistant, Dr. Rose, whom, behind his back, we called "Lurch"; he looked like the character, Lurch, from the TV series, *The Addams Family*. The secretary seemed to be the person running the school. The rest of the faculty consisted mostly of funeral directors, making extra money by teaching (some of them were very good), and teachers who would come over from the main campus of Wayne State University.

One of the instructors was Beaver Edwards, an artist who also taught restorative art on human remains. He sculptured most of the statues that are located in the large White Chapel Cemetery in the Detroit area. He told us he would make the statues in clay and have them shipped to France, where the molds were made that would be used to make the final bronze statues. He said that in his next life, he would choose to work in scrimshaw because he could keep everything he was working on in his pocket.

Most of the bodies that we practiced embalming on came from the Detroit City Morgue. Bodies that had been unclaimed in the morgue for at least two weeks would be sent to the school. We would embalm, dress, do the cosmetics for, and casket the remains; they would later be buried in a city cemetery known as a potter's field, a cemetery for indigents. Most of these remains were in bad condition when they arrived, not only because they had been dead for some time, but also because some had died violent deaths. Communicable diseases were always on our minds as we worked with the bodies.

Some of the bodies brought to the school came from funeral homes when they needed extra help. I do not think they paid for the embalming. The students always wanted to work on those remains because most of those had not been dead very long.

There was no school housing, so students who did not live in Detroit, often lived in and worked at local funeral homes for room and board. I worked for a funeral home for $30 a week, and I was provided a room that I shared with another student. We had a bunk bed, two small desks, and a bathroom with a shower. Because there was no eating facility in the funeral home, I had to eat all my meals out. Sometimes, I simply ate out of a can. Luckily, the year I was in mortuary school, there were gas wars going on and the price of gas got down to twenty-three cents per gallon. I lived about ten miles from school, drove an Opel Kadett, and paid three dollars per week for gas.

My roommate and I alternated nights on duty, which consisted of working during visitation hours in the evening and letting the removal company that delivered remains in the door at all hours of the night. I worked all holidays. Sometimes, on major holidays, I had a hard time finding a place to eat because most of the restaurants were closed. Once in a while, one of the full-time staff women would bring me a plate of food, and I really appreciated that. Fortunately, down the street from the funeral home was a small diner called the One Up. I got to know the owner and his family quite well, and they often gave me bigger portions; sometimes that would be my only meal for the day.

Upon completing mortuary school, students had to go to Lansing to take a two-day exam. The first day of the exam consisted of written exams, one each hour for eight hours. The next day, oral exams were given. During the oral exams, we were seated in an auditorium-type room, and, one by one, we would be called up to sit in front of one of the members of the state board of examiners, who would ask all kinds of questions, mostly about laws having to do with the funeral business. There were three examiners; one in particular was grueling, and we knew it. We prayed to God we would not get him—not so much because we did not know the answers, but because he would go on relentlessly, bringing up questions. Happily, I did not get that examiner. I sat across from a man who had done his funeral director apprentice training with my father years earlier. He asked me two questions: how my father was and if I knew my stuff. I told him my father was doing well and that I knew my stuff. He told me he believed that I did know my stuff and said I was done with the interview. It cannot hurt to know someone.

Once we had completed apprenticeship training, schooling, and exams, we received a license to practice mortuary science in the state of Michigan. Years ago, there were two licenses—one for embalming and another for funeral directing—but, now, a mortuary science licensee is a funeral director as well as an embalmer.

II.

LIFE and WORK in the FUNERAL HOME

DEATH CALLS and FUNERALS

First Family Served

*L*ike a lot of professions or trades, as a funeral director, you can do all the book learning in the world and serve a lot of time in an apprenticeship, but you don't really learn the business or trade until you are working on the job with no supervision, because there is no one to go to if there is a problem. You have to learn how to deal with every situation on your own. I learned very quickly. I had no sooner started working as a licensed funeral director when my father took a quick trip to Florida, leaving me alone to run the funeral home. While he was in Florida, he and his brother were involved in a car wreck and he ended up spending the entire month in Florida recuperating from his injuries.

I was confident I could do the job, but not so confident that I wasn't afraid of messing up. The first family I met with was the Vallier family. My problem was that Mrs. Vallier was Catholic, and even though I had assisted with Catholic funerals, I was not sure I knew all the liturgy or procedures of a Catholic funeral. I was petrified that I would make a mistake.

I met with Harry and Anna Edgecomb, whom I did not know. Anna was Mrs. Vallier's daughter. I escorted the Edgecombs to our arrangement office and we sat down at my desk, with them on two chairs facing me. The first person to speak was Harry. He said, "First of all, Mr. Rossell, we want to tell you that we are so glad that we have come to someone who truly knows what they are doing."

The only thing I could think to say was, "And who would that be, Mr. Edgecomb?"

Harry and his wife laughed and laughed, and then he spoke again. "Ralph, whatever you do, it will be fine with us." As the years went by, the three of us became great friends.

After making the arrangements, I called Father Charles Jacobs and told him my concerns about the procedures in the Catholic Church. Fr. Jacobs replied, "Ralph, most of my congregation does not have a clue what the procedures are, either. If there is a mistake, we will go along like that is how it should be, and no one will be the wiser."

What a great start for my career in the funeral business! That was a busy month for me, but with the kind words of Harry, Anna, and Fr. Jacobs, I had the confidence I needed to do my job.

The Pickers

Even in the late forties and early fifties, Flushing was still a rural agricultural town. During the harvest season, we had an influx of Mexican migrant workers who would come to pick fruits and vegetables. Once, an elder in this migrant group died and the family came to us for services. They said they had no money but the expenses would be paid before the funeral.

The man who died was beloved, and many people came to pay their respects, all dressed in black and the women wearing black veils. When mourners came into the funeral home, they went to the widow to express their condolences and then kneeled before the casket. They then made the sign of the cross, got up, and went to hug the son, who was standing by the door of the chapel. While hugging, they pressed money into his hand. Several times during the next few days, the son went to the office and put money on the desk. Before the funeral, all the expenses were paid.

Mrs. M

Mrs. M was a cook at a church camp that a group of kids from our church attended. She was easy for a kid to remember because she had a tattoo on her arm. Until I had seen her tattoo, the only other tattoo I had seen was Popeye's.

I was married and still living in the funeral home when Mrs. M's husband died. They had no family, had been out of circulation for a long time, and had few friends. The visitation was Christmas Day. I was in the foyer, ready to answer the door, when she came in. She went to the chapel where her husband was in the casket. A few minutes later, she came out and said she wanted me to spend Christmas with my family. She said, "Go upstairs with your family. If I need you, I will knock on your door. Please leave me alone now so I can spend Christmas with my husband."

Andrew

Once, a man in his late sixties came in to make funeral arrangements for his elderly father, who had just died. The man's mother could not come in because she was in a nursing facility. When he sat down across from my desk, he was trembling and appeared very nervous. I asked him if he was going to be all right. He told me he was embarrassed to tell me his problem, but then he proceeded.

He told me that his parents had never wanted him to suffer the pain of loss, so he had been shielded from anything that had to do with death. They had not taken him to any visitations, funerals, or memorial services, and he had not been allowed to go to his grandparents' funerals. He had never been to a visitation or a funeral. He said he had been afraid to meet with me because he had no idea what had to be done or what to expect.

Because he confided his concerns, I was glad to spend extra time explaining the entire funeral process to him. After the funeral was all over, the man came to me and told me it was a shame that he had missed so many visitations for family and friends. He said he had never known how many friends his parents had and how much he appreciated seeing them at the visitation and funeral. He told me that he would never miss the opportunity to do the same for others.

A Trip to Ireland

Jerrod grew up on his family's farm. By the time he married and had one son, his parents were too old to run the farm by themselves, so Jerrod stuck around to help. Because all of their weekends were spent working the farm and caring for his parents, Jerrod's family never took a vacation.

When Jerrod's mother died, she was 100 years old and her husband was 101. They had celebrated their seventy-first wedding anniversary together. Neither one had ever been in the hospital until the wife's recent illness. I was surprised when Jerrod's father came in alone to make the funeral arrangements and was more surprised when he told me he no longer believed in any god. When I asked him why, he told me that no compassionate god would take his wife away from him.

Normally, I would not have said anything, but this time, I did. I told him that he should pray and thank God for all the years He had given him and his wife together in good health, and that few people have had the opportunity to do so. The man was so overwhelmed by her death that he did not pay much attention to me.

During the visitation and service, I got to know Jerrod, who was already in his seventies, as well as his wife and son, quite well. I told him how I admired him and his family for taking care of his parents and giving his life to their care.

A year or two later, Jerrod stopped to see me. He told me he had only one cousin and that his cousin had called and asked if Jerrod and his wife would like to take a trip with him to Ireland to see where their ancestors had come from. Jerrod was so excited about this proposed trip because it had been his life's dream! By this time, his father had become feebler but was in good health and Jerrod did not know whether he should go on the trip. He said that he had talked to a local nursing home and had been told that his father could stay there until Jarrod's return from Ireland. Jerrod was concerned not only that his father had never been away from home before but also that his father might die while he was away. I told Jerrod if his father died while he was overseas, we could bring his father's remains to the funeral home, embalm them, and keep them until his return. I told him we would not announce the death until his return and no one would know the difference. He reluctantly agreed, arranged for the nursing home, and made plans to go to Ireland.

The night before Jarrod and his family and cousin were to head for the airport, Jerrod's father died. Jerrod was crushed — not only that his father had died but also that his trip, after all the planning, would have to be aborted. I told him, "You have taken care of your father all these years, and you now need to do something for yourself. God took your father now so you would not worry about him while on your vacation. We will stick to the plan. Your father will be embalmed and will keep just fine until your return from Ireland." I told him there would be no extra charges. He finally agreed and went on the trip.

When Jerrod and his family returned, he told me what an absolutely wonderful time they'd had. He told me he was grateful that we had made it possible for him to go. Sadly, Jerrod had a heart attack and died not six months later, but his wife and son both told me that they were grateful he had been able to fulfill his life dream of visiting Ireland.

Rusty

Rusty's dad always sat in his wheelchair in his front yard on Main Street, waving to friends and strangers as they drove by. He had many friends, and there were few days in the summer when he was not seen there. After Rusty's dad died while on vacation in Florida, Rusty walked in the back door of the funeral home and asked how we were going to get his dad back to Flushing.

We told him we would contract with a funeral home in Florida to embalm the remains, put them in a shipping casket, and arrange to have his father flown to Flint on a commercial flight. Rusty did not want that, however, and asked why he could not drive down to bring his father back. I told Rusty that he could, as long as his father was embalmed and he had the proper burial transit permits. We arranged to have his dad embalmed, to have permits waiting for him, and we loaned him a stretcher to put in his station wagon. Rusty drove straight through to Florida and back, stopping only to use the restroom and to buy coffee and gas. He told me that it was the least he could do for his father.

Oren

Oren was very sad when his wife died. He had no children and was very alone. It took a while, but he slowly got into a routine after her death. He and his wife had not had much money, but they had lived a simple but full life.

Just after I started working with my father in the funeral home, I decided to go over the records to get a feel for the business. As I looked at the cases, I discovered a mistake my father had made on the billing for Oren's wife's funeral: He had overcharged by $500. Neither our bookkeeper nor Oren had caught the mistake.

My father was horrified. He hurriedly wrote a check and made a trip out of town to Oren's small house to deliver the check. When my father explained the situation, and gave Oren the check, Oren started crying. He explained that he had been to the dentist and found that new teeth would cost him $500 and he had just been praying to God for help.

Back in Time

We received a call from Don, who lived in one of the upper-scale subdivisions outside of town. He had stopped at his ninety-year-old father's home earlier that morning to check on him and had discovered that his father had died. He had already notified the authorities, who had told him that the funeral director could make the removal. Don asked if I could come right away and said he would be waiting for me.

The address was in a remote area in the next county, in farming country, on a seldom-traveled dirt road. When I arrived, Don was waiting for me at the entrance to the two-track dirt drive leading up to the house. He wanted a private word with me before I proceeded. He wanted to assure me that he did not live the lifestyle his father lived. He told me that his father had chosen to live as he had in the old country. His father had worked his small farm mostly by hand.

It had not occurred to me I would have an opinion on how Don's father had chosen to live, but it was important to Don that I understood that it was not his own standard of living.

As I proceeded up the driveway, I saw an old, dilapidated gray outbuilding standing next to a shack covered with tar paper. A goat tied to a long rope was standing near the only opening into the shack. Don told me that his dad used the goat for milking.

As I stepped into the shack, I saw that the walls were made of cardboard. The insulation of wadded-up newspapers peeked through the seams. The floor was made from bare wooden planks. Standing in the middle of the room was an old-fashioned Franklin wood-burning stove. A plain square wood table and a single chair stood next to the stove. On the other side of the table, next to the wall, was a small bed where Don's father lay.

The house had no electricity and no plumbing. Near the bed was a galvanized bucket that was used as a toilet. The place was clean and tidy, and everything was in its place. When Don explained to me that his father had been taught to be self-sufficient and so had not wanted any modern conveniences, I told him that I didn't think anyone was going to judge his father's lifestyle and, if anything, would admire him for it.

Empty House

A man and his wife had raised their children in a medium-sized farmhouse just outside of town. The children were grown and their mother had died earlier, so when their father died, all the children came in to make funeral arrangements.

Although everything went well, I sensed there was tension within the family. This often happens when there are several children involved, with different ideas about what should be done, but it also can be due to the different ways each child deals with grief. Problems often occur when assets are involved and there is no will.

The family arranged for two days of visitation, with the funeral on the third day. On the day of the funeral, the family asked me to announce that there would be a luncheon at the farmhouse and everyone was invited to join them after the burial at the cemetery. The funeral was scheduled for 11:00 a.m. The minister, the friends, and all the family, except one of the sons, arrived by 11:00 a.m. This was a time before cell phones, so no one knew how to contact the son to ask where he was. The family decided there must have been some problem, so they said they would delay the start of the funeral for a few minutes.

The few minutes turned into an hour. Everybody in the funeral home was getting fidgety, so the family told us to go ahead with the proceedings. The sermon was long and there were several songs, so we did not leave for the cemetery much before 1:30 p.m. The son never showed up. I announced the luncheon while we were at the funeral home and also after the committal service at the cemetery.

A big shock awaited the family at the farmhouse. It was completely empty. Not one item was left in the house—not even the kitchen sink. A neighbor, who did not attend the funeral, said he thought it strange that while the funeral was being held, the son backed up a semitruck and, with some other people, emptied the entire house, including the food for the luncheon.

The Audit

When one family met a chaplain, who had ministered to their now deceased loved one in the hospital, they asked him to officiate at the funeral. He agreed. The funeral was set for 10:00 a.m. The day of the funeral came, but at 10:00 a.m., there was no chaplain. We waited. The minutes continued to tick away, and still no minister.

At 10:30, the chaplain called. He said he was about thirty minutes away. While driving, he had started daydreaming and had missed his exit.

Finally, after another lengthy wait, he finally showed up. He was apparently ill-prepared, too. After an opening prayer, he started jumping from one topic to another, none of which had anything to do with the deceased. Everyone was having a hard time trying to figure out what he was saying. He was not in the least coherent and said nothing about the deceased.

He kept stumbling on for well over an hour. The poor family was disappointed, but there was nothing to do. On the way to the cemetery, the chaplain was in the lead funeral car with my brother and said to my brother, "I guess I really screwed that up, didn't I?!"

My brother responded, jokingly, "Well, the son-in-law is an IRS auditor, and if anyone was going to be audited, it would be you."

After the committal service at the cemetery, a family member came up to my brother and asked if he had the chaplain's card. It was the IRS agent. He told my brother he thought the man was due for an audit!

Charlie Smith

Charlie was ninety-nine years old when he died, missing his hundredth birthday by just ten days. His only surviving relative was a great-nephew, who flew up from Florida to make funeral arrangements. Because there were no other relatives and few friends (Charlie had outlived them all), the great-nephew wanted to have a one-day period of visitation followed by an early-morning funeral the next day so he could catch a flight back to Florida. But then he remembered that when Charlie's wife had died, there had been two days of visitation and thought maybe he should do the same thing for Charlie.

It was in the fall of the year and the weather was unusually balmy, but there was a prediction of some snow, so the nephew wondered if he should go with his first plan and get back to Florida before the snow came. But then his conscience was going to bother him, so he went with two days of visitation.

No more than six people came to pay their respects in the whole two days of visitation for Charlie. The night after the second day of visitation, it did snow ... and snow, and snow, and snow — until there were about three feet of snow on the ground. Not only were all planes grounded, but the cemetery called and said it would be a week before they could get into the cemetery to open the grave. The great-nephew was stuck in Michigan and the funeral was delayed a week, but when Charlie was finally buried, it was the day of his hundredth birthday.

He's All Thumbs

The first thing I noticed was that this deceased man had no fingers on either hand, only thumbs. He had clearly not been born that way, so I was curious about how this had happened. I did not want to ask the family about it, but during the visitation, I overheard them talking.

The man had worked at the local lumberyard before there had been safety guards. At the lumberyard was a huge circular saw used to cut timbers into boards. It seems the man had gotten his hand too close to the saw blade and had cut the fingers off of one of his hands. A few years later, someone talking to him at the lumberyard asked him how he had lost his fingers. He had said, "Just like this," walked over to the saw, and passed his hand over the saw, getting too close and cutting off the fingers of the other hand. It turned out that he had been farsighted and had not worn glasses.

Loving Niece

The niece of a farmer and his wife had voluntarily given up having a personal life to care for her aunt and uncle because she loved them dearly. The farmer and his wife had also told her that if she would take care of them in their old age, they would leave her the farm. The farm was not large, but it supported them enough to meet their needs. The farmhouse, which stood in a clearing near the woods that edged up to the farm, was old but had been well maintained and had a landscaped lawn.

After her aunt died, the niece continued to care for her uncle for several more years, until he also died. The caregiving niece had lived with her aunt and uncle for most of her life and was in deep grief when she came to the funeral home to make funeral arrangements. She arranged for a two-day period of visitation, with a funeral following on the third day. Her uncle would be interred in the cemetery next to his wife. Her uncle had been old and had not gotten out much, so he had few friends. She knew the funeral would be small but made an effort to notify all of her cousins of the death, even though she did not think they would come because none of them had visited or kept in contact.

On the first evening of visitation, the other nieces and nephews showed up. They were all standing around the casket, saying what a great aunt and uncle they'd had and how much they would be missed. Then one of the nephews stood and announced that he would read the will he had in his possession. He read it loud and clear: The farm was to be sold and all the proceeds were to be split among all of the surviving nieces and nephews. He told the caregiving niece that she had to find a place to live because the "For Sale" sign would be put up immediately. He would be contacting the attorney in the morning to get the ball rolling.

The loving niece was in shock. Not only had she lost her uncle, whom she had dearly loved, but now she was going to lose her home, the only home she had known since she had left her childhood home. She was in tears.

On the second day of visitation, all of the nieces and nephews kept on and on, saying what great people their aunt and uncle had been. The caregiving niece sat in a corner and wept.

Later that evening, the attorney came to the funeral home, carrying a valise. The nephew who had read the will on the first night had contacted the attorney and told him that he wanted the estate settled straight away. As soon as he arrived at the funeral home, the attorney paid his respects at the casket, and then turned to face the people in the room. He said that before the aunt had died, she and her husband had come in to update their will. He pulled out some papers, announcing that he had the updated will and that the will stated that all of the uncle's possessions, including the farm and farmhouse, were to be left to the caregiving niece.

After that, all of the other nieces and nephews and their families filed out of the funeral home, never to return. The few people who attended the funeral were the caring niece, a few neighbors, and some close friends.

Holiday Motor Home

It was a beautiful sunny Saturday afternoon. I was looking out my office window facing the back area of the parking lot, when I saw a huge Holiday motor home making its way toward the building. It stopped fairly close to the back door. Three men, all wearing brightly colored Hawaiian shirts, stepped out and headed toward the back door. Recognizing one of the men, I stepped out of my office and into the back hallway to greet them. I asked them what was up.

The man I knew introduced me to his brothers and then said, "Dad is in the motor home. We went to Florida to bring our ninety-year-old father back to Flushing to care for him here. He died peacefully while we were passing through Georgia. We thought it would be easiest to bring him directly to you."

I gave them my sympathies for the loss of their father, and then I told them that several laws had been broken. When their father died, they should have stopped and notified the authorities. Then their father's remains should have been taken to the local morgue, where a medical examiner would pronounce their father dead and determine a cause of death. A death certificate would have had to be filed in the county of death so a burial transit permit could be obtained. Only then would the remains have been permitted to be taken out of the state of Georgia.

Of course, they had not done any of that.

One of the joys of living in a small community was that I happened to know one of the local county medical examiners who worked at Hurley Medical Center in Flint and also lived in Flushing. Because it was the weekend, I was hoping he was not on duty and was home.

Luckily, he was home when I called. After I explained the situation to him, he came right down to the funeral home and, after talking to the sons for a few minutes to make sure their story was plausible, went into the motor home, examined the remains, came out, and told us that it was an educated guess, but he thought their father had died about five minutes before he had arrived, of a myocardial infarction. He pronounced the man dead and recorded the time when the death had occurred in Flushing. He told me to prepare a death certificate and to bring it to his office on Monday for him to sign.

After it was signed, I filed the death certificate with the Genesee County Clerk and obtained a burial permit. Whew!

Angola, Indiana

In the forties, if you applied for a marriage license in Michigan, you had to wait at least three days before getting married. Many men were about to be shipped out during WWII, however, and wanted to tie the knot as soon as possible, so they went to Angola, Indiana, to be married because there was no waiting period.

Decades later, a widow came in with her children to make funeral arrangements for her husband. While I was gathering information for the obituary, the widow told me she and her husband had been married in Angola, Indiana. Because a lot of people now do not know why so many people had driven that far to get married before WWII, I glanced at the children and asked, "Do you know why your parents were married in Angola?"

Before they could answer, the widow blurted, "I was pregnant, so there!"

Apparently, the children had not heard that before, and my foot did not taste very good. I quickly changed the subject!

Woof!

In the funeral home, off the entryway into the funeral chapel, is an old oak staircase leading to an apartment. At the top of the stairs is a long banister along the hallway. My brother and his wife had a small cockapoo, Fred, that was always quiet and stayed at the top of the stairs while they were out. During one funeral, however, when one lady stepped out to sing a song in a high, shrill voice, we could hear Fred howling along with the song.

A Sad Ending

A very pleasant lady lived in a house down the street from the funeral home. She was always doing volunteer work and also always had a nice word to say. Her life was not easy. Her husband had been dead for some time, and her son was always in trouble with the law; no matter what she did, she could not control her son. There had been a lot of vandalism going on in town, and he was the main suspect. I am not sure what all he had done, but the sheriff and local police departments knew him well.

We received a call late at night telling us that the woman's son had been found in the middle of Mt. Morris Rd., a few miles outside of town. He had apparently been run over by a car that had not seen him and he was found lying in the middle of the road. Although there were no witnesses, it was suspected that he had been drunk and had stumbled into the road, where he had passed out. One of the officers told me that it was even speculated that someone had thrown him into the road, though this was never proven.

It was sad to see the mother grieving so deeply when no one else was grieving at all. The only people who came for the visitation and funeral, other than a few people from the church the mother attended, were police officers. One of the officers told me that most of the officers and detectives who came in were making sure the dead man was this troublemaker. Several of them told me that the world was now a safer place.

The Tie Man (a Memorable Funeral)

Mr. Tomasoski, nicknamed Tomo, was a beloved schoolteacher in New Lothrop, a small town not too far from Flushing. Tomo always wore a tie to school, but he rarely wore the same tie twice. This was noticed by everyone.

When he died way too young, his passion for ties was given attention. During the visitation, a colorful array of his ties was displayed all around the funeral chapel, and the pallbearers each chose one to wear to the funeral.

I recently talked to Mrs. Tomasoski, who told me that the family had kept all the ties in hopes of making a quilt out of them someday.

I have seen ties draped on Mr. Tomasoski's monument.

Doc Bigelow

Dr. Bigelow was a well-known and beloved veterinarian in Flushing. There are many wonderful stories about the doctor, his practice, and his community service. Dr. Bigelow was known for his staunch allegiance to his alma mater, Michigan State University, its football team, and all the Spartans. The doctor had a large brush pile out in the field behind his barn where he would let me dump yard waste (mostly branches and old shrubbery). He would burn the pile in the winter.

One time after I had just unloaded a truckload of debris, I noticed the doctor was in his barn, and I walked over to see what he was doing. As the doctor always did, he stopped what he was doing and invited me in. I saw he was working on a large float of some kind. When I got closer, I could see the face of Sparty, the mascot of the Michigan State Spartans, that he was sculpting out of large pieces of foam. He intended to take Sparty to football games and many other sporting events at MSU. While he worked on his project, the doctor told me, jokingly, that when he died, he wanted to be buried in a casket that looked like a football. I told him I could arrange that as soon as I found a kicker who could kick him from the funeral home to Flushing Cemetery. Later on, he also made a float of a large football.

Doc Bigelow and his lovely wife, Rita, enjoyed tailgating outside the football stadium before game time. As a joke, the doctor made a post from a six-by-six piece of wood with a water pipe running up from the ground to a water spigot and with an electrical pipe attached to an electrical outlet. Neither worked, but he had it rigged to look like it was hooked up to his electric grill, and he placed a half-full bucket of water under the spigot. He said people would walk by, give him a funny look, and often remark, "How come, no matter where you tailgate, you get water and electricity?"

Although when the doctor died, he was not buried in a football, he was buried in a green casket (green and white are the MSU colors). As Dr. Bigelow was put in the hearse, a friend played the Michigan State fight song on a trumpet.

After the committal service at the cemetery, I stepped up before the gathering and told them that the doctor might need water and electricity, and while the MSU fight song was being played again, I placed the tailgate post on his grave. The post stayed there for a long time and may still be there.

Seth

The phone rang about one a.m. It was Seth. He told me his elderly aunt was dying and he wanted me to go directly to the nursing home in Caro, Michigan, about fifty-five miles away, so I would be there when she died. He did not want her remains lying in the nursing home, waiting for someone to come retrieve them.

I told him to have the nursing home call me as soon as his aunt died and I would be on my way, but Seth did not like my answer. He told me that I did not understand; he wanted me there now. He started to get angry and told me he knew my father and wanted to talk to him.

By that time, my father had retired and was living in Florida. I gave him my father's telephone number. Unfamiliar with the area code, Seth asked me where a number like that was from. When I told him it was my father's retirement home in Florida, he was even unhappier, but he agreed not to call my father and to call me as soon as his aunt died.

Three years later, I answered the phone and heard a gentleman say that I would probably not remember him, but he had talked to me a few years earlier. I recognized his voice and asked, "Did your aunt die?"

He was surprised I remembered him and replied, "Yes, about an hour ago." He told me it would probably have been expensive for him if I had gone to Caro and waited for three years.

I answered, "Yes, it would have.", then told him I was on my way.

The Meanest Man

My office was located just inside the back door of the funeral home. This door was used mainly for the staff and flower delivery, but sometimes friends would stop by to say hello, find out the latest news, or just have a cup of coffee and talk.

One day I was in my office when a man came in the back door and into my office. We exchanged greetings, and then he sat down and proceeded to tell me that I was going to bury the meanest man in the world. I was pretty sure a joke was coming, but I was soon surprised when he assured me I was, in fact, going to bury the meanest man in the world. He told me that his stepfather had died the previous night and his mother wanted him to notify us of the death and start the funeral-arranging process. He added that his stepfather was not only mean but a despicable old cuss, too!

When the widow came in to finalize the arrangements, she told me right out that the funeral would be small because her husband had been an ornery man and nobody liked him. She said she could not remember for sure why she had married him and that her marriage had been a trial, but she wanted to do the right thing and have a decent funeral and burial for him. She then voiced her concern about a minister. She said her husband certainly was the most unchristian person she had ever met, and she wondered what minister would want to officiate at his funeral.

I told her not to worry; I would find a minister for her. Then I called a minister friend of mine and explained the situation to him and he agreed to officiate. He said he would keep the service light and would center his sermon on God's love for everyone.

During the visitation, almost everyone who came in qualified why they had come: They were there out of respect for the widow, not her husband.

Before the funeral, the minister met with the family in our private conference room to discuss the details of the service with them. When the very short meeting was over, the minister came back to my office and said, "That man must have been the meanest man in the world!"—the family had told him they would understand if he could not find anything good to say about the man.

A Bad Way to Start Funeral Arrangements

An elderly, healthy, and well-off widower in his early nineties, who lived in a nice home on a side street, was paid a visit by a friend who many people thought of as having a very negative attitude. After the friend left, the man fetched his twelve-gauge shotgun, put it in his mouth, and fired.

Two of the nephews of the deceased came in to make funeral arrangements. To be helpful, Ed, a cousin of the nephews, came in with them. After they were all seated and I started to ask the nephews questions about their uncle, the cousin interrupted and said he wanted to see the remains. I told him that he might not want to do that because of the nature of the injuries. He insisted, however, and even though the nephews did not want him to, they consented. I led Ed into our embalming and preparation room and lifted the sheet covering the remains.

Ed became very pale, turned around, and walked back to the arrangement office. He looked at the two nephews and, in a raised voice, said, "JESUS CHRIST!!! HE BLEW HIS F****** HEAD OFF!" This was not the help the nephews needed!

And He Will Raise You Up

A lady's husband died, and we brought his remains to the funeral home. When we called his widow to make an appointment for her to come in to make arrangements, she gave us explicit instructions to not embalm the body or do anything else to the remains because she was quite sure her husband's remains were going to be resurrected by the third day. This was the middle of July and it was very hot outside, the temperature in the nineties, and the man had already been dead for some time before we had brought him to the funeral home.

It would have been nice if we could have left the man's remains in the cooler at the hospital for three days, but the hospital did not have room and the widow did not want her husband's remains to be stuck in a cooler when he was resurrected.

Some bodies decompose faster than others, and this one was decomposing rapidly — and getting worse because of the temperature. The smell got worse by the minute, and the odor was starting to find its way into the public part of the funeral home. In desperation, I put the remains in a sealed plastic container, put them in a wooden box, and then took them to the garage not attached to the funeral home and locked the door, hoping that if the man's body were resurrected, it would find its way out of the garage.

After three days had passed, I checked to make sure the remains were still where I had left them. I was sure even before I could see them that they were still there, because the odor was unbearable. I called the widow to give her the news and to inform her that we could still embalm her husband's remains, but because they were in such a bad state of decomposition there would be no viewing. She instructed us not to embalm but to take her husband's remains directly to the grave. We were more than happy to do that.

When we arrived at the cemetery, the sexton helped us carry the casket to the grave. He asked, "What is that smell?"

From this story, I am reminded of the minister of a church in Flint who had convinced his congregation that when he died, his remains would be resurrected from the grave, so his congregation should be ready for his return. I talked to the funeral director who had buried that minister's remains and asked him what he thought about the resurrection. He told me the minister looked pretty dead to him and he expected him to remain so. The minister's congregation met for several more months, but slowly it dwindled to just a few people before the church was closed for good.

Detroit Drunk Lady

When I was in mortuary school at Wayne State University, I worked for a funeral home in Detroit. One day, a widow was in the funeral home, mourning the loss of her husband. She was dealing with her grief mostly by drinking whiskey right out of the bottle—in fact, several bottles. She was so drunk that she was incoherent and was stumbling around the chapel. Finally, the funeral director on duty told her she had to go home. She mumbled to him that she had no way to get home; a friend had dropped her off. Because I was the low man on the totem pole, my boss told me to take her home in my car. When I asked where she lived, I was told the woman would give me directions to her house while we were driving there.

It was very cold and snowing, the roads were bad, and I had to drive slowly. We were about five blocks away from the funeral home when I asked where I would be turning. She told me I would be turning in to a bar because she needed a drink before going home. She said she would tell me where she lived but I would have to buy her a drink first.

I figured if I said out loud what I was thinking, I might go to hell, so I kept my mouth shut and took her to a convenience store that sold liquor and said if she needed a drink, she could go buy one but I was waiting in the car. I also told her that if she did not tell me where she lived, I would be leaving her at the store. She stumbled into the store, bought a fifth of whiskey, got in the car, and slurred, "Take me home. You are no fun!"

Bird Lady

I got the call around eight p.m. The man on the phone said he and his wife had stopped to see his mother and had found her in bed, where she had died, apparently in her sleep. When I arrived at the woman's house, her son met me in the driveway. He told me that since his father had died, his mother had become a little odd; she was lonesome and had found a way to have companionship. He said it kind of apologetically. I knew this man from high school and knew he was hurting at the loss of his mother, but I also knew that, whatever was inside, he did not want everybody to know about.

When I walked in the door, the first things I noticed were white splotches everywhere. There were sheets on all the furniture that, at first, made it appear that someone was painting. Then I realized that all the pictures were still on the walls and they, too, were covered with splotches and, in fact, were heaped with splotches on the tops of the frames and everywhere else. It was then that I heard the *birds*.

The woman had found companionship with all of the robins she kept in her house, and the birds had free rein. Bird droppings were everywhere, including on her and her bed; all over the kitchen cupboards, pots, pans; and on all the doorknobs, not to mention the floor. The woman's son and his wife had pained expressions on their faces and looked like they needed me to understand. And I did. I assured them that I understood what they were going through and everything would be OK.

Because the woman had died at home, the local on-duty police officer had to come to the house to make sure that it had been a natural death and that there were no signs of foul play. He would report back to the medical examiner, and the medical examiner would contact the woman's doctor and make a determination as to the cause of death. If that could all be done on the phone, the woman would not have to be taken to Hurley Hospital for an autopsy.

I met the police officer, whom I knew, in the driveway and took him to the woman's bedside. He took a look around and then went to the kitchen to talk to the son and the son's wife. He also could feel the son's pain.

When I met the officer back out in the driveway, he looked at me and said, "Did you see that?!"

"Did I see what?", I asked.

He answered, "I didn't see anything."

"Neither did I.", I replied.

The woman had been under a doctor's care, and her doctor said her death was not totally unexpected since she had been suffering from various illnesses. The medical examiner released her remains to us, and the incident was never mentioned again.

Down's Syndrome

My apprentice and I arrived at the old farmhouse way out in the country north of town. After driving up the muddy two-track driveway, we noticed that the old farmhouse was in great need of repair, maybe beyond repair. There were only a few flakes of paint left on the side, and a few boards were swaying in the breeze. A few other boards had fallen to the ground. The front porch looked like it would cave in if someone ventured to step onto it. There was rusted farm machinery all about, and the yard had not been mowed for years.

We stepped onto a bale of hay in order to go into the house and into the kitchen. It smelled bad! Two sweet sisters and the husband of one (the other sister had never married) greeted us at the door very cordially. The style of the sisters' dresses and hair was from the 1930s. The family eked out a living by working the small farm their parents had started. They were really nice, but it was apparent that the clock had stopped for them when their parents had died years before.

They said they had lived in this house since they were born, and they told me that their brother, who had died, was in the bedroom.

Already, my apprentice and I knew this was not going to be pleasant. Not only did the place smell terrible, but junk was stacked to the ceiling and there was garbage everywhere.

I asked the women if their brother had been under a doctor's care, and they answered, "Heavens no. He has never been out of the house." Their brother, who had Down's syndrome, had been born in the house, and his birth had never been recorded. They thought he was in his forties.

When we stepped into the bedroom, we saw that the situation was worse than we had imagined. Their brother, who weighed about 350 pounds, was in an old bed. He was surrounded by hundreds of Coca-Cola cans. When we tried to move the mattress that he was lying on, it came apart from rot. I do not think the man had been out of bed for a very long time.

When my apprentice reached down to move some trash out of the way so we could try to get our stretcher into the room, a large rat — not a mouse — ran up his arm. My apprentice shot back and fell over trash and pop cans.

Behind all the trash, I noticed a beautiful old chest of drawers against the wall. It had to be an antique and was in very good condition. Out of curiosity, I opened one of the drawers. Inside were fine sheets of linen, and blankets that were perfectly folded and yellow with age. They had not been used in years.

The smell in the house was so bad that we worked as fast as we could to get out of there.

While bringing our stretcher out of the bedroom, I glanced into the living room. The trash was piled high, but there was beautiful furniture underneath it. The sisters told me they never went in there because, when their parents had been alive, they had not been allowed in the living room. The sisters had kept everything in that room as it was except for putting more stuff in there.

Trash seemed to have just crept in everywhere. It was apparent that the sisters and husband lived in the kitchen and the bedrooms, though I did not see the other bedrooms. I also saw no signs of running water.

Because the deceased was not under a doctor's care, we had to notify the sheriff's department, who, in turn, would contact the medical examiner to obtain a release to the funeral home. It was cold outside, so I opted to stay inside the house with the family while waiting for the sheriff's deputy to arrive. My apprentice decided to wait in the car.

When I saw the sheriff''s car making its way up the drive, I stepped outside to greet him. I explained the situation to him, telling him that the man had obviously died from natural causes and that the sheriff might better call the medical examiner from his car. He looked at me like I was an idiot. He told me he would go take a look and call the medical examiner from the house. He stepped onto the bale of hay and into the kitchen, then immediately stepped back out into the yard and said, "I'll call from my car."

When we arrived back at the funeral home, our overcoats and clothes smelled so bad that we had to disrobe in the garage, put on clean clothing, go home and shower, and put on another set of clean clothes. We put our suits and coats in plastic bags and took them to the cleaners, and we kept the windows in the removal car open overnight to air it out.

It took some time, but we cleaned the deceased brother up and put him in a new suit. He had a proper funeral and burial and was buried next to his parents in the old section of Flushing Cemetery. The family's clothing smelled bad; we kept the fans in the funeral home running.

A couple of months after the funeral of their brother, the sisters came in to purchase a headstone. They wanted the granite to match that used for their parents' headstone. I am usually good at matching the different types of granite and I thought I had this one right, but I didn't. When the headstone was delivered to the cemetery, we saw that the granite was nearly the same color but was of a different grain. It was not a match. I told the family it was my mistake. One of the sisters told me, "Don't replace it. It's just as well; our brother was quite different, too."

George, One of the Town Drunks

There were two "town drunks" in Flushing. There were probably more, but these two, both from decent families, were often seen stumbling down the street, sitting in doorways, or wandering down by the river.

One of the drunks would go into a bar, and when they kicked him out, he would weave down the street to the next bar. He was skinny as a flagpole. One time, I saw him facedown, crawling on the sidewalk, digging his fingernails into the cement, trying to get away from the demons that were chasing him.

The other drunk, George, was short and pudgy and was often seen weaving around the alleys and side streets. Once in a while, he would curl up in a store entryway and go to sleep.

The blizzard was getting worse by the minute. It was in the middle of the night when I got a call from Hurley Hospital informing me that a man had been brought to the emergency room, dead on arrival. He had no identification on him, but the local police knew who he was. It was George the drunk.

It was dark and the blizzard had already dropped more than a foot of snow when George had been making his way down Pierson Road in the tire tracks because the snow on the side of the road was too deep to walk in. George may not have known where he was going. The snow had still been coming down hard when a car had come along and run over him, unable to see him. George was always stooped over, and on this night, he was dressed in dark clothing and covered in snow, and he may have decided to curl up and take a nap, or he may have simply passed out.

I am not quite sure how I made it to the hospital to get George's remains, but I remember I had to stop the car and dig myself out several times. When I arrived back at the funeral home that night, I moved George onto our preparation embalming table. He was still dressed and was much bigger than I remembered him. It turned out he had on a heavy woolen coat, seven shirts, seven undershirts, seven pairs of pants, seven pairs of underwear, and seven pairs of socks.

I always check pockets, in case there are valuables that should be given to the family. I found nothing until I reached the last pair of pants. In one of the pockets was a package about the size of a large box of kitchen matches. It was covered in brown paper, that looked like it was from a grocery bag, and wrapped with rubber bands. I started unwrapping, taking off the first layer, and found another layer like the first. I kept unwrapping until I got down to the seventh layer. Inside the seventh layer were seven pennies. As far as anyone knows, George had all of his earthly possessions with him. He was buried with his seven pennies.

Was This a Test?

We made the removal from an old farmhouse. The old widower had died from natural causes, and his six sons were there, waiting for the priest to arrive to administer their father's last rites. After the priest had performed his duties, the sons gave me the clothing their father was to wear for the funeral and burial, which included the usual underwear, shirt and tie, socks and shoes, and a two-piece suit.

After the family came in to finalize the arrangements and choose a casket and burial vault, I started the process of dressing, cosmeticizing, and casketing the remains. As I was putting on the suit, I noticed, in the back pocket of the pants, folded up, six $100 bills.

When the sons came in for the first visitation, before they went into the chapel, I took them aside, showed them the money, and explained that I had found it in their father's suit pants pocket. Without a single word, the oldest son reached out and grabbed the money, and they all proceeded to the chapel.

I have always wondered if they were checking on my integrity.

The Great Wall

Mike and Margie came in to make arrangements for their mother. While they were doing so, it became very clear that the brother and sister did not care for each other. In fact, they did not even acknowledge each other's existence. I had to repeat everything because if I asked Mike a question and then turned to Margie, she would say she had not heard any question; if I asked Margie a question and then turned to Mike, he, also, would say that he had not heard me ask anything.

It took a while, but the arrangements were finalized. There was just one major detail to take care of: the funeral chapel where the visitation and funeral were to take place had to be divided by a plywood partition so the siblings would not have to look at each other!

When people came in for the visitation, we had to ask if they were friends of the daughter or of the son, and then tell them which side of the partition that sibling was on. If someone asked one of the siblings about the other, the response would be, "I have no sibling". For the funeral, we had to arrange chairs so each sibling could see the minister but not each other.

When the minister saw this, he said, "You have got to be kidding me!"

After the burial, Mike and Margie went their separate ways.

My Turd

When we arrived at the lady's home, she explained that her husband's remains were in his half of the house. The couple did not get along, so they had divided the house, and each had kept to his or her own part. She told us that he lived on the lower level and never came to her part of the house, which was on the main floor, and she never went to his part of the house.

Despite the fact that they hadn't gotten along, the widow was genuinely sad that her husband had died and she wanted a proper funeral for him. The funeral was in the funeral home and the burial was going to be in Saginaw, about forty miles away.

Usually, the casket spray (the floral arrangement that is placed on the casket) has a ribbon on it that says *husband, wife, father, mother, son, daughter, aunt, uncle, niece,* or *nephew*. Not on this casket. The ribbon on the spray said *My Turd*. When I placed it on the casket, I asked if maybe a mistake had been made. The widow said, "No. Turd was a term of endearment, and I always called him 'my turd'." It was interesting, and fun, to watch the expressions on the faces of the people who came in to pay their respects. The minister came to me and said, "Please tell me I do not have to refer to the deceased as Turd!"

Before the funeral, the widow told me to announce at the funeral home and at the cemetery that a funeral lunch would be served after the burial in her part of the house. Because the family was small and the visitation consisted mainly of neighbors and colleagues, I told her that usually if the burial was out of town, few people except relatives would wait to go to a luncheon. She insisted, however, that she wanted a grand funeral feast prepared in honor of her husband.

Two cars of people met at the cemetery for the committal service. When we returned to her house from the cemetery, only the caterers were there. There was food ready to be served to fifty people or more. There were several choices of entrees, including chicken and prime rib, but the only people there, other than a few family members, were me, one of my staff, and the caterers. There were a lot of leftovers.

Splitting up Dad

A man and his sister came to the funeral home to make funeral arrangements for their father. When I sat down with them, I sensed they were at odds with each other, and I asked if there was a problem I should know about. There was.

It turned out their father had been married and had a son, and they had lived in Flushing. The man's wife had died and was buried in Flushing Cemetery. After her death, he had moved to Florida where he had met another woman and married her. He and his second wife had a daughter together and lived in Florida. The man's second wife had also died and she was buried in Florida.

There was a headstone in Flushing Cemetery with his, as well as his first wife's, name on it. There was also a headstone in the Florida cemetery with his, as well as his second wife's, name on it. Both the son and daughter loved their father dearly, and until now, the two siblings had gotten along and had no problems with each other, but this was a big problem for them. Their father had not discussed with them where he should be interred.

The daughter thought their father should be buried with her mother, because he had been the one to buy the second headstone and put his as well as his wife's name on it. Her brother, however, felt that because their father had lived in the Flushing area the longest and had moved back to Flushing after his second wife's death, his remains should remain in his hometown and be buried next to his first wife.

Just as it looked like the discussion between the two of them was going to come to blows, I told them that I had a suggestion. When they both sat back and looked at me, I told them that after the visitation and funeral, they could have their father cremated and bury half his ashes in Flushing Cemetery and half his ashes in the Florida cemetery.

They were silent for a few minutes, letting the suggestion sink in. Then they looked at each other, looked at me, smiled, and said almost simultaneously, "Thank you." The idea had not occurred to them earlier because neither of them had equated cremation with a funeral and burial in a cemetery.

They rented a casket designed with a heavy-duty cardboard container inside that is removed after the funeral and used to transport the remains to the crematorium.

The two siblings have remained close to each other.

Lithuanian

One of the parishioners of the old — and only — Lithuanian church in Flint died. She was a sweet elderly lady who lived just outside of town. Her husband had died earlier, and she had no relatives. She and her neighbors had become good friends, and the neighbors always looked after her and helped with her affairs. When she died, what little she had, she left to the neighbors.

Her neighbors contacted us and said that her request was to have her funeral officiated by a Lithuanian priest, speaking in Lithuanian, in the Lithuanian church and then to be buried next to her husband in the Lithuanian section of the cemetery.

Over the years, the membership of the old Lithuanian church had dwindled to only a few very elderly Lithuanians. The young people had all moved away or joined English-speaking churches. The church could no longer afford to support a full-time priest, so a Lithuanian priest would have to drive ninety miles from Detroit for the service. It took a while to find the person who had the keys to the church and then to contact the priest from Detroit, but we had all the arrangements in place for the funeral Mass.

I had participated in many church ceremonies and funeral Masses, but never in a Lithuanian church. I had saved material from mortuary school regarding the different religious services, but there was nothing in it concerning the Lithuanians. Because I could not speak or understand Lithuanian, I was mainly concerned that I would not know when it was time for my assistant and me to come down the aisle after the service to bring the casket out with the mourners following, but the priest assured me there would be no problem. There was a large cross set in front of the casket, and he told me that when he stepped down and kissed the cross, the service would be over and my assistant and I could come down the aisle to escort the casket and the mourners out of the church. He said that while I was doing that, he would change into the robe he would be wearing at the cemetery.

It was a long service and everything was going well when, finally, the priest stepped down and kissed the cross. He then went back and into a little room. My assistant and I proceeded down the aisle, turned the casket around, and had the mourners follow us. The pallbearers had rolled the casket almost to the door of the church when the priest came rushing up to me and said the service was not over. I reminded him that he had told me that when he kissed the cross, the service was over. He raised his eyebrows and said something in Lithuanian, then shrugged and said, "I didn't tell you I kissed the cross two different times during the service." He said there was nothing to do but proceed to the cemetery and he would finish the prayers there. No one at the funeral, except the priest and I, knew a mistake had been made, because not one of the people attending, other than the priest, spoke or understood a word of Lithuanian.

One More Gray Hair

This funeral was being held in a very old Catholic church on the other side of Flint. The church was small and had a small parking lot. I parked the lead car so it blocked the main entrance, encouraging people to drive in from the back alley. This let us line the cars up tightly to get as many cars in as possible. There was only about an inch of snow on the ground, but during the service it started snowing hard and several more inches fell. After the funeral, the casket was put in the hearse, people were going to their cars, and the pallbearers were heading for my car. I reached into my pocket for the keys and discovered that there was a hole in the pocket of my overcoat. I thought the keys must have fallen on the ground and been covered by the snow. How was I going to find them? No one was going anywhere with my car blocking all the other cars!

I started to panic. Even though it was cold outside, I was sweating! The spare keys were ten miles away at the funeral home. I was kicking the snow out of the way from the car to the church when I heard a faint noise like keys clinking together. I reached down and discovered that the keys had fallen through the hole in my pocket and were stuck in the lining of my overcoat that was sewn shut. Talk about relief!

High-Rise in Detroit

I was working for and living in the Harris Funeral Home in Detroit when we received a call about a woman who had died in her high-rise apartment in downtown Detroit. Her doctor had released her remains to the funeral home, and her daughter was waiting in the apartment for us to come and make the removal. When we arrived at the complex, we took our stretcher up in the elevator to the seventeenth floor and found the apartment; the daughter invited us in.

She didn't offer any information about where her mother was, so after a few awkward moments, we asked. She said we would have to wait a few minutes and then she left and went into a room down the hallway. After about ten minutes, she came back out with a full set of clothing, including an overcoat and boots, and told us that these were her mother's clothes. It is not uncommon for people to have clothing set aside for the deceased to be buried in, so I told her we would take them with us, but she told me I misunderstood her.

She said she would bring the burial clothing to the funeral home when she came in to finalize the funeral arrangements, but the clothing she had just brought to us was what her mother wore when she went out. Her mother would never dream of going out with just a gown and robe on, the daughter told us, so we went in and dressed her mother so she would be ready to go out. The daughter then gave me lipstick and said it was what her mother wore when she went out.

During the visitation, as floral arrangements arrived, the daughter insisted that the flowers be arranged according to how close the person sending the arrangement had been to her mother. There were two rows of flower stands coming straight out from the casket, forming an aisle. The row of stands on the left (head) end of the casket was for arrangements sent by relatives, and the row on the right (foot) end of the casket was for arrangements from friends. I was put in charge of arranging the flowers. As floral arrangements came in, I would take them into the chapel and the daughter would take great care in deciding how close the person sending the arrangement had been to her mother. Sometimes I would stand there for five minutes waiting for a decision. If she decided that the flowers were from someone closer than those already received, I would have to move all the flowers down one stand to make room for the new arrangement. A few times, the daughter changed her mind and the process was repeated. Toward the end of the day, the aisle of flowers extended to the back of the chapel, nearly to the entrance, and it was taking longer and longer to place the arrangements. I prayed the next arrangement would be sent by a distant relative or a passing acquaintance of the deceased. I was glad when the visitation was finally over!

A Sad Story from the Tulip Festival

While I was working at the funeral home in Detroit, I encountered a sad, sad, sad situation.

A divorced man had a love of tulips. Every year, he made a pilgrimage to the Tulip Festival in Holland, Michigan. There, he met a woman who was from the Netherlands, who also had a great love for tulips and was also visiting Holland for the festival. They fell in love, and because she had no relatives, she decided not to return home. She and her tulip-loving boyfriend lived together for many years in Detroit, but they never married.

We got the call that the boyfriend had died in his home. When we got there, we found that the front yard was full of tulips, but the backyard was a mess. The inside of the house was in shambles. Apparently, they liked not only tulips but also their dachshunds—all twenty-nine of them. They liked the dogs so much that they gave the dachshunds the run of the house. It was very bad.

There is no common-law marriage in Michigan, so the girlfriend was not the legal next of kin. She spoke little English but said her boyfriend had an estranged son, a Baptist minister in Kentucky, whom she had never met.

Because he was the only legal next of kin, the son was contacted. He came to Detroit to make funeral arrangements, but before making arrangements he said, "The first thing I have to do is get that whore out of the house." He kicked her out, and he forbade her from coming to the funeral.

The son preached the funeral. He preached fire and brimstone and how only those who confess their sins are going to be saved and everyone else will burn in damnation. He did not say anything about helping people, forgiveness, or God's compassion, and he never mentioned his father or his father's companion of many years, who, after being kicked out of her home, became a homeless person with no job, no skills, no money, and no way to get back to the Netherlands—not that she had anywhere to go back to, anyway.

Who Done It?

Police found a young married woman dead in bed. The husband said he had returned home from work and found her there. The cause of death was apparent suffocation, though how the suffocation had occurred, no one knew.

When the husband came to the funeral home to make funeral arrangements, he was accompanied by a young teenage boy who never left his side. No one who came to the funeral home knew who this boy was. The husband seemed very cool about everything. He made arrangements for a day of visitation and the funeral the following day. They woman had no relatives, and very few people came to pay their respects. Those who did were acquaintances, not really friends.

I would not have remembered this story except that the evening before the funeral, just after the husband and the boy had left the funeral home, a police officer stopped by and asked if he could view the remains. I escorted him into the chapel. He stood before the casket for several minutes, then turned to me and said, " I know she was murdered, and I am pretty sure who did it, but there is absolutely no proof."

Hanging

The elderly widow did not want to suffer any more, so she strung up a rope and hung herself. Yes, there were rope marks, but we could cover them.

At one point during visitation hours, three elderly lady friends of the deceased were the only mourners in the funeral home. They were alone in the visitation room when I peeked around the door because I heard them whispering. All three of them were leaning way over into the casket, and one of them was saying, "I can't see any rope marks. Can you?"

Later in the day when there were many people in the visiting room, Ed, a large, boisterous person came up to me and in a loud voice, said, "Ralph, what did you do with the rope?!" Everyone was shocked at his comment.

New Mexico

Picture a man sitting on a bench under the porch of a stagecoach stop. It is hot and the streets are dusty, and the man is leaning back with his feet on the hitching post, his hat covering his eyes. The phone rings inside, and he wonders if it is worth his effort to get himself up and answer it. I am sure this was the man I was dealing with.

A man had died in New Mexico and his family had contacted us to have his remains transported to Flushing for the funeral. When someone dies out of state, we usually call a funeral home in the area where the person died to make the removal, do the embalming, and arrange to have the remains flown to Detroit Metro Airport. This person died, I believe, in a remote area because there were no funeral homes nearby to call; I'd had to call the medical examiner to ask if the remains had been released for removal and who I should call to make the arrangements on that end. The remains had been taken to a county morgue.

The phone rang and rang and rang.

Finally, a man answered, "Haallo."

"Is this the medical examiner's office?", I asked him.

He replied, "No medical examiner in these parts, only coroners." I asked if I could speak with the coroner. He told me I could call back when the coroner was on duty in an hour or so.

I called back in two hours.

The same man answered, " Haallo, coroner speaking."

"Aren't you the same man I was speaking to earlier?", I asked.

He said, "Yaaah."

I asked why he had not talked to me earlier, and he answered, "Wasn't on duty then."

I asked him if the body had been released and, if so, whom I should call to make the removal from the place of death to the nearest funeral home. He gave me a name of whom to call (I had to look up a phone number) and said I would also have to get a burial transit permit from the sheriff. He said I could call the sheriff after 4:00 p.m. You guessed it ... he was the sheriff, too — same man, different hat. And to get copies of the death certificate, I had to call the local clerk. Yep, it was the same man. Lesson learned: do not call him when he is not on duty.

Loud Music

The person who had died was elderly, so most of the people who came to the funeral were also elderly. My secretary who operated our music was gone, so I asked my wife to turn on the tape player and turn the volume up when it came time to play the music. Because the music would be played from the office, there was a button in the back of the chapel that I would push to alert her when to start the music. I did not tell her that she had to turn the music up only to 3 (the highest being 10). She turned the volume up, and it was LOUD! There was no way I could tell her to turn it down.

After the funeral, as people were walking out of the funeral home, a woman came up to me and said, "You have the most beautiful singing voice I have ever heard. Would you sing at my funeral?" Because our stereo speakers are located in the back of the chapel and I had been standing just outside the back door, people must have thought I was singing the song.

I answered the woman, "Thank you very much. If I am able, I will sing at your funeral."

She said, "Oh, thank you!"

I think for many of the hard of hearing, this was the first time in a long while that they were able to hear the songs being played at the funeral home.

Fire and Smoke

After my wife and I moved out, the apartment in the back of the funeral home had been empty for some time when a local florist friend approached me, saying he needed a place to live and asked if the apartment was available. I told him it needed some updating, but he said that if I would rent it to him, he would help me renovate. It took almost a year, but the kitchen was restored to its original beauty and the rest of the apartment was completely updated and redecorated. By that time, my friend had already moved in.

One Saturday night after that, my wife and I attended a one-person play at Buckham Alley Theater in Flint. The actor was a friend of ours, and after the play, we went to Paddy Magee's, a popular pub in Flint, to celebrate with our friend. We got back home around eleven p.m. It was a pleasant evening, and we left our window open when we went to bed around midnight. Around one a.m., my funeral home line rang and the town fire siren went off. I could smell smoke, and I had a very bad feeling. The person on the line told me the funeral home was on fire.

By the time we got to the funeral home, which was about five blocks away from our house, there were fire trucks from all over. Thanks to the quick thinking of an off-duty fire department volunteer who had seen smoke and immediately called it in, the fire was contained to the back of the building. The fire department already had it in their plans that if any major building in the downtown area was on fire, all area fire departments would be called immediately. The city hall and police department were located on the lot next to the funeral home; the fire chief later told me that if they had arrived fifteen minutes later, not only would the funeral home have been lost, but the fire would probably have spread to the buildings next door.

We learned that the fire had been caused by an extension cord that had become crimped when a credenza had been pushed against the wall. My friend had left the apartment to go out for the evening, and nobody else had been in the funeral home.

The fire destroyed all of the apartment and the offices that were under the apartment. There was a lot of smoke damage, especially on the third floor. There was, however, one miracle: I had built a special cabinet that held the funeral records of the funeral home dating back to 1906; although those records were in the office area, they had not been touched by the fire. (Later, I had the records put on microfilm and stored in a lockbox.)

The Flushing Fire Department did an excellent job of cleaning up and getting the smoke smell out of the rest of the funeral home. Other than the back end of the building, we were okay. The building inspector, however, said he was going to close us up because the wiring was in bad shape, so I called an electrician friend of mine and explained the situation to him. He came right over and had all the necessary repairs done within a few hours. Those few hours were the only time the funeral home had ever been closed.

We were back in business, so I called a builder friend of mine, Tom Staley, who started making repairs immediately. We set up a temporary office in the side foyer of the funeral home while repairs were being made.

The total damage repair cost was around $70,000. Happily, we were fully covered by insurance.

Two nights after the fire, in the middle of the night, I got a call from a family whose father had died at McLaren Hospital. They told me they wanted to, but were not going to use Rossell Funeral Home, because of the fire — they did not want the smell of smoke during the visitation and funeral. I did not know how to respond to this, so I just gave my condolences.

After hanging up the phone, I wondered why they would call to tell me such a thing instead of just calling another funeral home. Then I thought maybe they had called because they wanted reassurance that our funeral home would be okay to use, so I called McLaren Hospital. The family was still in the room with their deceased father. I spoke with one of them and said that if it was not too late, before they called another funeral home, I would like them to come see our facilities because, although we had had a fire and damage was visible in the back, everything was cleaned up and the restoration was in progress; the front of the facility was untouched. I told them the fire department had put huge fans in the building early on to blow the smoke out and had sprayed it with Ozium to neutralize smoke odors.

They told me it was not too late and they would come over early in the morning. When they arrived, I took them through the funeral home and they all agreed that it would be okay for their father's funeral, but what happened next dumbfounded me.

When the family came in for the first visitation, before going in to see their father, they told me they were heavy smokers and asked if we had a smoking lounge. They were pleased when I told them they could use the whole back end of the funeral home.

SHORT FUNERALS

Ten

The lady told me to call her minister and instruct him that the funeral be no more than ten minutes; if the minister could not say everything in ten minutes, she would get another. On the day of the funeral, the minster came in to greet the family. The widow looked at him and said, "You have ten minutes," and he assured her it would be a brief service.

When the time of the funeral came, the minister stepped up to the podium and started the service with a prayer—not a long prayer, but not short, either. After the prayer, he read some scripture from the Bible and said another prayer.

He started his message. He was about two minutes into the message when the widow stood up, pointed at her watch, and said, "Time's up!" She turned to the stunned audience and announced, "We are heading for the cemetery," then looked at me and said, "Ralph, let's go!"

She was definitely serious about the ten-minute time frame!

Not Much

The son of the deceased operated a small machine shop in Flint. He came in to make funeral arrangements for his father. He appeared to have come from his workplace, because he was wearing a dirty old beret and was dressed in greasy clothing. He had an unkempt beard and long, straggly hair. His hands were grimy with oil and grease. Even though he looked rough and tough, he was very pleasant.

When I asked him about a minister, he told me his father had never gone to any church and that his father's ex-wife had asked if he would officiate at the funeral.

There were other children and other ex-wives, and all of them had their own friends, so there were a lot of people at the funeral. We were getting a little worried when the time of the funeral drew nearer and the son who was to officiate had not yet appeared. About a minute before the funeral was to start, he walked in, dressed the same as when he had come in to make arrangements. He said he would have come in a bit earlier but he had been busy at his shop.

Everybody was seated and it was quiet when the son walked up to the podium. He looked up at the audience and said, "Well, I guess there isn't much that can be said, so I think we might as well go to the cemetery."

That's All, Folks

There was a new Episcopalian priest in town. The small Episcopalian church had been around a long time and the congregation was deeply rooted in the history of Flushing. Among the members were many well-known and influential Flushing people.

When one of the members — a lady known for her volunteer work not only in the church but also in the community — died, the family did not request a Mass in the church but preferred to have the funeral in the funeral home.

The deceased had been active in many service organizations, and, as expected, there was a crowd for the funeral. Cars were lined up in the parking lot and into the street. All of the chairs the funeral home had were all occupied. Everyone was anticipating a wonderful celebration of the long life of a woman who had devoted herself to helping others.

The priest arrived at the funeral home just as the service was to begin. He walked up to the podium, read two verses from the Bible, and said a benediction. That was all. The service was less than five minutes. As we dismissed the stunned mourners, we heard a lot of unhappy murmuring. Upon leaving, the priest told me he wasn't much into funerals. That was very apparent.

Short? Not!

The man had lived for one hundred years, and his longtime friend was asked to stand and say a few words at his funeral. We knew we were in trouble when the man informed the audience that he had met his friend in the year nineteen aught six and then proceeded to tell the story of their friendship year by year.

MEMORIAL SERVICES GONE BAD

Many fraternal, service, and veteran organizations provide a memorial service at the funeral home, usually held the evening before the funeral or at the graveside. This is a tribute to show the family and public their respect for their fellow brother, volunteer, or comrade. When this is done properly, mourners very much appreciate the effort. Sometimes these services do not go so well, however.

The Forty & Eight

The Forty & Eight is an organization that began with WWI veterans of the US armed forces. The official name is "Societé des Quarante Hommes et Huit Chevaux," which is French for "The Society of Forty Men and Eight Horses." Now, it is an honor organization dedicated to charity and patriotism. Participation is open to US veterans and is by invitation only. The group in the Flint area often showed up to participate in Independence Day parades driving a black vehicle that looked like a train and fired a small carbide cannon off the back of the car. When I was a kid, it always scared me when it went off.

As the veterans got older, the ranks thinned, but the survivors still wanted their presence known. Some days, though, they should have "stayed in the barracks."

The Forty & Eight in Flint wanted people to know that they were available to provide an honor guard at the casket as well as a memorial service for WWI veterans, so the person in charge of publicity put an ad in the *Flint Journal* that the Forty & Eight would provide free funerals for veterans of the US armed forces. What he meant to say was that the Forty & Eight, as a service to the community, would provide, for free, an honor guard and memorial service for deceased veterans.

Several families of veterans who had read the ad regarding the free funeral came for our services and told us to send the bill to the Forty & Eight. When I called the Forty & Eight about it, I heard, "Oh my God, that is not what we meant!"

Most of the families were very upset and thought I was lying about the Forty & Eight providing only an honor guard. One of the families, however, decided to let the Forty & Eight conduct a memorial service and provide an honor guard at the casket at the funeral home the night before the funeral. The service was scheduled on a summer night at the funeral home. Prior to the service, I heard some yelling in the back of the parking lot and went to see what the fuss was about. There stood two old men in their ceremonial uniforms, facing each other, both holding one ceremonial rifle, pulling it back and forth, and shouting at each other.

"I am holding the gun!", yelled the man on the left.

The veteran on the right pulled on the gun and said, "No, I am holding the gun!"

Then, a little bit louder from the left came, "I am holding the gun!"

Then, a little bit louder from the right came, "I told you, I get to hold the gun!"

Before it came to blows, I told them they should go home. They looked at me in disbelief, one of them saying, "We are here to do a solemn tribute to the dead."

Veterans of Foreign Wars

21 Guns

The Veterans of Foreign Wars (VFW) detail was at attention about twenty yards from the grave site, prepared for the gun salute. Seven veterans dressed in their uniforms were standing at ease, their rifles in hand. They were to fire three shots each, representing the twenty-one-gun salute.

When the minister had finished saying the committal prayers, I nodded to the commander in charge and he nodded to the sergeant.

The sergeant stepped up and said in a loud voice, "Ready!" The men snapped their rifles up. "Aim ... fire!" The guns went off in unison.

The sergeant then said, "Aim ... fire!" The guns went off in unison.

The sergeant said, "Aim ... " The guns went off in unison.

Why, I do not know, but the sergeant yelled, "I DIDN'T SAY FIRE!"

The veterans met at a business that was next door to the funeral home to get ready for the memorial service scheduled for 7:00 p.m. at the funeral home. They all arrived to the business early so they would have time to drink with their fellow comrades. By the time of the service, they were well under the influence.

They marched over to the funeral home and formed a slightly staggered line in front of the casket. Other than a few slurred words, however, the service went well, until...

At the end of the service, one of the more inebriated men broke rank and stumbled two steps forward and center. He then reached deep into his pocket and pulled out a crumpled sheet of paper. He straightened the paper, adjusted his glasses, held the paper in front of his face, and slurred, "This will conclude our services!" He then crumpled the paper into a ball, threw it off to the side, and stepped back.

This scenario played out at several other memorial services until a young Vietnam veteran joined the post and, after hearing our complaints, made sure this did not happen again. From then on, all the services were practiced and done perfectly.

The American Legion

The American Legion twenty-one-gun salute was to follow the interment service at the cemetery. I told the person in charge of the American Legion that the funeral Mass was at 11:00 a.m. at St. Robert Catholic Church and would last about an hour. Because the cemetery was in the next county, I told him it would take us about forty-five minutes to arrive at the cemetery, so the men should be at the cemetery and in place no later than 12:30 p.m.

As many of the old cemeteries were often located on land that could not easily be farmed, the cemetery was out in the country, located on a large hill surrounded by gravel roads.

When we arrived, the priest and family followed the casket to the grave site, which was located on one side of the hill. There were no signs of any military veterans.

It was a beautiful summer day with enough breeze, coming in small gusts of wind, to make it comfortable. The priest had no sooner begun his prayers than I noticed a cloud of dust in the distance. I realized that the veterans were coming in several cars, and at a great rate of speed down the dirt road. They skidded to a stop on the other side of the hill, kicking up even more dust. Because they were on the other side of the hill, we could only hear them. We heard car doors slamming, then yelling, and then gunfire. They were running up the hill from the other side and stumbling, causing the guns to go off. Everyone standing around the grave was stunned. The priest glanced at me and asked, "Are we being attacked?"

Once the priest had finished the prayers, the ragtag team of veterans stumbled down the hill for the salute.

Apparently, the men from the American Legion had decided to stop at a nearby bar to wait for the funeral procession to arrive. They had been drinking heavily and having a pretty good time—a time that had gotten away from them. They had remembered the funeral only when someone had walked into the bar and said they had seen a funeral procession go by several minutes earlier.

Fraternal Groups

While attending mortuary school in Detroit, I lived in and was employed by the R.G. and G.R. Harris Funeral Home in Harper Woods. These events happened while I was on duty.

They Put the Final Nail in His Coffin

The family had chosen a very expensive casket, either solid oak or mahogany. As the service was coming to a close and the funeral director walked toward the front to dismiss people, one of the members of the fraternal group grabbed a hammer out of a satchel, pushed his way past the funeral director, went to the casket, and nailed a hat into the top of the casket.

Horrified, the director turned toward the family, but they raised their hands and said it was okay. Apparently, this was a tradition of the fraternal group.

Odd Fellows

The arrangements were for a prominent member of the community who was a member of the Independent Order of Odd Fellows. A memorial service was scheduled for 7:30 p.m. at the funeral home. Expecting a large turnout, we set up the chapel with extra chairs to accommodate the crowd.

As the participants of the Odd Fellows service came into the funeral home, they were ushered into a side room to organize themselves and prepare for the service. There were many people in the chapel when, at about 6:50 p.m., all of the family and friends of the deceased walked out of the chapel and out of the funeral home. No one knew why. At 7:30 p.m., twenty or so Odd Fellows filed in around the casket. The head of the group looked out and asked where everybody was, but no one knew where the others were. The Odd Fellows went ahead with their service but were very upset and perplexed about why everyone else had left. The head of the group said, "After all, we are doing this service for the benefit of the family."

The widow, family and friends all returned to the funeral home at 8:00 p.m., not long after the memorial service had ended. When asked why they had all left, the widow explained that her husband had told her that the Independent Order of the Odd Fellows was a secret organization, so she had thought this must be a secret service and had told everyone they had to leave while it was going on.

DISPOSITION of HUMAN REMAINS: Cemeteries, Crematoriums, Body Donations

Cemetery Fall

The weather was cold, but bearable, when we arrived at the cemetery. It had been snowing, so the cemetery personnel had cleared a path to the grave the best they could. There was just enough ice on the ground to make it slippery. The path was on a slight incline. My brother was assisting the widow from the car to the grave site when she slipped and her feet went out from under her. Luckily, my brother caught her and righted her, no harm done.

We gathered around the grave, and the minister began the committal service. "Let us pray to the one who keeps us from falling.", he intoned.

Everyone looked at my brother.

A Chinese Custom

As I have mentioned previously, I lived in and worked at a funeral home in Detroit while I was going to Wayne State University's College of Mortuary Science. This funeral home had several locations, one of which was near downtown Detroit where there was a small Chinese community. The funeral home often served those families when there was a death.

It is a Chinese custom when the services of the funeral home are complete, which is usually after the committal service at the cemetery, for a family member to present one of the funeral directors with a silver dollar wrapped in a white cloth to represent the purity of the funeral contract and the proper rendering of services. The person then gives a nickel and a piece of candy to one of the funeral director's assistants as a token of good luck. The funeral director's assistants, therefore, always tried to get as close to the Chinese families as possible so they would get the token of good luck.

At one such service, the limousine driver received the token of good luck and was happy to accept the nickel and the candy. When the driver of the limousine pulled out from the cemetery, however, he was T-boned by a car that had lost control, completely wrecking the limousine. Nobody was hurt, but the limousine driver was seen throwing the nickel out the window. He ate the candy.

Cronk Cemetery

There is a little country cemetery on Beecher Rd. near River Rd. The cemetery is named Cronk Cemetery, probably after the family who either owned the land or started the cemetery. The longtime sexton of Cronk Cemetery was an elderly lady who, being from the old school, insisted on hand-digging the graves. Until she died, she took care of all the details concerning the cemetery: maintenance, record keeping and grave digging.

Although the funeral home did not have many burials in this cemetery because most of the burial spaces had been purchased and used long ago, we once conducted a funeral for a man who was to be buried there. We called the sexton and made the arrangements for the grave service to be held after the funeral.

The deceased had belonged to Hope United Methodist Church located on Beecher Rd., down the road from the cemetery. The minister from the church was to officiate at the funeral and graveside service. On the day of the funeral, the minister arrived early at the funeral home, riding his large Harley-Davidson motorcycle. He explained that he had planned a motorcycle trip for quite some time and that right after the graveside service, he was going to head out on the cycle to meet up with his fellow cyclists who would be waiting for him before starting on their journey. Right after the funeral, he would go ahead of the funeral procession on his motorcycle, park his bike in the back of the cemetery, and then meet us at the grave site located toward the front of the cemetery.

But when the minister turned in to the cemetery with his "hog", the sexton took off after him with a shovel. She yelled at him to get out of her cemetery and stay out. She didn't want any motorcycle gangs hanging around "her" cemetery.

The minister tried to explain the situation to her, but she would hear none of it. When the funeral procession arrived at the cemetery, we found the sexton at the grave site with shovel in hand, and the minister some distance down the road, waiting for someone to explain to her who he was.

Bendle Cemetery

Everyone called Mr. Sexton "the sea captain" because that was what he looked like. The elderly Mr. Sexton was the sexton of the small and very old country cemetery called Bendle Cemetery, which was operated by Clayton Township, the next township over from Flushing Township. Mr. Sexton knew the cemetery better than he knew the back of his hand. It was always a pleasure for us to work with Mr. Sexton because, even though the old cemetery records were sketchy, he knew where everyone was buried and if there were empty spaces for relatives on family lots. He kept the township records but also had his own records going back years and years.

When Mr. Sexton eventually died, the township officials scrambled to find someone to take his place. In the meantime, Mr. Sexton's wife, who was also elderly, filled in.

One of my clients was in the process of purchasing a grave marker that was to be placed in Bendle Cemetery, but the client wasn't sure where the grave space was. Since I would be conducting a graveside service at the cemetery that week, I knew I would be seeing Mrs. Sexton and I could ask her the location of the grave site.

After the committal service was over, I approached Mrs. Sexton and asked if she knew where the gravesite was for my client.

She replied, "Yes, I do.", so I asked if she could show me.

"I am not doing that today.", she replied.

When I asked her why, she said, "You will have to call for an appointment."

I asked her if I could make the appointment right then and she replied, "I am not taking appointments at the moment. You will have to call."

I gave up. I called her the next day and said I needed an appointment for her to show me the grave site for my client. Mrs. Sexton told me she could meet me at the cemetery on Monday the following week at 10:00 a.m. sharp and warned me, "Be on time!"

When I arrived at the cemetery, Mrs. Sexton was standing next to the grave we had used the previous week. I asked her where the grave site was for my client.

She pointed and said, "Right there!"

It was one grave plot from where we had been the week before. I asked her why she hadn't told me that the previous week, and she replied, "You didn't have an appointment last week."

When Clayton Township finally found a replacement sexton and requested that Mrs. Sexton turn over the cemetery records, she said that the records had belonged to her husband and that since she was his heir, she would *not* turn them over. She was certainly a controlling person!

Flushing Cemetery

Flushing Cemetery existed long before Flushing became a city. In the old part of the cemetery are buried early missionaries who came to minister to the Native Americans who camped along the Flint River. The old part of the cemetery is divided up in sections, then lots, and finally gravesites. Each lot has eight burial spaces numbered from one to eight, starting with the north grave. Long ago, families tended to be large and rarely left the area, so when a resident died, the family would be given eight grave spaces.

The cemetery is a beautiful cemetery, but it has had problems, major problems! Early on, the record keeping was not that important because most of the families put gravestones on the graves soon after burial. It was common for people to visit the cemetery after church services on Sunday, not only to mourn but also to visit with other families;

it was something of a social event as there wasn't much else to do on Sunday. Huge monuments, a sign of wealth, were often erected by families to try to outdo the families in the other sections of the cemetery.

The problem arose when families started moving out of the area before having placed markers. It was discovered years later that whoever had been in charge of the cemetery record keeping had not been recording the burials in the correct grave spaces. If a body was to be buried in grave number 5 and the body was the first one to be buried on the lot, the record keeper wrote, "buried in grave number 1," instead of "buried in grave number 5." It made sense to him because, after all, it was the first burial on the site. If the grave was not marked with a stone, no one could tell where the burial had been. When a family needed a grave space, and wanted the burial to be in grave 1, they were told someone was already buried in grave 1. If the family then decided to use grave 5, they were shocked to discover that someone was already buried there, and they wanted to know the person's identity and when the burial had occurred.

As people moved away from the area, few returned to bury their family members on family plots, leaving many of the eight grave spaces of each plot empty, never to be used. Much-needed grave space, therefore, remained empty unless relatives could be found who were willing to sell their grave spaces.

Because the cemetery was running out of room, a farmer's field across the road was purchased to allow for expansion of the cemetery. This area became the new part of the cemetery. To add further confusion, the graves in this area were numbered from 1 to 8, but this time starting from the south. The gravediggers then often became confused and when grave 1 was to be used for a burial, they might instead use grave 8.

One of the early sextons of the cemetery was Claude Fenner. His son, Chuck, helped, and when Claude died, Chuck took over. Claude had kept records on the maintenance garage wall with the idea that he would eventually transfer them to the record book kept at city hall. The maintenance garage burned down before he had gotten around to the transfer, so quite often, without a cemetery marker or the good memory of a family member, no one knew where anyone was buried. The cemetery workers therefore took to using a thin metal rod to probe the ground to determine if there had been a burial on a particular grave space.

Eventually, Ray Rushing was hired by the Flushing Department of Works and was given the job of being the cemetery's sexton. Ray took it upon himself to reconstruct the old records as best he could by talking to people and using the markers that had already been placed on the graves. The people of the City of Flushing should know what a monumental task that was and what a good deed he did for the city!

Unfortunately, although Ray was well-intentioned, he lacked tact. I met Ray at the cemetery with a recently widowed lady to pick out a grave space for her husband. While we were standing there, Ray asked me when the funeral was going to be. I told him Saturday. Without thinking, Ray blurted out, "Gee, that wrecks my weekend!" The widow, as astonished as I was, looked him in the eye and replied, "I don't think as much as mine is."

Later, the head of the department of Public Works for the City of Flushing, Mr. P, was responsible for the maintenance of the cemetery. He decided it was too much trouble to trim around all the monuments in the summer, so he wanted the city to make an ordinance banning upright monuments in the remainder of the unsold plots so they could mow right over the ground-level monuments. I do not think he knew that by mowing over them, and not trimming them, they would eventually be overgrown by grass and would require edging like on sidewalks.

There was a public outcry because it was a tradition in the cemetery to be able to install upright monuments. People who already had family members interred in the cemetery wanted to be able to match the monuments they already had purchased and placed elsewhere in the cemetery. I agreed and was also vocal about my concerns. I think

Mr. P told the city council that the only reason I did not want the ordinance was because I sold monuments. (For the record, I also sold flush markers.) The council passed the proposal. They drew a line in the cemetery beyond which no one was allowed to install upright monuments.

Not long after the ordinance was passed, the wife of a wealthy man died. The husband and I met Ray at the cemetery so the husband could purchase grave spaces. The wealthy man bought an entire lot of eight graves because, he told us, he wanted to install a large monument in the middle with the family name on it. Ray should have been aware that the plot was located in the new area that did not allow monuments.

When the large monument was delivered and Mr. P became aware of it, he wanted the monument removed, but the man who purchased the grave contended that Ray had never told him about the ordinance, even though he had told Ray he was going to place a monument on the grave. The widower then threatened a lawsuit, and the ordinance was rescinded. The rest of the cemetery is now full of upright monuments.

***

There was another problem when the City, deciding that it was too expensive for their workers to be paid overtime to work on burials, passed an ordinance that there would be no burials on Saturdays, Sundays, or holidays. When Mr. Rushing died, the family wanted the burial on Saturday, so I requested a waiver from the City to make an exception for Ray because he had been the sexton for many years. They refused.

When Mr. P died, however, they made an exception, and Mr. P was buried on a Saturday. I called the City to see if they had changed their regulations; they said "No", and would not comment further.

St. Robert Cemetery

St. Robert Bellarmine Catholic Church has always been a large part of the history of Flushing. The church owned a cemetery located in Flushing Township. Cemeteries often allow only evergreens to be planted in the cemetery because the root systems are close to the ground and don't interfere with grave digging. St. Robert had only one very large maple tree, located near the back of the cemetery.

I met the sexton of the cemetery with a widow who was purchasing a grave space. There were two vacant graves under the tree, she commented how nice it would be for her husband to be buried under the shade of the tree, and she purchased them. When we arrived at the cemetery after the funeral, however, we discovered that the sexton had cut the tree to the ground because the roots had been in the way when he had dug the grave. The widow was horrified.

***

A man came to me to purchase a small granite cemetery marker for his baby, who had been stillborn many years previously when the young couple could not afford a marker. I contacted the sexton of St. Robert Cemetery who told me that when babies were buried, they were only recorded as baby 1, baby 2, baby 3, etc., right on down the line, in the section they called Baby Land. Unless the family had placed a monument on the grave as soon as the baby was buried, he could not determine where this baby had been interred, so, sadly, this father was not able to mark the grave of his infant.

***

The church hired a man to take over the job of digging the graves. He did a good job, and when his son was older, the son came to help his father. We arrived at the cemetery in procession from the funeral home. The son stood in the road, directing cars into the cemetery while wearing a sweatshirt with the arms cut off to his shoulders, along with jeans with the legs cut off at his crotch, sandals, and large beads around his neck. The widow asked, "Who the hell is that guy?" I later told the sexton that I did not want to see his son at the cemetery while we were there unless he was dressed appropriately. The sexton was so mad that his son could not "express himself" that he quit as sexton that day.

Flint Area for Profit Cemetery

Years ago, FAFPC sent an army of salespeople out into the Flint area and convinced people that there was going to be a great shortage of land for cemeteries and if they wanted to ensure that their families would be buried in the same grave lot, they should purchase the graves as soon as possible. Many people bought into that.

Years later, to increase their profits, the cemetery started to charge higher fees than most cemeteries were charging for opening and closing graves. The burial vault companies, who delivered burial vaults, would not charge extra for the placement of the vault, but FAFPC told them to just drop off the vaults and FAFPC would charge for the placement. A grave marker could be purchased anywhere, and prices were competitive; the standard size for a single grave marker is one foot by two feet. FAFPC required a grave marker that was a bit larger. The cemetery had them available at a higher price than the standard, but less expensive than a special order from another monument company would be.

For exercise, I often swam in the pool at the YMCA in Flint. I once met a man there who did not know I was a funeral director and told me he was a salesperson for FAFPC. He said the cemetery personnel would call county residences to ask people their marital status and whether they were permanent residents of the county; a few weeks later, the permanent residents would receive a letter saying they were eligible to receive a free grave space. If the people receiving the letter did not respond, this salesman was to go to their home and tell them whatever they needed to hear to make the sale. If he did not meet a quota, he would be fired.

Not long after that conversation, I received one of those letters. When I called and told the cemetery I wanted to know the location of my free space so I could donate it to someone, I was told that in order to get the one free space, I had to buy a second space; the free space could only be used for my burial and the second space had to be for a member of my family.

One time, I received a call from a widow of one of my clients. She was most upset because while she had been visiting her husband's grave on Memorial Day at FAFPC, a salesperson from FAFPC had approached her and told her that if she loved her husband, she should have the cement foundation for the headstone removed and replaced with a granite foundation. No one, of course, would ever see the foundation. She had been so distraught, she had purchased the expensive granite. I took some hassle from the cemetery, but I finally got her money back.

When people started to realize how expensive this cemetery had become, they started calling me to see if I could find people to buy their grave spaces, but I told them that people could go to most other cemeteries and purchase grave spaces for sometimes half the price of the opening and closing fees charged by FAFPC.

***

Although FAFPC is one of the most expensive cemeteries, they do not always provide good service, and I have had many bad experiences there. For example, one time when I arrived in procession, the man waiting at the gate to lead us to the gravesite was sound asleep in his car. I had to get out of the lead car and wake him up.

Sometimes, especially in bad weather, the committal services are held in the cemetery mausoleum. One time, the cemetery person led the procession to the mausoleum, only to discover that the doors were locked and no one knew who had the key.

Another time, when we arrived at the grave, the cemetery workers were just starting to dig the grave and we had to wait until they were done. One of the men even took a break to talk on his cell phone. Then, when I told the workers that the family had paid to have a tent set up for the committal service, the worker told me they did not set up tents. I asked him about the other tents that were set up in the cemetery, and, unbelievably, he told me that was how each tent was stored. When I questioned him about the committal services being held under some of the tents, he replied that he wasn't in charge of that. My family didn't get a tent, a refund, or an apology.

***

Over the years, FAFPC has had several owners and there has been some but not much improvement. I hear from many people how unhappy they are with the high prices and poor service.

Crematoriums

In Michigan, funeral homes are not allowed to own cemeteries or crematoriums. For a cremation, a funeral director is required to make the removal from the place of death, put the remains in a sanitary container, and deliver the remains to the crematorium. The funeral director also meets with the family, completes the death certificate, and obtains a cremation permit from the county where the death occurred. Most crematoriums require the remains to be inside a minimum container of either cardboard or wood, or a combination of both. In Michigan, it is illegal to reuse a casket, so often, people are cremated in the casket used for the visitation and funeral. After the cremated remains are retrieved, if a metal casket was used, the metal from the casket is discarded. Most crematoriums, however, do not allow metal caskets anymore.

The alternative to being cremated in the conventional casket used for viewing and visitation is to use a rental casket for viewing and visitation.

The rental casket has a removable interior surrounded by cardboard that is removed with the deceased and taken to the crematorium. A new interior surrounded by cardboard is then put in the casket so the casket can be used again. Since it is illegal to reuse a casket, funeral directors refer to this casket as a "rental unit" because the cardboard insert becomes the cremation casket and the exterior is rented.

For many years, there was only one cemetery near Flushing (about ten miles away) that operated a crematorium. We used this crematorium (FAFPC) for a while, but I started to get a bad feeling about how the place was run after delivering remains there during the winter and noticing some kids sliding down a hill in the back of the cemetery—on the inverted tops of previously cremated caskets. After that, we always took remains to a first-rate cemetery in Clarkston. We did not charge extra for the mileage, and I could sleep nights knowing that the process was done in a dignified manner.

Fortunately, Sunset Hills Cemetery, a nonprofit cemetery located not far from our funeral home, built a crematorium and I felt very comfortable using them. At the time, they were charging $150.00 for the cremation process.

One day, I was in my office when my secretary told me a man from a crematorium in Ypsilanti, a town near Ann Arbor, had a proposition for me. The man told me that his crematorium would charge $100.00 per cremation and we would not have to deliver the remains to them; they would pick up the remains from our funeral home and return the cremated remains to us. He told me a lot of funeral homes were using him, charging the family $150.00, and pocketing $50.00.

When I asked how he could afford to do this, he said they operated on volume and that he had a large van with compartments that allowed him to make a trip through Michigan every day to pick up the bodies that were to be cremated. I told him that the next time I was in the Ann Arbor area, I would swing over to Ypsilanti to see his facility, and he told me that before I came, I would have to call him first so he could be sure to meet me at the facility.

I did not call him first.

When I arrived in Ypsilanti, I had trouble finding the facility because I was expecting a more modern building; the building I found looked like an old warehouse. When I walked into the building, I saw, off to the left of what looked like an old bump shop, a small, dingy and dusty office with a beaten-up metal desk and a couple of dented filing cabinets. An older woman was sitting behind the desk. The desk was piled with papers, and all around the office were boxes and boxes of cremated remains that appeared to be in no particular order.

The woman was apparently surprised to see someone in the building and asked what I was doing there. I told her I was from a funeral home in Flushing and wanted to inspect the crematorium facility, and she told me very abruptly that I could not inspect anything without her boss being there.

Then I asked her if I could use the restroom. She pointed to a room across from her office. When I entered the bathroom, I was glad I was a guy. I would not touch anything in there, even to flush the toilet, because it was so dirty.

I walked out of the building, got in my car, and decided to drive around back to see what I could see. It was like driving around old vacant warehouses that were attached to each other. I spotted a small door in the back corner of the building and got out of my car to check it out. When I discovered it was unlocked, I went in. The place was fairly clean and organized, but I saw only one retort (the place where bodies are cremated), which made me think that if this guy was doing the volume of cremations he said he was doing, he might be cremating more than one person at a time and commingling the cremated remains.

I was not impressed by what I saw, and I decided I did not want his services. I was certain the families I was serving would rather spend the extra $50.00.

It wasn't long after I made that visit to Ypsilanti that TV news reported that a crematorium in a mid-southern state had been receiving remains but not cremating them. There were bodies stacked up everywhere, many of them in advanced stages of decomposition. Who knew what had been delivered to families as cremated remains? The operator of the crematorium had been indicted for fraud.

A few weeks later, I happened to be at Sunset Hills Cemetery and asked the groundskeeper how their new crematorium was doing. He said that after the news of the crematorium in the South, their business had increased a lot because many of the funeral directors in the area had been using the Ypsilanti crematorium and had had second thoughts.

Body Donations

Bodies may be donated for scientific study; some are given to medical schools for dissection. Although some bodies used to be used for study in car-crash tests, I think they use robots now. Sometimes, visitation and a funeral take place before the body is taken to the body-donation facility, usually a hospital at a major university; other times, the remains are taken directly to the donation facility shortly after death.

Once at a research facility, the body is "super-embalmed," meaning it is injected with a strong formaldehyde solution using high pressure and no drainage. Afterward, the body resembles a balloon figure, probably not recognizable to most people. Typically, the body is then used by medical students for anatomical studies, including dissection, and after a year, what is left of the remains is cremated and either returned to the family or buried in a cemetery. Sometimes, bones are saved for future anatomical study.

In mortuary school, we had a box full of various bones that we could use to study, and occasionally, a chicken or a beef bone would show up in there!

CASKETS

Purchasing a casket can be stressful because it enforces the finality of life. This may also be one of the first steps leading toward accepting the death of a loved one.

In mortuary school, our casket-sales training course lasted about two minutes. Our instructor walked into the classroom and told us that the way to sell a casket is to go to the casket you want to sell and put your hand on it. Supposedly, this would lead the client to purchase that particular unit; that was it.

Thus, the task of training a funeral director in the sale of caskets was left to the middle man: the casket salesman. Early in my career, dozens of casket companies around the country tried to convince funeral directors that their products were superior to those of other casket companies. There were maybe a dozen casket salespeople who came to our business several times each year, most of them representing small, independent casket manufacturers. Basically, these manufacturers would purchase the shell of the casket from a metal stamping or a woodworking company and, upon delivery, customize the casket to the funeral director's specifications. The salesman came to the funeral home with samples of the gauges of the metal, typically 20-gauge (the lightest) and 18- and 16-gauge. There were also samples of velvet and crepe fabric in many different colors to be used for the interior. The salesman also had samples of the more expensive copper and bronze caskets. Later, stainless steel caskets also became available. There was always a wide variety of wood caskets. We typically purchased wood that people were familiar with, such as solid (rather than veneer) oak, mahogany, walnut, and maple.

Softer woods such as pine and poplar were considered inferior for caskets, until people wanted something simpler. When talking about their deaths, people often would tell me, "When I die, just put me in a plain pine box." Sometimes families making funeral arrangements, also told me that their loved one wished to be placed in a pine box. My brother and I thought that maybe if we could convince a company to make a nice pine casket, it would appeal to those clients who wanted something simpler. We started asking the different companies if they would consider offering one. With the exception of one company, all the other companies were opposed to the idea. Hutton Casket Company took on the challenge. They came up with a fine polished pine casket with medium-dark stain and a simple crepe interior.

The casket was a big success. When families looked at our caskets, they gravitated to the pine, saying, "Perfect, just what he would have wanted." It wasn't long before all the major casket manufacturers were offering pine caskets, and later, southern poplar was also used to make nice-looking caskets.

Families sometimes chose inexpensive caskets simply because they could not afford more expensive ones. There are inexpensive caskets that are made cheaply and look cheap. Many funeral homes showed these not to get people to buy them, but to steer clients to the high-end caskets instead. There are also inexpensive caskets that are made well and look dignified. I have always wanted families to not feel embarrassed because of their financial situations, so I encourage them to purchase the inexpensive but well-made caskets.

A funeral director has a profit margin when selling caskets, but it is always important to me that a family purchases a casket that meets their needs. I want people to choose a casket that they are satisfied with and is within their budget, so I try not to sway their opinion on how much to spend or what to purchase. I do usually explain why one casket is more expensive than another and show the different features, and I also point out that all of the caskets we offer are of high quality but some are more expensive because of the materials that are used. I then leave the family in the casket showroom and let them look around and make a decision. If they have other questions, I am, of course, available in the next room.

Several stories tend to come to my mind when I talk about and selling caskets.

Mahogany

One of the premier casket manufacturers makes wood caskets exclusively. One is a mahogany casket called the Presidential because some presidents of the United States have been buried in it. Mahogany is one of the more expensive woods, so this is one of the most expensive wood caskets we offer.

Usually while I escort the family around the casket showroom, explaining the different features of the caskets, a family will either say they like one or will move on to the next. Rarely do they say, "I hate that one. Who would buy such a monstrosity, yet alone spend that much money for it?", however, that is what one family did. I had just shown them a very expensive solid-mahogany casket made by one of the elite casket manufacturers. The family members were so vocal about their distaste for the casket that I thought I should defend it. I told them that this casket was popular because it reflected a lifestyle. I explained that my parents' furniture had all been mahogany: a mahogany headboard for their bed, mahogany dressers and chest of drawers, and mahogany shadow boxes on the walls. Even the davenport had been framed in mahogany. Again, I said, it was a matter of lifestyle.

Then I continued showing them the rest of the caskets and describing the different features, but they gave no indication whether they liked a particular casket. I told them I would return to the arrangement office and when they had made their decision, they could come and get me to show me what they had chosen.

After about half an hour had passed, the family walked into the office and looked at me, and then the son of the deceased said, "You are absolutely right. All of our parents' furniture is mahogany, even the furniture at the family cottage. We'll take the mahogany casket."

Another time, a woman came in to make arrangements for her mother's cremation. She told me that because they had not lived in the area long and her mother's family and friends were all deceased, there would be no visitation or service, and she wanted her mother to be cremated. I explained to the woman that we provided an inexpensive cardboard wood sanitary container for the remains to be transported to the crematorium and the container is cremated with the deceased. The woman looked at me and told me she wanted her mother to be placed in a solid mahogany casket to be cremated in. When I explained that no one would see the casket and that it was very expensive, she told me that money was not the issue—every piece of furniture her mother owned was mahogany, and she wanted her mother to go out in mahogany. The daughter also purchased a solid mahogany cremation urn that was interred in the family plot in the cemetery.

Prepared for the Next Life

People often ask me if they can put items in the casket of the deceased. For centuries, people have sent their loved ones away with treasures. We have put in golf clubs, pictures, books, toolboxes, cigarettes and cigars, bottles of booze, fishing gear, money, jewelry, the cremated remains of animals, balls and bats, letters written to the deceased — and the list goes on. One young boy even requested that he have a portable radio put in the casket with him.

We have also displayed many things next to caskets, including sports equipment — golf clubs, baseball bats and gloves, footballs, and fishing tackle — quilts, artwork, military uniforms, and more. Maybe the largest items we have displayed were a motorcycle and a John Deere tractor.

Unusual Caskets

In the late sixties and early seventies, my father and mother renovated the funeral home and built a large addition. Because the funeral home is located downtown, the community took an interest in the construction process. After the completion of the project, we were pleased with the results and so we scheduled an open house. Admittedly, going to a funeral home open house might seem like an odd thing, but in a small town, some people think of the funeral home as an extension of their own homes.

Another funeral director suggested that we do something unusual to lighten the atmosphere for the open house, so we purchased some fairly outrageous, expensive caskets. One was an attractive but very artsy casket. It was wooden and had flat surfaces and a macramé interior. Another, we called the moon ship simply because it looked like a rocket. It was made from stainless steel and was shaped like a cylinder, flat on the ends, and its interior was trimmed with a plain powder-blue velvet. The third casket was made of metal and was airbrushed a brilliant red, white, and blue. The interior was made from bright red, white, and blue velvet. To say the least, it stuck out. All three caskets became conversational pieces.

After the open house, we wondered who would ever buy those caskets. We thought maybe the artsy casket would be used for an artist; the red, white, and blue might be used for a veteran, a very patriotic person, or a younger and more flamboyant person; but we had no idea who would ever purchase the moon ship.

The first of these to sell was the artsy casket. A lady died, and her daughter, who was, in fact, an artist, chose that casket for her mother. The widower did not necessarily care for it, but the daughter's insistence won out.

Eventually, a lady in her nineties died, and the whole family came in to make the arrangements: children, grandchildren, brothers, sisters, nieces, and nephews. When they all walked into the casket display room, they looked at each other and, without hesitation, said, "Grandma loved roses! We'll take the red, white and blue one!"

The large family had little money and when the husband and father died, they could only afford an inexpensive, cloth-covered wooden casket and a simple concrete grave box for the casket to be buried in. Years later, the man's widow, now very elderly, died. It is common for family members to buy something similar to what was purchased for the first deceased spouse, so we thought this family would do that. There were several sons and daughters, and I asked if they intended to buy the same as they had for their father. They said they probably would, but they wanted to see all of the caskets anyway. Some of the children lived a somewhat bohemian lifestyle and, while making arrangements, one of them said they did not want one of the old-fashioned Catholic prayer cards printed up. Instead, they wanted something more "contemporary" that had lots of color. I told them I could arrange for that.

When it was time to show them the caskets, I walked around the room, explaining the different features. When I got to the moon ship, I could not keep myself from saying, "If you want contemporary, this would be the one." I thought they would smile at my joke, like a lot of people had, because it was such an unusual casket, but they looked, nodded, and moved on, saying nothing. After showing them the last of the caskets, I left them alone so they could look around and then make a decision, telling them to take all the time they needed.

This may have been a mistake. After half an hour, I went in and asked if they had any questions. They said no, they were still looking. Another half hour passed and I went in and again was told that they were still looking. I noticed one of the children was on his back, looking at the bottom of one of the caskets; another was looking under the mattress of a different casket. I didn't ask any questions; I left the room and waited. After another hour went by, I went back in and they told me they needed a few more minutes. About half an hour later, they walked in and said they had made a decision. They would take the "contemporary" casket.

Hot Pink

There is a small family-owned funeral home in the northern part of the lower peninsula of Michigan. This funeral home was the only funeral home for miles around, so when a death occurred, this was the funeral home called. There was a service organization, a fraternal group, in town that had decided when the fraternal brothers died, they would be buried in the same type of casket: a casket painted hot pink, with a hot-pink interior. They never offered an explanation for the color choice. When the first brother died after that choice had been made, the family told the director, that, yes, they wanted to go along with the lodge's request. The funeral was delayed a couple of days because the casket had to be ordered. The next time a lodge member died, he, too, was buried in a hot-pink casket and his funeral was held up until the casket could be ordered and delivered.

The members of this particular lodge were all getting on in years, so the funeral director decided he'd better have some of those hot-pink caskets available so the funerals would no longer have to be delayed. He ordered six hot pink caskets.

When the next lodge member died, the funeral director was glad to tell the widow that she did not have to wait for a hot-pink casket to be delivered, because he had one in stock. The widow told him that she thought a hot-pink casket was the stupidest thing she had ever heard of, and no way was her husband going to be buried in one.

It turned out, all the rest of the lodge members' wives felt the same way, so the funeral director had six hot-pink caskets stored away for a very long time. He may still have them.

Sir Graves Ghastly

On Saturday afternoons when I was in high school, the Sir Graves Ghastly show was on a local television station showing old horror movies. The show opened with the host, Sir Graves Ghastly, slowly opening the lid of the casket he was in and welcoming the viewer to the show. The casket was a cloth-covered wooden casket called the Doeskin and was manufactured by one of our casket suppliers, the Opportunity Casket Company in Saginaw. I heard from one of the employees that the owner of the company was worried because he did not want anyone to know that he had provided the casket to the TV show. He thought his company would get a bad name, however, I am pretty sure he was paid handsomely

Checking out the Casket

One of my colleagues took a group of women around the showroom and left them alone to choose the casket they wanted for their mother. When they had not come back to the office for a while to tell her what they had chosen, she went to them to ask if there were any questions. As she entered the room, she saw one of the daughters getting into one of the caskets to see if it would be comfortable enough for her mother. The daughters finally picked the one they thought would be most comfortable. Then, when the daughters came in for visitation, one of them approached the casket and sprayed glitter all over the inside of the casket, including on her mother. She really sparkled.

Casket Companies to Avoid

Years ago, there were a lot of privately owned local casket manufacturers. Slowly over time, the small casket companies either merged with larger companies or closed, so eventually, only around six or eight salesmen stopped by the funeral home to show their wares.

The major casket manufacturers make their products much like automobile manufacturers do, in that people have a limited choice of styles and colors. Unlike cars, however, when people custom-order caskets, it does not take much time for delivery. There are warehouses around the country with literally hundreds of unfinished caskets for this purpose.

Years ago, when there were many casket salesmen, I was used to dealing with the same salesmen representing companies that had good products. Once in a while, however, I talked to a new salesman representing a new casket manufacturer. One day, such a salesman rang the doorbell. He told me that he represented a new casket company located in the Detroit area. He seemed like a nice individual and seemed to know his product fairly well, so I ordered one casket from him. In a few days, the casket arrived. Upon inspection, I noticed that the lugs holding the handles on the casket were rusted, so I called the company and told them to come and get the casket because I was not going to pay for it. The same salesman came to the phone and told me he would simply send me new lugs. I was insistent that I was not going to keep the casket and that he should come get it. I also implied that this would be the last transaction I would make with him. About two months later, I read in the *Detroit Free Press* that that casket company and a funeral home were being sued because a family had purchased one of the caskets and as the pallbearers were carrying it to the grave at the cemetery, the bottom of the casket had fallen out. After that incident, I became more suspicious of casket companies.

China

Recently, casket distributors have started showing up all over the country, selling cheap caskets made in China that are knockoffs of the ones made in the United States. Some funeral directors have bought these and sold them either for the same price as the premium caskets made in this country or slightly cheaper, to attract customers. Some cemeteries and big box stores, I suspect, were also selling these products.

Every year, the Michigan Funeral Director Association organizes a convention, at which they have meetings and exhibits. Exhibits include vendors showing their funeral wares, from memorial folders, register books, computer software, and insurance all the way to caskets, burial vaults, hearses, and limousines. The first year that caskets made in China were on display, the paint on one of the caskets started to bubble and peel off. This was seen by a number of funeral directors before the vendor could remove the casket. Still, they did a brisk business. Greed is a strong incentive!

BURIAL VAULTS

There is a myth that a burial vault is required by law. I do not know of any place where a burial vault is required by law. By definition, a burial vault is a water-resistant sealed container that a casket is placed in for burial. There are many kinds of burial vaults: some are made from steel, and others are made from concrete with plastic, copper, or bronze liners. Usually the vault is placed in the grave, the casket is lowered into the vault, and the lid placed on top. The base of the steel vault is placed in the grave, the casket is lowered onto the base, and the top is lowered over the casket. Air pressure alone keeps water from entering the grave, much like a diving bell.

Although most cemeteries require a container that will keep the grave from caving in when and if the casket deteriorates, the required container is not necessarily a burial vault. Before burial vaults were readily available, it was common to put a casket in a wooden rough box. The box was made from rough sawn wood and looked a lot like a shipping container. Years later, when the rough box deteriorated along with the casket, the grave sank in and the cemetery had to remove the sod, fill the grave with dirt, and re-sod. It is much more efficient to require a container that will not allow that to happen. A vault will serve the purpose, but the minimum requirement is a concrete grave liner, a plain concrete box that is not sealed and has drain holes in the bottom. Many people want a sealed burial vault to keep the elements from getting into the casket.

***

Years ago, when my uncle owned a funeral home in Kent County, Michigan, a man made a cement burial vault that he claimed would never take on water, and he said he would prove it. The townspeople showed up while the vault was lowered into the river, where it would stay for a week. The man had put a pack of cigarettes in the vault and said he would smoke the cigarettes when the vault was opened. A week later, the vault was hauled out of the water, but they had a tough time getting it up because of the weight of the water inside.

***

In the 1970s or 1980s, a company was formed in Michigan that made a burial vault entirely out of fiberglass. It was inexpensive, light, and easy to handle, and it was completely sealed. There was a major problem, though: When it rained and the ground became saturated, the fiberglass vault would float out of the grave. The company thought it could solve this problem by placing a boulder on top of the vault once it was in the grave, then cover the boulder with dirt; but no one wanted to handle boulders, and, if a bolder was dropped, it would shatter the fiberglass.

ALONG the WAY, SMELL the FLOWERS

Believe me when I say that sending flowers, even if only a single rose, to a bereaved family says everything without you having to say anything.

Sometimes, however, people go a bit quirky with what they send. This chapter is about some of the more extreme examples.

The arrangement placed near the casket consisted of a 24" x 12" piece of Styrofoam with blue plastic flowers around the edges. Glued on the right side of the face of the Styrofoam was a blue toy princess telephone with the receiver hanging off the hook. To the left of the telephone were large gold stickers spelling out "Jesus Called." I told my staff, "If the phone rings, think twice before answering."

A lady had been killed while riding her bicycle. On top of the floral spray was a bent bicycle made from pipe cleaners.

The cause of death was alcoholism. The huge arrangement of flowers placed at the head of the casket in the Presbyterian church was in the shape of a giant Budweiser beer bottle.

The remains of a Buick executive were in state at a Presbyterian church in Flint. Above his casket was a huge ribbon of flowers that spelled out "BUICK". The minister wondered if General Motors always advertised at funerals.

Too Big of an Order

A young woman who had been active in several organizations in the area died, and I received a call from a woman in one of those organizations. She told me that a young tree that had not yet blossomed would be delivered to the funeral home; she wanted it placed near the casket, and the local florist would then come to the funeral home to decorate the tree with flowers. I thought maybe it would be an indoor tree. It was not. A nursery delivered a ten- or twelve-foot tree with a root ball that more than likely weighed several hundred pounds. The root ball was not wrapped in any way. The nursery dropped the tree off near the back door of the funeral home, in front of the garage door. There was no way we could move it without making a dirty mess. I called the woman and told her she would have to come and get the tree — and that maybe it would be a good idea to deliver the tree to the home of the deceased, where it could be planted. The woman was most upset and told me she could not understand why I would not accommodate her. She sent her husband and another man to the funeral home to retrieve the tree, and I watched out my office window as they tried to lift the tree onto the back of a pickup. After not being able get hold of the root ball, they left and came back with a 4' x 8' piece of plywood. The two men wrestled the root ball onto the plywood but could not lift the plywood. After calling several other men to help, they built a ramp and pushed the tree onto the bed of the pickup. A pile of dirt was left in the driveway.

Missing Flowers

When we go in procession to a cemetery, we often take any cut floral arrangements with us to put around the grave. After the committal service and when the cemetery workers finish filling in the grave, the workers arrange the flowers on the grave; the flowers stay there until they wilt, at which time the cemetery workers remove them.

When we started getting calls from families the day after the burial wanting to know why fresh flowers were missing from their loved ones' graves in Flushing Cemetery, I called the City of Flushing and was assured that workers were not removing them.

Because we had no answers, the police staked out the cemetery after a burial. Just as it was turning to dusk, an elderly lady who lived in an apartment across the street from the cemetery walked over to the grave and started taking some of the fresher flowers. The police approached her and asked what she thought she was doing, and she exclaimed, "If these flowers are left here, they will die right away. Why shouldn't someone enjoy them for a little while longer?" The police left her alone. After we explained to families what was happening, no one complained anymore.

***

On Memorial Day, it is common for people to buy flowers or plants to put on the graves of their loved ones. During this holiday period, a vendor was doing a brisk business selling flowers and plants out of his flatbed trailer while it was parked just outside the gates of Flint Memorial Park, a large cemetery.

Some families who had purchased plants or flowers and placed them on their loved ones' graves informed their relatives that these had been placed, so the relatives would not have to buy and place any. When the relatives arrived, however, they would find nothing on the graves. They complained to the cemetery. It was discovered that the vendor had a partner who was following families to the graves; once the families left, he removed the flowers and plants and took them back to the vendor so they could be sold again.

MONUMENTS

Harding Family

A lot of people knew Joe Gage and his family; they were beloved by everyone. Joe had a barbershop and was a volunteer fireman; his wife worked in a downtown hotel. When Joe died, we knew his funeral would be too big to be held in the funeral home, so it was held in the community center, next to the funeral home. There was standing room only; people were even standing outside.

Most people think Joe and his wife were the only black people to live in Flushing, but there was another black family living there, also. I will call them the Harding family. They lived not far from where Joe and his wife lived. They were poor and quiet people, and very proud. They moved away after they had buried some of their relatives in Flushing Cemetery. I had only heard about this family; I had never met them.

I had not been working in the funeral home for very long when Ray, the sexton of Flushing Cemetery brought up the subject of this family. He told me that a man from Flint had come to the City of Flushing, wanting to buy a grave for himself in Flushing Cemetery. Although the graves cost quite a bit more for nonresidents, the man told Ray that he had never been to Flushing before but, no matter the cost, wanted to buy. Ray had asked the man why he wanted to be buried in Flushing Cemetery, and the man had told him that he did not like black people and did not want to be buried next to black people, which he was afraid might happen if he was buried in a Flint cemetery.

Ray told me that he had been so upset about this man's prejudice that he had sold the man a grave next to the Harding family's plot. The man later died and was buried there.

I do not know why Ray told me the story; maybe he simply needed to tell someone.

Not two weeks after I heard that story, the doorbell of the funeral home rang, and my secretary went to answer it. A few minutes later, she came to my office and told me that a whole roomful of black people wanted to see me. They were the Harding family.

Since moving out of town, they prospered, very successfully, in several fields. They told me they had family members buried in Flushing Cemetery and when those family members died, there had not been enough money for headstones to be placed on the graves. They asked if I would assist them in purchasing them.

They were surprised that I knew exactly where their grave spaces were located. We were able to figure out which grave space each of their deceased family members was buried in, and I suggested to them that, in honor of their heritage, they should buy black granite headstones. They did.

When they noticed a light-gray granite headstone next to their family plot and wondered who that man was, I told them I had no idea.

Train Wreck

It was a beautiful, sunny summer day. An elderly, fragile widow told me she wanted to go to the monument company to pick out a monument for herself and her deceased husband. On our way there, we were traveling on a main highway and approaching a railroad track that had red lights flashing. We saw a car coming from the other direction and could tell the person was not going to stop. Just as the train arrived, we heard a horrible crash. The train was not going very fast, and we could see the front end of the car attached to the front of the train. I thought my client was going to have a heart attack.

When the train backed up to clear the road, what we saw was quite remarkable. The driver of the other car, a woman, had been driving her husband's new Suburban. The front of the Suburban was gone, and she was sitting in the front seat with the steering wheel in her hand, muttering that her husband was going to kill her. I thought I might be selling two grave stones.

Flushing Businesspeople

Almost all of the small-town mom-and-pop stores—the stores you went to and dealt directly with the owner—are now gone. Some of the stores and owners were memorable.

Arthur "Dude" MacArthur owned the Flushing Bakery. His donuts were the best in the county. He baked a lot of other things, but I remember the donuts. He was the person to call when Thanksgiving came around, because, if you did not want to roast your turkey at home, he would roast it in the bakery. Dude was proud of his Scottish heritage, so his widow wanted a headstone for his grave with a picture of a bagpiper. I told her that because Dude had been such a part of the community, it would be nice to also etch a picture of the bakery on his headstone. She agreed. Dude is buried in the Flushing Cemetery: look for a headstone with a picture of the Flushing Bakery with a bagpiper next to it.

There were two mom-and-pop hardware stores in the downtown

block, one on each side of the street. When those two stores closed, the hardware store of choice was Flushing Hardware and Lumber. The proprietor, John Bulger, had just about anything a person would need. He was always there and knew where everything was. The lumberyard had been in the same location for many years and consisted of old wooden barnlike buildings, some of which were sagging. The hardware store had character with its old uneven wooden floors. If you needed lumber, you could go out to the lumber barn and either load up yourself or have one of the local young men, whom John had hired, help you. Then you went inside the store and John totaled the bill for you. The lumberyard was passed down to his son. (The old lumberyard has since been torn down; now, the large Bueche's Food World stands on the site.) When John died, I suggested that the family put a picture of Flushing Hardware and Lumber on his headstone, and they did. It is a tribute not only to John but also to the memory of a hometown lumberyard and hardware store.

Inflation

The family owned a car dealership. The father had started the business near the downtown block but later built a new modern building, and the sons had taken over the business when their father had died.

The family had come from the little town of Burt in Saginaw County. If you drove through the country and blinked when you went through Burt, you missed it. In the very old cemetery in Burt is a very large monument with the family name etched into it.

When one of the uncles of the owners of the car dealership died, the widow came to me to purchase a cemetery monument to be placed in Flushing Cemetery, where her husband was buried. She wanted one to exactly match the family monument in Burt cemetery.

When I went to the Burt cemetery to get the dimensions, type of granite, type and size of lettering, and pictures to show the style of the monument, I was excited because I knew this was going to be a big sale with a big commission. After talking to the monument company and making sure they could match the granite and style, I called the widow and made an appointment so she could sign a contract. When I quoted the price to her (it was in the thousands), I thought she was going to have a heart attack.

When she had caught her breath, she told me that the price was absurd. She said the monument in Burt cemetery had cost only $400. I asked her when that monument was purchased. She said in 1909, so I told her I would sell her the monument for $400.

She gulped and replied, "You will?"

I said, "Yes, if I can go to your nephew's car dealership and purchase a new car for what a car cost in 1909." She said that would not be the same, because the monument was only stone that had come out of the ground and should not increase in price. When I replied that a car was mostly metal that came out of the ground, she purchased the monument at the quoted price.

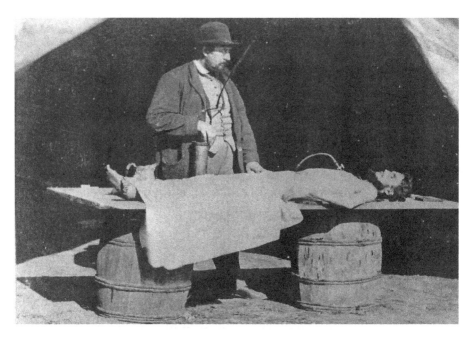

Dr. Burr, Embalming Surgeon, Civil War, 1864 (photo courtesy of Jack Deo, Superior View, Marquette, Michigan)

Early Funeral Home (the former Niles residence, Wheeler Funeral Home and then Rossell Funeral Home)

New Hearse

New Addition (with new wrought iron railings

Rossell Funeral Home as it is today (in the same location)

Author with new Enchroma (colorblind) glasses

Stace

CLERGY and CHURCHES — HOLY and NOT SO HOLY

One thing I have found over all these many years is that all churches (the people) are looking for much the same thing. They want to know that there is life after death and that they will see their deceased relatives once again, preferably in heaven. I have also learned, even though ministers and priests are supposed to be up on a pedestal and saintlier than everyone else, that they aren't. If any minister or priest says they are anything but human beings, struggling just like the rest of us, he or she is lying.

I am not saying that there are not outstanding clergy. There are. What I *am* saying is that most of the clergy I have met are down-to-earth people trying to do the best job they can to lead their flocks. Just like there are some hardworking and outstanding clergy, there are some who perhaps should have had some other calling.

Priests and ministers come and go. Some are beloved by their congregations, and some are not. These are a few I have met during my career.

Catholic

Father Frank and his Associate Father Samuel

Most clergy meet with and try to get to know families who are dealing with the loss of a loved one, but some do not. When we called Father Frank, he rarely asked the name of the deceased and would not talk to the family about when the funeral Mass would be convenient for them, instead telling them when it would be convenient for him — that is, unless the deceased's family happened to be big financial supporters of the church, in which case, he would bend over backward to meet their demands.

Upon our arrival for a funeral Mass at the Catholic church, as we brought the casket into the church, Father Frank always came up to me and asked me the name of the deceased. One time, when I told him the name of the deceased was "John", Father Frank thought I said "Don". All through the Mass, he called the deceased "Don". The family wondered who he was talking about.

Father Frank never came to the funeral home to officiate the Rosary service, which was usually scheduled the evening before the funeral Mass. He would, instead, send his elderly associate priest, Father Samuel. It was assumed that Father Samuel had a drinking problem, because he always slurred through the Rosary service and many could not understand what he was saying. He would often leave out words and phrases. One time, just after the Rosary service, when one of the parishioners asked Father Samuel why he skipped over the words, the priest replied, "I did?"

The Scripture service, often used in place of the Rosary service, uses the same prayers every time. The prayer book that Father Samuel read from was written like this: "And may the Lord bless the soul of (his or her name), and may …" All the priest had to do was insert the name of the deceased. At every service, however, Father Samuel would read, "May the Lord bless the soul of his or her name, and may …", instead of inserting the person's name.

After the Vatican II met, a lot changed in the Catholic church. I went to Hartland, Michigan, with a few young priest friends of mine to a meeting called by the Catholic diocese to go over the new liturgy. We learned that it had been decreed by the Vatican that all Catholic funeral masses would be conducted in the same manner, no matter what parish or church. It had also been decreed that there would be no more public Rosary service; the Rosary would, instead, be said privately, and the Rosary service was to be replaced by a Scripture service. My priest friends and I were all excited because everyone would be on the same page regarding Catholic funerals.

After the all-day seminar, materials were handed out so we could show the parishioners the changes. The morning following the seminar, Father Frank called me on the phone and said, "What you learned yesterday at the seminar might be okay for other churches, but not in my parish. Things will be done as I say."

Rosary Service

Catholics had been taught to pray the rosary, but after Vatican II, the Catholic Church wanted me to tell its parishioners there would be no public Rosary for funerals and that the Scripture service would take its place. Unfortunately, this information had not been passed on to the parishioners of the church. None of them had heard about the seminar in Hartland, so when families came in to arrange Catholic funerals, they were still requesting Rosary services. Even after I showed the families the brochures we had been given, they did not believe me, saying they had recently attended a Rosary at another funeral home and wondered if it was *my* rule.

One family, for example, insisted that some priests might not say the Rosary but *their* priest would. When I called *their* priest, he told me to insist on a Scripture service. The families of that particular church started blaming me for not meeting their wants. I finally got tired of battling families, so when a family requested a Rosary service, I told them they would have to notify the priest and that the priest could let me know the time of the service. It wasn't long before the priest tired of it all. Now, Rosary services are done in the funeral home and Scripture services are rarely mentioned.

I'm Hungry

I don't know if they do it now, but at one time, Catholics did not eat before a funeral Mass. After one funeral Mass at St. Robert Catholic Church, we escorted the casket out to the funeral coach, and the families to their cars. Father Wiley, who had performed the Mass, then removed his robe, walked over to the rectory, which was situated right next to the funeral procession, and sat at his breakfast table. We watched as he read the morning paper and his housekeeper prepared his breakfast.

After enjoying a leisurely breakfast and finishing his coffee, Father Wiley returned to the church, put on his robe, walked out to the funeral car, and said, "Let's go." People had been waiting in their cars all the while.

What Are You Looking At?

I was standing outside the church, waiting for the priest to come out so I could escort him to the car that he would be riding in to the cemetery. He came out the door, stopped a minute, and stared across the street at an attractive woman walking by.

I kiddingly said, "I didn't think you were supposed to be looking at a woman like that."

He replied, "Just because I am on a diet does not mean I can't look at the menu."

What a Waste!

Father Key, a young priest, came to town. He was tall, dark, and very handsome. He had a million-dollar smile. Everybody liked him.

When a young married man died an untimely death and we took his remains to Detroit for the funeral Mass, Father Key officiated. After the Mass was over and as I escorted the young widow out to the funeral car, she looked at me and said, "What a waste!"

I replied, "Yes, your husband died way too soon."

She then exclaimed, while looking at Father Key, "Not that! It's a shame he's a priest!"

***

I not only liked Father Key but also greatly respected his ministry. When he was transferred to a very poor parish in a bad part of another town, he drove a junk car. He had driven a very nice car before, so I asked him what had happened to his car. He told me that the people he now served could not relate to him if he were driving his previous car, so "I drive a car that is like the ones they drive."

Father Key went on to lead a large parish in another part of the state and remains well liked.

Father King

Father King was liked by most people. He had a nice personality and was a good speaker, but I always felt he was arrogant. I was once told by a parishioner that while he shook the priest's hand at the door following Mass, the priest would be scanning all the people and when he spotted a big donor to the church, he would immediately excuse himself and fawn over the big donor.

When I escorted Father King to the car that would take him to the cemetery, he always told me that a competitor funeral home would put him in a limousine instead of a sedan.

It was always apparent that Father King needed a lot of attention. When the local Catholic cemetery built a huge and beautiful mausoleum, Father King arranged for his family to be entombed in the front, where everyone could see his family name when walking into the mausoleum.

I was disheartened to find out that Father King was not only arrogant but also unethical. Once, Father King told me about the cottage he and his brother had purchased on a lake. A widow had asked him for advice about the cottage that she and her husband had owned. She didn't think she would be using it anymore and asked the priest what he thought she should do, so Father King told her that she would not get much money for it and that it would drain her financially if she kept it. He then suggested that he would take it off her hands; he and his brother paid a fraction of the value of the cabin.

Eventually, Father King was transferred to a larger church. He had been there for a few years when a former acolyte from our local Catholic church approached him and told Father King that he should make amends for molesting him as a child. Father King told the man that he—the former molested acolyte—needed to see a counselor and to get over it. It had been hard for this man to expose himself as being a victim of child abuse, but he had had the courage to do so; later it was revealed that several others had also been molested, some of whom had their lives ruined as a result of the abuse. The statute of limitations for being tried for molestation had passed years before, so Father King could not be tried for his crimes. It was on an Easter Sunday when Father King stood before his congregation and told them that he had been accused of child abuse and would be leaving the priesthood. Parishioners left the Easter service confused and disgusted.

Detroit Priest

Once when I was going to mortuary school in Detroit, many people were gathered in the chapel and waiting for a Rosary service to start. The priest arrived at the front door of the funeral home, as usual, fifteen minutes before the Rosary was to begin. He walked through the front door, extended his hand to the greeter and said, "Good evening", then dropped dead.

The funeral home greeters dragged his body into the reception office, then called an ambulance and the church. Luckily, there was another priest available to officiate at the Rosary service. The family of the deceased never knew what happened.

Father Jacobs

We were in procession to Flint Memorial Park Cemetery, about ten miles away. Father Jacobs always liked to drive his car in the procession and was following the lead car. I was behind him in the hearse. We were crossing a major four-lane highway. The lead car had just gone into the intersection, and I was looking both ways. I saw in the near distance a car coming toward us at a high rate of speed with a police car in hot pursuit. I thought Father Jacobs would surely stop, but he was only looking straight forward. He never knew how close that car came to hitting him; it missed him by inches.

At the cemetery, I told him he had better be more careful and look both ways before entering an intersection, even when he was in a funeral procession. He told me not to worry because he had God riding in the car with him. I replied that next time, he should let God ride with me because he might kill God. Father Jacobs only looked at me.

Presbyterian

Reverend Jay

Rev. Jay had been a chaplain in the US Army and had been the minister of the local Presbyterian church for many years. He was pleasant and congenial, but very unorganized, forgetful, and absentminded. We called him "Jittery Jay".

Jittery Jay could never remember names. Although I knew him for years, I do not think he called me the same name twice. He officiated at funerals and rarely called the deceased or any of the other family by their correct names.

The night before a funeral, when the visitation period was over and the funeral home was about to close, Rev. Jay would walk in to meet the family and go over the details of the funeral service. He would carry a clipboard with several forms to be filled out.

The family was usually tired and wanted to go home, but Rev. Jay was oblivious to that. He brought out the questionnaire for the family and made copious notes about them and the deceased. He kept the family there for well over an hour, which also delayed the cleaning up of the funeral home. Unfortunately, Rev. Jay rarely remembered anything he had written on his chart.

The day of the funeral, Rev. Jay would arrive with a schedule of service. He would hand one copy to the director and another to the secretary of the funeral home. There would be a prayer, followed by a song (played on our tape player from the office), and then a scripture reading. He told us he would sit down when the song needed to be played so we would know when to play the music. After the scripture reading, there would be the eulogy followed by another song, his sermon, and a closing prayer. It was always a very thought-out service, but it never played out as planned.

At the start of the funeral, Rev. Jay would pray, go to sit down, and then step back to the podium to read scripture. The music would already be playing. He'd say, "Oops", and sit down. After the song, he would read scripture and announce that a song would now be played. Then he'd say, "No, that comes after the eulogy.", and then he would do the eulogy. He would then go right into his sermon, then would stop and say, "Messed up again; there will be another song." — while the song was already playing. After the funeral, he would come out to the office and say, as he usually did, "I guess I screwed that up!"

What could we say? This happened at every funeral.

During every funeral, Rev. Jay told the congregation that Mr. Rossell had told him that the funeral home had never had so many flowers for a deceased. He said this even if there were less than a dozen arrangements. Also, during every funeral, he looked at a large scenic picture we had hanging on the far wall and exclaimed that that picture was the most beautiful and peaceful picture he had ever seen.

Rev. Jay was a likable guy and his few parishioners overlooked his faults. After he left to go to another parish, the church hired a more dynamic minister who built the membership to overflowing.

Reverend Harry

Rev. Harry was hired by the local Presbyterian church, whose membership had fallen to only a few families. Harry was outgoing and dynamic, his wife was a talented piano player, and he had two clean-cut sons, one of whom became an Eagle Scout. Little by little, Rev. Harry built his congregation until the pews were full every Sunday. One of the ways he built his congregation was by officiating at funerals of nonparishioners. Many people did not belong to churches and after he ministered to them during their time of grief, they often joined his church. My family also joined this church because we liked Rev. Harry.

Then it all came crashing down. One of the deaconesses notified the regional head of the church organization that after she had divorced her husband, she had been having a sexual affair with Rev. Harry. It had started, she said, when she called to ask if he would come to her house to counsel her.

The regional head of the Lake Huron Presbytery (we called him High Noon because he always wore a large ten-gallon hat and cowboy boots and was arrogant) showed up at the church and announced that Rev. Harry would no longer be the minister and would be leaving the Presbytery entirely. The following Sunday, during the regular service, a member of the Presbytery stepped up to the pulpit and described the lurid details of the affair, right in front of all the families with young children and teenagers present.

When some parishioners asked the leaders of the Presbytery why they were not using more discretion, they were told the leadership was going to make an example of Rev. Harry to all the other ministers. It was well known that High Noon did not like Rev. Harry, probably because of an incident that had happened at the funeral home. In that case, a local businessman's wife had been killed in an automobile accident. She had been a member of High Noon's church in Flint, so he was called to do the funeral. After High Noon met with the family at the funeral home, the husband, who had not been a member of the church, came out and told me he wanted a minister, not a cowboy. Rev. Harry had officiated at the funeral instead, and that infuriated High Noon.

The congregation was split over the affair: some wanted to forgive Rev. Harry and let him remain, others thought he should be banned from the ministry, and the rest simply left the church. The choir director was the most vocal of the group who wanted Rev. Harry to stay. Of course, the heads of the Presbytery would not allow Rev. Harry to remain, so the choir director left and joined another church. Later, it was found out that the choir director had also been cheating on his wife, and soon after that, he and his wife divorced.

Sadly, I think many of the young people who Rev. Harry trained and confirmed left the church and never returned or joined another church. The congregation dwindled because the young people did not stay.

I was amazed that the church did nothing to console or to counsel the distraught members. Rev. Harry was not only my minister but also my friend. At the next deacon meeting, I proposed that we form a group of people to call on all the parishioners. I thought the goals of this group would be to restore the parishioners' faith in the church and to try to get them to remain members. I was told by the head deaconess — and everyone agreed except me — that the only jobs of the deacons were to visit the sick, send flowers to the sick, and prepare funeral dinners for the families of parishioners who died. I left the church.

Reverend Ms. Black

For funerals held in Presbyterian churches, it is customary to have an open casket at the altar. Rev. Ms. Black told me that if viewing was necessary, it would have to be in the foyer until just before the funeral, and then the casket would be closed and taken to the altar. She told me she felt very uneasy around dead people.

Episcopalian

Father Carl

When Father Carl came to town, he came to the funeral home to discuss with me how funeral arrangements were to be made for his parishioners. He told me he would make all the decisions that his parishioners had to make regarding the purchase of funeral merchandise (casket and burial vault) and that he was to be notified when I was meeting with the families so he could be there to direct the details.

His assistant priest, who was with him, told him, "You've got nerve to tell this fine gentleman how to run his funeral home."

I never did call Rev. Carl when a parishioner died — not until the arrangements had already been made.

On the day of one funeral, the grieving family was standing around the casket in tears. I was glad the priest would be arriving soon, because the family needed some words of comfort. Father Carl did not arrive early, however; he arrived just minutes before the funeral was to start. He walked to the chapel door, where he saw the family and the casket, then made an abrupt turn and walked back into the foyer, where he walked up to me and said, "You are going to have to go in and close that casket before I can do the funeral. Dead bodies give me the creeps!"

Father Carl did a lot to drive people away from the church. The church had a very active youth organization of which the parishioners were very proud. The youth did a lot of fundraising activities like washing cars and selling candy and other items to fund their own activities. The church also had an active men's club. The club put on a community spaghetti dinner every year that also raised funds for the community. Father Carl told both groups that any money raised would have to go into the general fund to be used only for running the church. The fundraising activities ceased, and the church lost their youth and many of the active members.

Adding to turning people away was Father Carl's habit with people wanting to get married in the church. When a young couple came to him to ask to be married in the church, Father Carl would ask them what sexual experiences they had had. His assistant priest told me that he told Father Carl he was a jerk for asking such a thing.

Father Carl is now gone and the church still exists, but it has never regained the congregation it once had.

Father Eiger

Father Eiger had been the priest of an Episcopalian church in Flint for many years. He was a jolly priest, and people loved and respected him.

After the funeral that Father Eiger officiated, the family of the deceased invited Father Eiger and me to the informal luncheon at their home. It was a beautiful day, so a lot of us were drinking our refreshments outside. As Father Eiger leaned on a split rail fence, the fence gave way and the priest went flying over backward. On his way down he yelled, "Goddamn! Jesus Christ!"

Methodist

Reverend Ellsworth

There were a lot of people attending the morning funeral. Usually, Rev. Ellsworth, the well-liked Methodist minister, arrived at least fifteen minutes before a funeral, but not this time. The funeral was to start at ten o'clock. Ten o'clock came, but no Rev. Ellsworth. He had not called to say he would be late, so we called his home, but there was no answer. After waiting fifteen more minutes for him to appear, we decided something must have gone wrong, so my father went to his house and rang the doorbell. Rev. Ellsworth came to the door with a towel wrapped around his waist and shaving cream on his face, greeting my father by saying, "Good morning! Why are you here?"

We thought he had forgotten about the funeral, but we were wrong. Apparently, the power had gone off at his house during the night and then had come back on without him knowing it. The clocks were off by more than an hour. When we had called, he had been in the shower and hadn't heard the phone ringing.

When he realized he was late, he hustled around, got ready, and came to the funeral home. All the people thought it was funny because the deceased in this instance had always been late for everything.

This story reminds me of when the father of Walt Parkhurst, one of our employees, died. On the way to the cemetery, the hearse had not one but two flat tires, and everyone laughed because Walt's dad always rode on bad tires and hardly went anywhere without having a flat.

Reverend Bradley

When Rev. Bradley came to town, he contacted me and told me he would not do any funerals for anybody who was not an active and financial supporter of his church. He told me that he was to be called "The Reverend Joseph Bradley" in all obituaries and printed matter and also when anybody addressed him. He further told me there would be a charge to the family whenever he was asked to officiate at a funeral. Most families offer an unsolicited honorarium to the minister; it is usually substantial but is whatever they can afford. The Reverend Joseph Bradley wanted to be paid the same amount every time, in advance.

Once, there was a blizzard with almost whiteout conditions, and the snow was falling at a great rate. No way was anybody going to keep up the task of clearing snow until the storm let up. The family we were serving was small and decided they would not cancel the visitation because they doubted many people would show up even if it had not been snowing. The family was already in the funeral home and was quite content. As soon as the Reverend Joseph Bradley arrived, he came right to my office and demanded that I do something about our parking lot. He said one of his ninety-year-old parishioners was out there in the blizzard, trying to make her way into the funeral home with a walker. He turned, walked out of my office and into the foyer, and stood next to the fireplace. Three things came to my mind: (1) Why was he not helping her? (2) What was a ninety-year-old woman with a walker doing out in a blizzard where the snow was blowing sideways? and (3) What did he expect me to do about a blizzard?

Lutheran

The family members were a rough group. We would say they came from the other side of the tracks. They were big and mean. We had received the call that a young man who had returned from Vietnam the day before had gone out drinking with his two brothers. They had drunk most of the night and then headed for home. The driver had swerved off the road and hit a large oak tree, killing the veteran.

The father, mother, and two brothers came to the funeral home in shock and grief. Before making any arrangements, I asked them if they had other family or friends who would be with them. They said they had no other family and no friends. They were loners and had no use for anybody — until now, that was. I asked if they had any church affiliation. They said no, but they knew they needed someone to give them some words of comfort. The mother told me that one time, several years earlier, a neighbor had invited her to a Christmas program at her church, and the people of the church had been nice and she had felt very comfortable there. She wondered if maybe the minister from that church would come and talk to them and officiate at the funeral. The church was a Lutheran church.

At this particular church, it was policy that if you were not an active, "dues paying" member, they would not marry you or bury you. I knew this but called the church anyway. The church was between permanent ministers and had an interim minister who happened to be one of the higher-ups in the synod of the church. As expected, when I called, he told me it was obvious that the deceased young man was already in hell and that he could not possibly do the funeral.

I was shocked and mad. All I could think to say — and it was probably out of line — was, "This may be the only time these people are searching for answers. Churches do all kinds of things to get new members, but the one time they come to you, you turn them away. You call yourself a minister and a man of God? I am ashamed of you." Then I hung up the phone.

There were several minister friends of mine whom I knew would have been more than happy to minister to this family, but I was busy and did not call someone else right away. About an hour later, the Lutheran minister I had spoken with called and asked to speak to me. He told me that after I had hung up on him, he had been frozen at his desk. He asked me, if it was not too late, could he minister to this family, saying that he did not think he could help the dead boy but knew he could help the family. I was hesitant, but I told him it was not too late and that he could talk to the family.

I don't know how the family turned out over time, but I do know that they heard about God, about hope, about forgiveness, and about salvation. The minister was warm to them and did an outstanding job of giving comfort to them. I do not know if the policies of the Lutheran church have changed, but at least, this one time, they did, and it made a difference.

Iowa

The Lutheran minister was riding with me in the lead car to the cemetery. He had not been in Michigan for very long, and he was telling me his observations of the Flint area. He said that there was a strange phenomenon here: when the economy was good, church attendance plummeted; General Motors took care of its people; they got weekends and holidays off, plus overtime pay, health and death insurance, and hefty pensions. When the economy was bad, followed by layoffs and few available jobs, church attendance rose, because that was when people looked to God to take care of them.

He told me he was from Iowa, a farming state, and that Iowans are people of the earth and depend on God and earth for their livelihood. When they have a bountiful crop, they praise God; when they do not, they ask God to guide them.

Son of a Bitch

The minister started out fairly well, but the more he talked, the more he started to ramble. In fact, he got off on tangents that had nothing to do with the deceased, funeral, or religion. He started telling stories about his own life experiences that had no relevance. He went on for over an hour.

When the service was finally over, everybody filed by the casket, paid their last respects, and then stepped out to their cars. The family spent a few minutes at the casket, and then they, too, were escorted to their cars. The casket was brought out to the pallbearers. With the minister leading, the casket was carried to the hearse and secured.

The pallbearers got in the back two rows of seats of the limousine. Unbeknownst to one of the pallbearers in the back seat, the minister got in the front seat. We had not yet started the procession to the cemetery, when one of the pallbearers in the back seat said, "Damn! That was a long-winded son of a bitch!"

It was silent all the way to the cemetery.

Baptist

Several ministers in town told me they would never get air conditioning in their churches. Our minister told me that if he was going to preach hellfire and brimstone, he wanted his parishioners to sweat. One Sunday at the church I formerly attended, the Baptist church, it was so very hot that the deacons had placed two large fans in the front facing the congregation, providing some relief. It was the first time parishioners had vied for seats in the front. After the church announcements, a song, and a prayer, and just before the sermon, the minister stepped up to both fans and switched them off. It was too late to remove our Sunday suit coats. I knew then we were in hell!

Our congregation wanted an air conditioner, but the minister wanted a new church more. Years later, he told me he had kept making up excuses why the church could not have an air conditioner: he believed the congregation would be too comfortable with air conditioning, which would stall any plans for a new church. A family in the church even donated money in memory of their son—one of my friends who was killed in a car crash—to put in air conditioning, but the minister said, "Only when we get a new church will we have air conditioning." The minister eventually got his wish for a new church.

***

One thing I cannot deny about the Baptist churches in town is that they have the best homemade pies at their funeral luncheons!

Another Church: Rev. John

Rev. John was a minister we called when a family did not have a minister but needed words of comfort. He met with the family, personalized the funeral, and gave a message of hope. We always asked the family to give the minister an honorarium of $200, though he did not require one.

One day, the minister came in the back door of the funeral home and asked us to omit his name from obituaries, memorial folders, and any other printed material unless the deceased was a member of his church. I, of course, asked him why, and he told me that certain members of his congregation said he was not paid to work for nonmembers and he should not be making money by serving other families. Rev. John deserves credit for continuing his ministry by reaching out to families in need.

OH, DEATH!

We all remember the "good ole days" when life seemed a lot simpler and carefree, but those days did not have all of the advancements in medical treatment that have been made and are continuing to be made, all which have increased our life expectancy.

Below are some of the more interesting causes of death I've seen in the old funeral-home records, followed by some of my favorites.

Consumption

While I was growing up, very little was known about cancer and other diseases, and, often, doctors could only treat symptoms because there were no cures. About the only thing they could do was try to control pain and keep the patient as comfortable as possible. When someone died from an unknown disease, there was a blanket cause of death: consumption, which was a progressive wasting away of the body. The term *consumption* was also often used when someone died from tuberculosis.

Tuberculosis

In Flint, there used to be a tuberculosis sanitarium. It was thought that people who suffered from tuberculosis needed to be in dark and quiet quarters if they were ever to recover. Many years passed before it was determined that sunlight destroys the tubercle bacillus, the bacteria that causes tuberculosis.

Carcinoma

When someone died from cancer, it was a taboo subject and people referred to it as "the big C." So little was known about the disease that people simply didn't want to talk about it. The cause of death was rarely diagnosed as a specific type of cancer; the term was "carcinoma" of whatever part of the body was affected.

Old Age and ASHD

In the early records of my funeral home, "old age" was a common cause of death. Later, the State of Michigan did not think "old age" was a medical cause of death and wanted something more descriptive. "Old age" was then often described as ASHD (arteriosclerotic heart disease). Even into the 1970s and 1980s, when doctors were asked to sign a death certificate and an autopsy was not performed, leaving them in doubt of the cause of death, they often recorded the cause of death as ASHD. That covered a lot of symptoms. Later, the State of Michigan ruled that the doctors would not only have to spell out ASHD but add, "as a result of ..."

Infant Death

All through my years growing up in the funeral home and even after I was a licensed funeral director, up to 10 percent of the deaths we handled were infants. It was so common that we added a display room that showed only infant caskets. In these cases, death was often recorded simply as "infant death."

Thankfully, medical science and prenatal care have come so far today that we rarely have infant funerals.

Two of My Favorite Causes of Death Recorded on Death Certificates

Broken Heart

It is uncanny how many people die within six months of their spouses. Many times, after being married and in love for many years, the surviving spouses lost the will to go on, and they soon fell into despair and stopped eating and taking care of themselves properly. Soon after, the immune system stopped working, followed by sickness and death.

Fatal Wound

With this diagnosis, the doctor, coroner, or medical examiner gave no further information about the type or cause of the "fatal wound."

Scary Causes of Death

Acquired Immune Deficiency Syndrome

When we first started hearing about AIDS (acquired immune deficiency syndrome), it had the same stigma that cancer had once had. Funeral directors were afraid to embalm people who had AIDS because they did not know how contagious the disease was. As soon as people were educated about the disease, however, fears subsided.

Creutzfeldt-Jakob Disease

This is a rare disease that affects the nervous system. Scientists believe that it is caused by a protein that cannot be destroyed and that the incubation period may last for up to fifty years. People can get the disease when there is no apparent risk factor and the disease is very contagious if a person is exposed to brain or nervous tissue. This can be very dangerous for doctors, lab technicians, and embalmers.

There is no treatment for the disease. When death occurs from this disease, direct burial or cremation is recommended. The body can be embalmed, but the entire embalming room has to be covered in plastic and the embalmer has to wear a hazmat suit; after the procedure, all plastic, clothing, and instruments involved have to be burned. Plastic embalming instruments are made for this purpose.

***

Some families do not disclose that their loved one had a particular disease, and, usually, we do not learn of it until the death certificate has been signed by the doctor. The State of Michigan, therefore, made it a law that all hospitals, if they are aware of a patient's communicable disease, are required to notify the funeral home before the deceased is removed from the hospital. As soon as the law went into effect, the hospitals sent letters to the funeral homes stating that it should be assumed that all patients could have a communicable disease and precautions should be taken.

Suicide

What I have learned is that when someone takes their own life, there are no what-ifs.

I believe people who decide to end their own lives truly feel that others are better off without them — or do not think about others at all.

I also think the pain, anguish, and suffering these people feel cause them to look at suicide as the only way to feel better.

There is attempted suicide where people, except in rare cases, do not succeed. Those people are calling out for help. When someone ends his or her life purposely, their loved ones should not feel guilty about it; there is little that could have stopped the suicide.

Untimely Death

A lot of bad things happen everywhere, but when a death—especially an untimely or unusual death—happens to residents of a small town, it affects the community. These are a few examples of the deaths of Flushing people. Things like this are *not* supposed to happen to our neighbors.

The Realty Managers

A married couple decided to go into the rental property management business. One day, they visited a house in Flint Township to collect back rent. When they arrived, only the adult son was in the house. He invited them in, went to another room, came out with a .22-caliber pistol, and killed them both.

The Drug Buy

A young man told his mother that he was going to run out and buy some refreshments at the convenience store. Instead, he went to Flint to buy drugs. A witness said he had seen him staggering across the road, heading for a house, when, all of a sudden, he fell to the ground. He had a wound from a sword that had entered his lower abdomen and exited the back of his shoulder.

Death by Sex

Before modern-day nursing homes, there was what we called an old folks' home on Elm St., located one block from the main downtown area. This was an old house where people, who could no longer care for themselves, resided with the owner of the home. The owner also hired aides to assist in the elderly care. I was not older than twelve when my father received the call that an elderly man had died in the home. My father needed help, so I went with him.

Entering the house, I noticed a faint smell of urine, which was common in such places. The decor was drab and the carpet was worn. We were led to a small bedroom where an elderly deceased man was lying in a bed with just a pajama top on. It was the first time I had ever seen a condom on a penis, but I knew it must be one of the "rubbers" that I had heard older boys talk about. I knew my father was embarrassed for me to see this. He gently reached down, removed the condom, and wrapped it in the sheet. Nothing was said, but I suspected the man died happily. I have always wondered if he was with another resident or one of the workers.

Sports

A big event in Michigan was the smelt run. Smelt from the Great Lakes came along the shore to spawn in the spring when the water started to warm. They came in by the thousands, usually after dark, when the water was the right temperature. People would stand in the water and scoop hundreds of the fish with a net. Putting full-body waders on over warm clothes, you could usually get smelt by wading out to about waist level. Hundreds of people from around Michigan would gather on the shores of Lake Huron, a favorite spot being at the Singing Bridge in the Tawas area, as the smelt made their way along the shore to the river.

Sadly, not everyone realized there was a sharp drop-off not too far from shore, just before the mouth of the river. Two young married men from Flushing made the annual trip to get smelt; one of them ventured toward the river and stepped into the drop-off. His waders quickly filled with water and pulled him under. His friend saw what had happened and quickly went to his friend's aid. He stepped too close and also went under. Sadly, they both drowned. It is almost impossible to get out of waders when they are full of water.

***

Another big event in Michigan is the opening of deer hunting season. Hundreds of men and women head to the north woods for the hunt. Two young brothers decided to go "up north" for the hunt, leaving late at night so they would be in the woods at first light. One brother was sleeping, it was dark out, and the truck was warm. Apparently, the brother driving fell asleep at the wheel and the truck veered off the road and crashed into a tree. The two brothers were laid out in the funeral home, their caskets together in the chapel. For the next two days, there was a continuous line of people paying their respects.

***

Many men head to the snow-covered fields to hunt. A lot of them sit behind desks for most of the year and get little exercise. Then they get out in the cold, usually after having a couple of beers, and try to drag a dead deer back to camp. Almost every year, we receive a call that a hunter has died of a heart attack.

***

The family lived just outside of town, on a large piece of land that had woods. The father was very happy that his boy was finally old enough—maybe thirteen or fourteen—to go deer hunting with him on their property. He told his son to wait in the blind on one side of the woods while he went to the other side to flush deer toward him. The man told his son to shoot in only one direction. Apparently, he forgot which direction he had told his son to shoot in. The boy's shot missed the deer, but the buckshot caught his father in the femoral artery. He bled to death before the ambulance could get there.

***

A friend of the General Motors executive convinced the executive to go duck hunting. They were in their duck blind when a bird went up. Just as the friend was bringing his gun around and firing, the executive stood to take a shot. He was killed instantly.

***

Another big sport in Michigan is snowmobiling. Sometimes the excitement of the season causes people to forget precautions. A family headed to the trails. One of the members of the group had never been on a snowmobile before and was at the back of the pack, following the others who knew the trail. It was a beautiful afternoon. Because of the cold, the snow on the trail was a fine powder. As the snowmobiles rounded a corner, they threw up snow, causing a whiteout for the young man in the back. He did not see the turn in time, crashed the snowmobile into a tree, and flew off the snowmobile, hitting the trunk of the tree. His ribs broke, puncturing a lung and an artery. He was conscious and said he was okay. His companions were able to get him to a main road where an ambulance was waiting. While the paramedics were wrapping the young man in bandages, he was talking to them when his eyes closed and he died. The cause of death was internal bleeding.

***

When I was growing up, pheasant and rabbit hunting were popular sports. This was when Flushing was surrounded by woods and farmland and there were no subdivisions. It was not uncommon for people to have their shotguns ready for the hunt. One day, some teenagers got together for camaraderie in the home of one of them. They had been out back, practice shooting a .410 shotgun, using slugs as ammunition. When they were finished, they had come back into the living room, and one of the boys had unloaded the gun and set it in the corner. Then they all went back outside. A brother of the boy who lived there came home and saw the shotgun in the corner and the shells on the table. He reloaded the shotgun and put it back in the corner, then left the room. When the other boys came back for refreshments, one of them picked up the shotgun, thinking it was unloaded, pointed it at his friend and fired, shooting him right between the eyes, killing him instantly.

A Simple Request

It was a warm, sunny summer day. People were outside enjoying the day, some planting flowers, others mowing. In a quiet subdivision, a man was trying to line up his tractor to the hitch on his trailer. He enlisted the assistance of his neighbor, a family man who was mowing his own lawn. He asked his neighbor to hold the trailer hitch while he backed up. Somehow, the driver's foot slipped off the clutch and the tractor lurched backwards, driving the tractor hitch into his neighbor's chest, killing him instantly.

The Farm

For many years, the Flushing area was peppered with small farms, often containing silos standing next to red barns. Before many of these farms became subdivisions, it was common to see tractors being driven in the downtown area on Saturday mornings.

Surprisingly, there were few fatal farm accidents, but I remember one well because I saw my father preparing the body for the funeral. The eighty-year-old farmer had had no intention of retiring. He had been harvesting his crop when he had fallen into a corn picker, which ripped his spine out of his body. That is not something you forget seeing.

Out Driving

It was a freezing-cold night, at ten degrees below zero. Two young men had been out for the evening and were driving to the home of one of the men when the car veered off the road, rolled over, and hit a tree, killing the driver. It was not long before someone discovered the wreck and called the police. They did not realize that two men had been in the car because the passenger had been thrown out of the car and into some weeds, where he had been knocked out but was otherwise okay.

It wasn't until the second man's family heard about the death of their son's friend that they started looking for their son. They went to the scene of the accident and found his body yards away from the wreck. He had frozen to death.

Conflagration

It happened a few blocks away from the funeral home. A man and his wife were cleaning their oily basement floor and decided that gasoline would be a good solvent. After they had cleaned part of the floor, the husband saw they were not going to have enough gas and left the house to get more. When the fumes hit the pilot light of the furnace, the wife was caught in a fiery inferno.

Oh My!

It was a slow day. My secretary and some of the staff were sitting in the office, talking, when the doorbell rang. It is unusual for someone to ring the bell outside during the day because the door opens into a foyer and a bell rings when the door opens. Outside the door stood a woman in ragged clothes, with hair that was not combed and looked like it had not been washed in a long time. She smelled badly of body odor and sweat, and she said she needed to talk to the undertaker.

My secretary took her to the lounge because my office is small and she knew I would not be able to stand the woman's smell. I sat at the table with the woman, who told me that her husband was dead and she did not know what needed to be done. I thought maybe she was on her way home from the hospital and we had not yet been notified, so I asked her where her husband was and when he had died. She said, "Oh, he's home in bed. He died two or three days ago. It has been hard for me to sleep with him next to me, but I didn't know what to do."

Knock, Knock

Mr. Ellsworth was a regular kind of man. I got to know him at the local morning coffee group that met at Skip's Come Back Inn. I had met his wife only a few times, when they had come to the funeral home for a visitation, but I knew she was several cards short of a full deck. She was very old-fashioned, wore no makeup, and her clothing looked like it was from the 1920s. She always had a befuddled look. Mr. Ellsworth told the coffee group stories of weird things she did, but, he said, she had always been faithful to him and he would never leave her. He didn't offer an explanation of why they slept in different rooms that were adjacent to each other.

One morning, the men at coffee wondered where Mr. Ellsworth was. Normally, if he was going to miss the coffee group, he would have told us so the previous day. Late in the afternoon of the day Mr. Ellsworth missed the coffee group, the funeral home received a call that Mrs. Ellsworth had found her husband dead on the floor in his bedroom, against the wall next to her bedroom. She explained that a knocking noise had kept her up all night and she had planned to mention it to her husband in the morning. When she had gotten up and didn't see him, she assumed he had probably already gone for coffee. When he didn't return from having coffee, she went to look for him and discovered him dead in his room.

The authorities think Mr. Ellsworth had gotten up in the night, fallen on the floor, crawled across the room to the wall opposite his wife's bedroom, and started knocking on the wall for help.

Mistaken Identity

One of two businessmen had a membership to the athletic club of the YMCA. He loaned his entry card to a coworker who was his friend. While the friend was playing paddleball, he suffered a heart attack and died on the court. At the hospital, where he was identified by the membership card, he was pronounced dead. The hospital called the wife of the YMCA member to notify her of her husband's death. Of course, she was in shock, but she rushed to the hospital with her two young children, only to find out that it was not her husband who had died.

Dream Vacation Gone Bad

The two married couples were finally living their dream to fly to a remote island located in a large lake in the north of Canada to fish. The float plane flew in to the lake and taxied to an island that was outfitted with a rustic cabin and a small boat; there was no form of communication to the outside world. The couples had brought all of their own food and bedding. The plane would return in two weeks to pick them up. They all bedded down in bunks for their first night in the cabin. In the morning, they discovered that one of the men had died in his sleep. The three survivors did not know what to do. The widow did not want to bury her husband, for fear that animals would dig him up.

They were in an area that was usually cool, but there was a heat spell going on. Decomposition was taking its toll on the remains, and the smell was unbearable, but the widow insisted that her husband not be taken from the cabin. The other couple made a makeshift shelter outside. There they remained, cooking outside and sleeping in their shelter until the plane arrived.

Luckily, the weather permitted the plane to land. The remains were in such a state of decomposition that the pilot would not bring them on board. Once the three survivors had returned to civilization, a rescue team retrieved the remains. By this time, the remains were in worse condition. The people in charge obtained a Ziegler case, a hermetically sealed metal container that is completely sealed and soldered shut. There were no roads to this area, and there was no one to fly the remains back to Michigan. I had a friend who owned a small plane and he offered to go because it would be a new experience for him. If he had only known what was in store for him, he would probably not have gone!

He flew to Sault Sainte Marie in the northern part of Michigan, and, from there, he flew into Canada and hopscotched to the remote area. Later, he told me that he flew for hours without seeing anything but trees. He said that if he'd had an emergency, there would have been no place to land and he would never have been found.

Upon his return, he had to go through customs at the Canadian/US border. When the customs officer saw the Ziegler case, he told my friend that he would have to open it and inspect the inside. When my friend showed him the permit to bring human remains into the United States, the officer said he still had to inspect the inside. My friend told him that would be OK but that he would taxi the plane down to the end of the runway and remove the container, then taxi back while the container was opened and inspected, and once the container was sealed again, he would retrieve it. The officer immediately stamped my friend's passport and told him to fly on out.

All I Want for Christmas

His wife loved having a live Christmas tree, even though she was highly allergic to pine trees. They considered purchasing an artificial tree, but, although her allergies had worsened, she insisted on a real tree. A few days before Christmas, he and the children went to a Christmas tree farm and bought the perfect Christmas tree. They brought it home, set it up, and waited for his wife to come home to decorate it.

She was very pleased with the tree, and the family got out the decorations and started decorating. It wasn't long before the wife started having trouble breathing. She insisted she would be all right, but, a little while later, she collapsed and died.

Part-Time Resident

The man had two homes: a house trailer on his property in the country, and a small apartment in the city. He would live in the city for a while and then go back out to the country for a while. When he was not at his trailer, people assumed he was in town, and vice versa, so no one checked on him regularly. When he had not shown up for work after he had been off a while, people started looking for him.

They found him in his trailer. He apparently had preheated his oven, placed a potpie in there, had a heart attack and fallen into the oven. When they found him, his head was burned to a crisp and the rest of the body was full of maggots. A swarm of flies came out of the trailer when the door was pried open.

Mary Sunshine

This was the night that changed Flushing forever. We were busy at the funeral home because we had been preparing for two funerals. It was past dinnertime when I called my wife and told her that on the way home, I would stop at the Mary Sunshine store and pick up some ice cream for a treat. I was leaving my apprentice, who was living in the funeral home apartment, in charge of the funeral home.

I was walking out the door when he asked me if I would mind waiting a few minutes while he went down to the local A&W to get some hot dogs and a root beer. I told him to go ahead.

After he returned, I drove directly to the Mary Sunshine store near my house. The police had just arrived because there had been a robbery and three people had been shot to death. The only witnesses were some kids who had been in a car, waiting for their friend. They had seen two men run out of the store, get into a car, and take off.

If my apprentice had not asked if I could wait, I, more than likely, would have been in that store when everyone inside was killed.

Residents of Flushing started locking their doors, waiting for the murderers to be caught. The three victims—two women and a teenage boy—were brought to the funeral home. For the next several days, we worked around the clock. People from all over came to pay their respects. Flowers came in by the hundreds; after the first day of the visitations, we stopped trying to place the flowers near the rooms where the deceased were lying in state; we placed them wherever we could find room. On the night of a rosary service, people were packed in the funeral home like sardines. The families received hundreds of letters and phone calls. It was truly a sad time. When the funerals were over, there were so many flowers that it took us more than a week to deliver or dispose of them.

The last funeral scheduled during this time was not for one of the murder victims, but for an old bachelor who had lived with his brother and sister-in-law. I was so tired, I hardly knew what was going on. On the way to the cemetery, I drove the minister and pallbearers in the lead car. As we approached a railroad crossing, the minister began shaking me and telling me to put on the brakes. I had fallen asleep at the wheel and we just missed hitting the train. Everyone in the car knew what we all had been through, so no one except the minister said anything. He simply said, "I think you dozed off."

The two men who committed the murders were caught. They had recently been let out of prison for good behavior. They killed three people and stole less than one hundred dollars. They were convicted and received life sentences without parole.

Carbon Monoxide, the Silent Killer

I hope this paragraph will save a few lives. It is amazing how many people do not have carbon monoxide detectors in their houses and garages. Every time the power goes out for an extended period, I think of the people I have buried who thought it would be okay to bring a gas-powered generator into their house or garage. Often, people working in garages think they can run their car, lawn mower, or snowblower as long as the garage door is open, but that is not true: carbon monoxide can build up even when the door is open. Please don't operate a gas-powered machine in an enclosed area. Also, invest in a quality carbon monoxide detector.

A Broken Heart

The woman brought her children up in the 1960s and they got into the hippie movement. One of her sons experimented with drugs and became addicted to the point that he was not able to function. He had been a bright man with a lot of potential, but now his mother and father were watching him fade away. She was so heartbroken that she no longer saw a reason to continue living.

I heard that people of her ethnic origin were known to commit suicide the way she did. She drank a bottle of Drano and it took a week for her to die. She suffered horribly, but the doctors could do little for her other than keeping her as comfortable as possible. She was a bright woman and a friend. Although she had been extremely distraught, no one expected her to commit suicide.

Cause of Death and Funeral Home Policy

When there is a death in a small town, it is not unusual for people to want to know what caused the death and the circumstances surrounding it. Unless this information is on the news, people look to the funeral director for answers. Some families do not care that people know what caused the death, but many do not want it discussed.

When I started out, some of my friends would be the first to call to find out what was going on. Out of respect for the privacy of the families, however, I do not give out this information. At first, to avoid offending anyone, I would simply answer that I had not yet seen the death certificate and did not know the cause of death, and that it would take a few days before a certificate was signed and filed. People became aware of what my stock answer would be and stopped asking. I also tell my staff to follow this procedure.

HOSPITALS

There are several hospitals in the Flint and Flushing area, some being better than others. These are some of my experiences with these hospitals.

Flint General Hospital

This hospital no longer exists, but it is still memorable. Of all the hospitals I've gone to, Flint General Hospital had the most unusual way to get to their emergency room. First, we had to park the ambulance on North Saginaw Street, a main thoroughfare. Then we wheeled the stretcher through the front door into the foyer. To the left was the reception area, and straight ahead was the elevator. We continued through the foyer and then pushed the elevator button. We had to wait for the elevator to come down to the main level. When the elevator arrived, the front door and the rear door of the elevator would open and we could push our stretcher through the elevator to get to the emergency room that was on the other side.

Flint Osteopathic Hospital

One night around one a.m., the phone rang. It was the admitting office at Flint Osteopathic Hospital, reporting that a man had died in their hospital and the family had released his remains to us.

When I arrived at the hospital, I went to the admitting office, where it was procedure for me to sign papers before we went to the morgue to retrieve the human remains, but this night, when I arrived at the admitting office, the woman behind the desk was frantic and told me she did not have time for me. She told me she did not care what I did because, "We lost a patient."

"You mean someone died unexpectedly?", I asked.

She said, "No, the woman was brought into the emergency room this morning, and sometime after she was admitted and before she arrived to her room, she disappeared."

The hospital had discovered that the patient was missing when her family had called to ask how she was and if they could talk to her. Everyone in the office was in a panic! They were running all over, looking for the woman. I had to wait for more than an hour before someone would let me finally sign the papers to take away the dead body I had been called to collect.

What I found out later was that after the hospital had admitted the woman and assigned her a room, she had been sent to get x-rays before going to her room. The x-ray department had been busy, so an orderly had shoved her gurney, with her on it, into a side closet to wait for a nurse to come and get her. He had closed the door and had not told anyone where she was. She had been in there for several hours when she decided she had had enough. She got off the gurney, got dressed (her clothes were under the gurney), went to the lobby, called a taxicab, and went home.

***

The son had stopped at his elderly father's house to check on the man and found his father lying on the floor next to his bed, barely conscious, so he called his father's doctor. The doctor said he would come over to the house but that the son should call the ambulance. My father and I arrived in the ambulance at about the same time the doctor arrived.

The doctor called Flint Osteopathic Hospital to say that one of his patients was coming to the emergency room, and, apparently, the hospital asked what the problem was. The doctor lowered the phone from his ear and looked at my father to ask, "What do you think is wrong with him?"

My father responded, "First of all, he is dehydrated."

Without another word, the doctor put the phone back to his ear and said, "Treat him for dehydration." Then the doctor put down the phone and said, "I have to go." Even though he was a local doctor, I never went to him for treatment after hearing that.

Genocide Hospital

"Genocide Hospital" is the term some of the area funeral directors use to refer to a certain hospital because we have heard so many stories of poor treatment and of families believing that the poor treatment was the reason their loved ones died.

My in-laws' doctor worked out of Genocide, so my in-laws went there when they needed treatment. Once, my mother-in-law suddenly had a heart attack and then had several more. Her heart was operating at only about 10 percent of its capacity. Although my mother-in-law had an advanced medical directive, the hospital basically ignored it and insisted that she be intubated. When my wife questioned them about performing this procedure, they refused to give her any information about it or whether they would ever remove the apparatus. My mother-in-law could no longer talk to anyone and was on a respirator when a nurse came in with a big smile and a menu in her hand. She looked at my mother-in-law, who was barely conscious, and asked, "Now what are we going to have for breakfast tomorrow?" My mother-in-law died a short time later.

My elderly, very independent father-in-law had a stroke and was 95 percent incapacitated, with no hope for recovery. He not only had very good health insurance, but also had a directive should he become incapacitated; it stated that he wanted to be kept comfortable but did not want any treatment. The stroke happened in the Upper Peninsula of Michigan, so we had him flown to Genocide because his regular doctor practiced there. The doctor my wife met, who was supposedly the top neurologist at the hospital, told her that he wanted her father to go directly to rehab. When my wife asked him what kind of lifestyle her father would have if he had rehab, the doctor said her father would remain at least 90 percent incapacitated. My wife then asked what would be the point of rehab, and the doctor replied that rehab was what was normally done. When my wife explained her father's directive, the doctor said, "So you want him to die. You don't want him fed, given water, given his diabetes meds, etc." My wife firmly told him that she wanted her father to be kept comfortable. She explained to the doctor that she was dissatisfied with the care her father was receiving at the hospital: he hadn't been washed or shaved, and he had terrific back pain, but they would only give him Tylenol for pain. The doctor, who was irritated that my wife would not agree to send him to rehab, told her, "You will have to get him out of here and into hospice because he isn't making us any money."

My wife couldn't believe what she was hearing. We made arrangements for her father to be taken to Avalon Hospice, where, indeed, they washed and shaved him, and gave him the pain meds he needed. They kept him comfortable until he died a peaceful death a few days later.

Somewhat General Hospital

Usually, when a patient died at Somewhat General Hospital, the hospital staff would ask the family to what funeral home they wanted their loved one transferred. After the family told the hospital what funeral home should be called, the hospital would tell them that they would notify the funeral home and, consequently, the funeral home would then call the family to set up an appointment to make funeral arrangements. The hospital, however, rarely notified us in a timely manner, if at all.

We would find out about the death after a family member called, wondering why we hadn't contacted them. One family used another funeral home because they were furious we had not called them. We had not yet been notified of the death, but when I called the family back, they told me that the hospital had told them they would call us and they believed that the hospital had done so.

I once called the hospital after a family notified me of the death of their loved one that had occurred eight hours previously. I asked the hospital why we had not been notified and the person in admitting told me they were busy and then added, "We are interested in live people, not dead people." Because of what happened to this family, when speaking before a group, I often tell the audience that if one of their loved ones dies at Somewhat General Hospital, they should call us directly, even if they are told that the hospital will call the funeral home.

***

When a person dies, a doctor or medical examiner has to confirm the cause of death and sign the death certificate. When hospitals call us, they always give us the name of the attending physician who is supposed to certify the time and cause of death. I am guessing that at least 60 percent of the time when we contacted the doctor whom Somewhat General Hospital informed us would sign the death certificate, the doctor told us he had never heard of the patient or hadn't seen him in years. We would have to call Somewhat General back and try to find a doctor who actually had something to do with the patient. Sometimes, we had to call the medical examiner because the hospital did not have a name for us. This is the only hospital where we still have this problem.

***

Somewhat General Hospital called the funeral home around one a.m. They told us that John Scott had died and we could come and make the removal. They also informed us that the family wished to be called in the morning. The hospital gave me the family's phone number.

When I called the family in the morning, I expressed my sympathies to the widow and asked when she would like to come in to make arrangements. The phone was silent. Then she said, "I just came from the hospital, and my husband was fine. What happened?" I knew then that the hospital had made a dreadful mistake, so I called the hospital.

I learned that two men with the same name had been admitted to the hospital. When the woman in the admitting department had been notified of the death, she had punched the name into her computer and had given me the number of the first *John Scott* listed, even though the computer did not show that he was deceased.

When I told the hospital personnel to call Mrs. Scott and apologize, they refused, telling me it was an honest mistake.

MEDICAL EXAMINERS and PATHOLOGISTS

I have rarely met a coroner or pathologist I did not like. Almost always, they have been cooperative and in touch with the needs of the next of kin. Once in a while, however, things do not go so well.

Optimist Club Lunch Meeting

One of my duties as the Lieutenant Governor of the Michigan District Optimist Club, a local service organization, was to visit the clubs in my zone to make sure everything was going all right and to see if they needed any assistance. I decided to attend the luncheon meeting of one of the clubs that was being held in the dining room of a Flint hotel. The guest speaker was Dr. Mueller, the beloved medical examiner for Genesee County. He reminded me of Quincy, M.E., from the TV show of the same name.

It is customary for this club to serve lunch for the first half hour and then introduce the speaker, who gives a presentation for the second half hour. Dr. Mueller chose to bring his collection of some of the most gruesome deaths that he had encountered, including photo slides of the autopsies from crash victims, burn victims, suicides, and murder victims. During the presentation, at least six men left in a hurry to run to the restroom and throw up their lunch.

MFDA Dinner Meeting

The Michigan Funeral Directors Association organized the district meeting to be at Zehnder's Restaurant in Frankenmuth, Michigan, a very large restaurant renowned for its family-style chicken dinners. The meeting was more a festive event rather than a business affair, so the wives and families of the directors were invited.

The meeting was in a lovely room, the service was good and the food excellent. The speaker was Dr. Spitz, the famed medical examiner who had been involved with the O.J. Simpson murder investigation, the Jon Benét Ramsey case, and other high-profile murders. He brought his slides of mutilated deceased people and of their autopsies.

Such a program would have been very interesting to other forensic specialists, but not to this group of funeral directors who brought their families with them. As I looked around the room, I saw a lot of the guests turning a peculiar shade of green. Many of them excused themselves.

The doctor talked on as if he were talking about the weather. Fortunately, no outsiders peeked into the room during the presentation!

AMBULANCE, REMOVALS, and TRIPS

Years ago, hearses were outfitted to be converted into ambulances because in small towns and remote areas there were no ambulances. Since funeral directors were always on duty, they were available to respond to medical emergencies.

The Babies

When I was growing up, we never knew what the next call would be: a death call or an ambulance call. There were some men in town whom my dad recruited to assist him on ambulance calls, but, this time, I went with him. I think I was about fourteen years old. The man who had called had said his wife was getting ready to have a baby and he was boiling water. (Doctors used to tell soon-to-be fathers to boil water, on the pretext that utensils might have to be sterilized, but mainly to keep them out of the way.)

When we arrived, the man met us in the yard and told us the water was boiling in the kitchen. We went into the house and he pointed at a door and said, "She is in there." At this point, my memory of the details becomes a bit foggy, but what I do remember has stayed with me my whole life. For the first time, I saw a new human being come into the world—a healthy, pink crying baby. I was completely and totally awestruck! Years later, when she was in her teens, I met the girl who had been born that day. She was just as beautiful as on the day she had been born.

***

There was a raging blizzard going on when we got the call: A woman was in labor and needed to get to the hospital. My father called Rusty McIntosh, who worked for the city, and explained the situation. Rusty got a bulldozer—I am not sure from where—and plowed a path down the road so we could get the woman to the hospital.

***

As we were rushing a woman in labor to the hospital, the barrier arm on the railroad track went down. It was a slow-moving freight train. As the train went by, the engineer spotted the flashing lights on the ambulance. He stopped the train and men got off and separated the train at the crossing to let us by. We made it to the hospital just in time!

Drunk

One night we received a call from a man requesting an ambulance for his father; we knew the caller because he had called so many other times. We assumed the father was intoxicated again—not in the normal sense, but poisoned by alcohol.

The son was desperate, he said his father was really bad this time and had to get to the hospital right away. That night, there was a treacherous storm going on. The streets were glazed with solid ice, and the weather was getting worse as the night progressed. The minute the ambulance came out of the garage, the rain hitting the ambulance turned to ice. My father and I pulled onto Main St. and very gingerly made our way up to Seymour Rd. The studs on the tires helped somewhat, but we were still swerving all over the road and it was hard to see because of the ice on the windshield.

When we finally arrived at the house, the son was waiting for us on the porch and started yelling profanities because we had taken so long to get there. He did not stop his tirade even as we were getting the stretcher out of the car.

Suddenly, my father pushed the stretcher back into the ambulance and headed for the driver's seat. When the man demanded to know what he was doing, my father said we were going back home to enjoy Christmas Eve with the rest of our family. The man yelled at my father, "You cannot do that!" My father told him that he did not use profanity and he did not want to hear his; he also reminded the son that we had not been paid for the last two trips to take the father to the hospital to get dried out.

The son then apologized and pleaded for us to take his father to the hospital. He even got his checkbook and wrote a check for the previous two trips and this one.

We took his father to the hospital, but it was not the last time he rode in the ambulance. His last trip was to the funeral home, dead, from alcohol poisoning.

Heavy

It was dark and rainy when we arrived at the old farmhouse. The man, who was most distraught, had called for the ambulance. His wife had fallen out of bed and was having difficulty breathing.

When we entered their bedroom, we realized right away we had a major problem. The woman who had fallen weighed about 500 pounds and both her legs had been amputated at the hip. We could not get under her or around her.

My father had a plan. He gathered all the pillows and cushions in the house. First, he piled some next to her and rolled her up onto them, then he made a higher pile and rolled her onto that. He kept doing that until, finally, we got her onto the bed. Then we rolled her onto the stretcher. Sadly, she died as we were taking her to the ambulance.

Sex?

While a woman's boyfriend was visiting, she started bleeding profusely from her vagina, so he called for an ambulance. It was dark outside when we arrived at a very small farmhouse out in the country. We loaded the woman onto the stretcher and put her in the ambulance. The man insisted he ride in the back with her. There is only one seat back there, but because the woman seemed to be stabilized and the bleeding had subsided somewhat, my father agreed.

We were just going through town, heading for Hurley Hospital in Flint, when we heard some shaking in the back. The streetlights were bright, so we could see into the back. The woman's boyfriend had crawled on top of her and was trying to have sexual intercourse with her.

Naked

The woman called often; usually seeking help for a fall or an illness. When the police or ambulance arrived, she was always naked.

On this particular call, which was before portable phones, she had somehow managed to make a call from the bathtub, where her toe had gotten stuck in the water spigot.

Jell-O

The woman had been making a large bowl of Jell-O salad for a wedding rehearsal dinner that was to be held that day at the home of her backyard neighbor. She had gotten up early to make the salad and was still in her bathrobe. Before getting cleaned up, she decided to hop the five-foot fence to take the salad over to the neighbor. While she was climbing the fence, however, her foot got caught in the top of the chain link fence. She went over backward, tearing her robe off and dumping the salad all over her.

When we arrived, she was hanging from the fence, stark naked, covered in Jell-O, with a twisted ankle. It was hard not to laugh!

A Bad Day at the Detroit City Morgue

When I was a student at mortuary school and working for a funeral home in Detroit, I once went out with one of the funeral directors to make a removal of remains from the Detroit City Morgue. The morgue was located downtown, in a large building that sat next to the street. To get into the building, we had to park on the street and roll our stretcher to an outdoor ramp. At the top of the ramp was a door leading to the body storage facility.

The man we had come to get had had a full autopsy. The zipper had broken on the body bag, so we just overlapped the edges over the deceased's face. The funeral director I was with did not wait for me to help get the stretcher down the ramp; he just started pushing the stretcher headfirst down the ramp. Suddenly, the front wheels of the stretcher gave way, jerking the stretcher out of the director's hands. The stretcher flew down the ramp, over the sidewalk, and into the street. When it hit the curb, the stretcher stopped, but the body didn't.

When the man's head hit the pavement, the calvarium (top of the skull) came off and blood flowed into the street.

In shocked horror the director yelled, "Get this body into the hearse! Let's get out of here!" As we left, there was still a pool of blood on the street and I wondered if it was a common sight in some parts of the city.

Port Huron

I hadn't been working for the R.G. and G.R. Harris Funeral Home for very long when my roommate, Stan, and I were asked to take the hearse to make a removal at a hospital in Port Huron, some sixty miles away. When we arrived at the hospital, the woman in the admitting department took us to the morgue, where eight bodies were on their own gurneys.

We went to the first one, moved the body onto our stretcher, and left the hospital. It was late at night and we were almost back in Detroit when I asked Stan, "You did check the toe tag to make sure we had the right body?"

He replied, "No, I thought you did."

I hadn't, and I knew the admitting woman hadn't. We were sure we were going to have to return to Port Huron to get the right body, so Stan pulled over on I-94 (a major highway), and I crawled into the back of the hearse, unzipped the body bag, and looked at the toe tag. We had the right body!

I have always remembered the name of the deceased, Roy Rogers!

A Flat

Many families came from the South to Michigan to work for the auto industry. Fairly often, a family would request that their loved one be taken back to their hometown for a second funeral and to be interred in the family cemetery. This story takes place before fast transportation.

I was still in high school when my father and I put human remains in the funeral home's station wagon for transportation to Kentucky: this was before air conditioning in cars and before interstate highways. On our way, we had to navigate through a fairly large town. The temperature outside was in the nineties, humidity was close to 100 percent, and traffic was slow. Then disaster struck!

We were in the middle of the town when a tire blew out. The spare tire was in a compartment under the casket, so we had to pull over, set the funeral flowers that were surrounding the casket on the curb, pull the casket out, and set the casket on the sidewalk. We worked as fast as we could, sweltering in our suits.

The lug nuts on the tires did not come off easily. The sweat—not just from the heat and humidity, but also from the stress of the situation—rolled off my body, soaking my clothing. No one stopped to help, but everyone was bug-eyed as they inched forward in the slow-moving traffic. Pedestrians were standing around, just watching.

We often used the station wagon as a makeshift ambulance, and we had a flashing light that could be attached by a magnet to the top of the car and plugged into the cigarette lighter. After we finished changing the flat and loading the casket and flowers back into the station wagon, my father put the flashing light on the car as we eased back into traffic. He then blew the horn and said, "Let's get the heck out of here!" Cars pulled over and we got out of town in a jiffy. It was a good thing we did not encounter a police car that would have wanted to escort us to a hospital!

When we finally arrived at the funeral home that was to take over the arrangements, the director took one look at us soaked with sweat and with grimy hands and asked, "What in the hell happened to you?" We told him he didn't want to know. We did not want the family to hear that their father had spent part of the day on the sidewalk of a busy street.

Trip to the North

I was driving a station wagon with a casket in the back, taking human remains for burial in a remote cemetery located next to an old country church in northern Michigan. I arrived in a small town, the nearest to the cemetery, around lunchtime, and I was hungry. I did not want to be conspicuous, so I parked behind an insurance office that appeared to be closed, walked out to the main street, and went into a Dairy Queen. Because I was the only one in there with a suit on, everyone glanced at me. While I was waiting in line to give my order, a cook in the back was looking out a window and yelled out, "That must be George in the wagon parked back there. They are going to bury him this afternoon!" Everyone stared at me. I could only shrug.

I took my food with me, drove down the block and ate in the car. I arrived at the cemetery early. I left the deceased in the car because the pallbearers would be carrying the casket to the grave. Since the committal service was scheduled for a bit later, I went into the church, adjacent to the cemetery, where women were preparing tables for the dinner that was going to be served after the burial. One of the women saw me come in and said, "We have been waiting for you. Gladys saw you drive into town and called us. We figured you must be hungry, so we prepared a lunch for you." There was a plate piled high with food at one of the tables. I was already full, but to be polite, I ate all of it. I was really full afterward; it was not a lunch — more like a Sunday dinner!

Country No-Name Cemetery

Whenever we have a funeral procession to a cemetery I am not familiar with, I take a ride to the cemetery ahead of time to check the route. On one occasion, the cemetery was about forty miles away and I was busy and did not have time to check it out. I usually do not go that far in procession, but, in this case, the family insisted, so I told the son of the deceased that I needed precise directions. He told me to take the main highway to Williamson Rd., turn right onto Williamson and go exactly 5.7 miles, and there would be a small unmarked dirt road that you could only turn right onto. He said I was to go exactly 6.2 miles on that road and turn left, and he told me there would be no signs because the cemetery was an old family cemetery.

I was driving the lead car, and the minister was riding in the hearse with me. I found Williamson Rd, and turned right, then went exactly 5.7 miles and spotted the small dirt road. I drove the 6.2 miles on that road and then turned left onto a two-track road. After I turned, my heart sank. To the left of me was an old farmhouse and barn, and before me was a field of pigs running every which way.

I was thinking it was too late to back up, but then the minister pointed up and said, "Look!" Way in the distance was a small hill with trees. We could see maybe six headstones on top of the hill. That was the cemetery. We had to drive through the field full of pigs to get to the grave.

Going Back to the Old Country

A man from Israel was visiting relatives in Michigan when he died. The family wanted his remains taken back to Israel for burial. Before we could ship the remains, though, we had to contact the Israeli Burial Society to make sure the family owned burial plots there. We also had to contact the Israeli consulate to get the required transfer and burial permits.

I called the nearest consulate, located in Chicago, and asked them what the procedure would be. The woman I spoke with was kind and gave me two options. She said I could come to Chicago to start the paperwork and that it would take about two weeks to complete, or I could contact a man at a certain phone number and pay him $600, and everything would be taken care of in three days. I asked her if this was the normal procedure and she told me it was; the man knew how to get around a lot of bureaucracy.

I explained to the family the arrangements would cost an additional $600. Then I called the Chicago phone number the woman had given me. The man answered the phone promptly but did not readily identify himself. I explained what I needed, and he replied that all the permits and the flight arrangements to Israel would be made. He said he would meet me at Detroit Metropolitan Airport at the airline freight terminal and that I should bring a check for $600, made out to him.

There was one other problem, a Catch-22. When remains are shipped overseas, security agents have to inspect the inside of the casket to check for contraband, explosives, or weapons — but there is also a rule that the remains have to be in a hermetically sealed container. This container cannot be opened until it has reached its destination. I asked this man how we could get around the dilemma, but he said not to worry and that he had everything under control.

Three days later, I delivered the casket with the remains to Detroit Metropolitan Airport at the predetermined freight terminal. The man was there and had all the paperwork. The remains were boarded on the plane to begin their way to Israel.

When I paid the man, and asked him how he had gotten into this business, he was up front with me. He said there were so many rules and regulations when shipping human remains overseas that funeral directors did not have the time to learn about or deal with all the paperwork. He saw a job opportunity and decided to learn all he could about what was required to ship remains to many countries and how to make the process go faster. He told me the consulates were happy with this arrangement because it saved them time explaining the regulations to funeral directors; they simply referred the directors to him.

I WANT a JOB

Over the years, I have hired many part-time people who serve as greeters. Many of them have worked for me for ten years or more, some over twenty years. They also clean the funeral home after visitations and funerals, park cars, go on trips to deliver or retrieve human remains, deliver flowers, and perform a host of other jobs that make my job easier. Most of these people work not necessarily for the money, but to have something to do after retiring. However, it does give them some extra spending money. The majority of these people who have worked for me have lived in the community and I have served their families. It is good for our clients to come in the funeral home and see their friends serving them. The following stories are about some of these employees.

Mary Ellen Zellers

Shortly after buying the business from my brother, I was short of staff, especially greeters. While standing in line waiting to sign up to donate blood at a blood drive at the local Presbyterian church, I was assisted by a volunteer, Mary Ellen. I had served Mary Ellen's family when her husband had died several years earlier, and she sang in the choir and was a member of the church I attended. I said hello to her and asked her if she would consider working at the funeral home, and she replied, "Yes.".

Mary Ellen worked for me for twenty-six years and retired in 2015. She treated every family we served with grace and compassion. When it came time for cleaning or setting up for visitations and funerals, she went right to work. She also filled in for other workers who needed time off or were sick. She never complained about anything. She has always been a first-class lady.

I have employed many people like Mary Ellen who helped the funeral home run smoothly.

Sergeant Major Robert Fate

Almost all of the independent funeral directors/owners have what I call a Bob Fate. Bob Fate worked for me for years and was my right-hand man. No matter the chore, he did it and never complained. Even though he may have not always agreed with what I was doing, he did as I asked.

Keep in mind, I pay only a tad over minimum wage. Bob had retired from the military and then worked for the city of Flushing. He had done a lot of jobs for the city, one of them being a gravedigger at Flushing Cemetery. After retiring from the city, he had come in the back door of the funeral home one day, looked in my office, and told me that he had always enjoyed being a gravedigger but now wanted to be on the front end of the funeral process.

I will never forget the first day Bob worked for me. It was very busy. We had two funerals that day and two to get ready for. Every time Bob came to me, I gave him a job to do, but he had already done it. For example, when I told him the flowers in the garage had to be delivered to the local nursing home, Bob replied, "I thought you would want that done, so I already did it." The chairs in the side chapel needed to be taken down and the chapel swept, but, again, when I suggested it, he replied, "I thought you would want that done, so I already did it." The cars needed to be taken to the car wash and to the gas station to be filled up. "I thought you would want that done, so I already did it." Finally, I told him to take a break.

For the next seventeen years that he was with me, I rarely had to ask him to do anything; he instinctively knew what had to be done.

Don Bolesta

There is an elevator lift in the garage attached to the back of the funeral home. We use this to bring not only bodies in and out, but also caskets, supplies, and flowers. It had been in use for many years when it finally refused to operate. I had no idea who to contact to fix it, so my wife found an elevator repairman in Detroit, whom I called. He told me to take the end unit off the motor and ship it to him, and he could probably get it back to me in about three weeks. This was not an acceptable option.

My neighbor, Don, had been a troubleshooter in the factory and had recently retired. When I went home for lunch that afternoon, he was out in his driveway, tinkering with his car. When I went over to see him, he said "Hello", and then I started telling him my story of woe. He listened to me for a few minutes and then asked if I would mind if he looked at the elevator. I told him to go ahead.

The next day, he came down and carried his tools into the garage. Around noon, I took a peek in and saw that he had parts scattered all over the floor. I decided not to say anything. Around 4:30 in the afternoon, he came to my office and told me it was all fixed and I owed him for the part that was needed. He said it would be sixty-eight cents. Then he said, "Never mind, I had the part in my toolbox." I asked him if he wanted a job.

He worked for me for many years.

Frank Pendell

I wondered why Frank kept working for us. The day he started, we had three funerals scheduled for the day. His job was to line up cars for the funerals. It started out cold and rainy, and, as the day progressed, the weather grew steadily worse. It started to snow hard along with the rain. The parking lot piled up with slush about four inches deep. Throughout the day, it alternated between rain and snow.

After the funerals, we were cold and soaked to the skin, but we still had to deliver cars full of flowers, some to the homes of the families and some that the families wanted donated to the local nursing home. The day finally ended at ten p.m. Frank looked totally wiped out. When I said I would not blame him for not returning to work, he looked at me and said, "I signed up to work. Didn't I do okay? After today, the job can only get better."

Frank was a keeper; he stayed on for many years and was a wonderful employee.

A Special Employee: The Snowplow Man

When it snowed, the first priority was the shoveling of the sidewalks and the driveway of the funeral home. When I was in school, my brother and I listened to the radio, hoping for a snow day, with the false belief that we could sleep in. As soon as it was light, however, we had to get out and clear the snow.

I think Rossell Funeral Home was always the first business in town to have its walks cleared. The driveway and parking lot were another matter, however. Because City of Flushing offices shared our driveway, once in a while, Rusty MacIntosh, a city employee, would drive the city snowplow through to clear the snow. It wasn't long, though, before someone saw him doing it and complained to the city council that if he did it for Rossells, he should do it for everybody. That ended that.

After that, my father hired Mr. Neff, a man who had a tractor with a plow. Helping Mr. Neff was fourteen-year-old Jerry Todd, who owned a tractor with a board attached to the back that he used to plow snow by backing up. After Mr. Neff could no longer clear the snow, Jerry kept at it. Along the way, Jerry obtained a bigger tractor and then a truck with a snowplow attached to it. Much later, he added a salting rig to the back of the truck.

Jerry is a man of many talents. He has been a cattle farmer, an automotive production worker, a cement contractor, and also an accomplished chef. More than fifty-five years later, Jerry is still plowing snow for Rossell Funeral Home.

***

In my years as a funeral director, I have also hired a few people who did not work out so well.

Victor

I hired a man, Victor, who had worked in a factory and had also been a committee man for the union. Victor was a local man, and I thought he would work well with my staff. I soon learned that hiring him was a mistake.

Just about every time I asked Victor to do any task, he told me how much he could get in a lawsuit if he injured himself. For example, one time I told him we needed to deliver some funeral flowers to a family. He replied that if he fell while loading them, cut himself on a glass vase, or twisted his back, a lawsuit would greatly reward him. When moving caskets, he told me if he hurt his back, my insurance company would be in trouble. Once, when we had to work into the night, he informed me how much it would have cost me in overtime if this was a union job.

I knew that if I fired Victor, he would find a way to collect unemployment and to bad-mouth me and the business. Luckily, something came up in his life that would not give him the time for this job.

When he came to me and told me how sorry he was that he was going to have to quit, I told him it would be hard to replace a man like him—and I meant it.

Ford

Ford was a good guy, but that was not why we called him one of the good guys; we called him that because he always wore a white cowboy hat. At the time, there was an ad on TV for a car dealership where all the employees wore white cowboy hats, and they called themselves "the good guys." We could not tell Ford to wear a black hat because we knew, when we hired him, that he wore the white hat all the time. People would not recognize him without it.

Although Ford was a nice man and tried to do his best, I sometimes wondered how he made it through the day. One day, we were sitting in the office when my father asked Ford to go out to the garage and get out the black Buick Electra to put it in front of the funeral procession for the funeral that day. A couple of minutes later, we heard a terrible squealing noise and a tremendous crash. When we went out the back door, we saw Ford walking toward the office. He said, "Geeeeeee, I put on the brake, and the car went flying through the back of the garage."

Another time, he was vacuuming in the chapel of the funeral home when we heard a screeching noise and started to smell something burning. Ford came into the office and said, "I hear a terrible noise and I can smell something burning." He didn't realize that the vacuum had run over the cord; the cord had become entangled under the vacuum, causing the cord to burn and the vacuum to screech.

We kept Ford on because he was a "good guy". Even though he made mistakes, he was a hard worker who always meant well.

Allan

I hired a man who had been a foreman in the factory at Buick. He was a good worker, but one day, I told him to go to the garage and get our station wagon, put the seats down, load the flowers left over from the funeral, and deliver the flowers to the nursing home. That should have taken him no more than forty-five minutes. After about an hour and a half, I started to wonder what had happened to him and thought maybe he'd had to make a stop somewhere. After about two hours, he came in the back door of the funeral home and said, "Say, how do you put the back seats down in the station wagon?"

Leonard

Leonard, retired from the factory and wanting something to do, heard that working at Rossell Funeral Home was a good job. When I interviewed him, he was clean, was neat, and had a good personality; it appeared he would fit in well with my staff. He worked as we needed him for two or three months.

I was very busy when Leonard told me he had to talk to me in private. I thought, *Uh-oh! He's got someone mad at him or he wrecked the car or broke something.* We went to my office and closed the door, and then Leonard proceeded to tell me how disappointed he was to be working for me. He said he had thought he and I would become pals and sometimes go for coffee and maybe go to lunch together. Then he told me that I rarely sought him out to say hello or to ask about his family. I explained that even though we worked together as a family, we had a job to do and I hired him to help get the job done. We often do not have time to socialize.

He replied that he was sorry but he could not work under those circumstances. He never returned.

Marvin

Quick learner, energetic, eager to learn new skills, Marvin was who I was looking for. I told him I would pay for him to take the class so he could take the exam to be able to sell funeral insurance. Then I received an e-mail from the State of Michigan saying he could not take the exam because he had been arrested.

I called Marvin into my office and asked him what that was all about. He said he had failed to tell me that he was going to be sentenced in two weeks because he thought I would not hire him if I had known.

Bye, Marvin.

Alice

We needed a secretary. A woman was working at J. C. Penney but she needed to work more hours, so applied for the job. She was neat, smartly dressed, and had secretarial skills. After a few weeks of working at the funeral home, she came to me and said, "I'm quitting. I'm not meeting any men here."

***

Over the years, some of my new employees have lasted only a day, for various reasons.

George

One young girl's car blew up when she was rear-ended by another car; she burned to death. I had to go to the hospital to retrieve her remains and I asked the new man to assist me. He had worked in nursing homes, so I thought he would be able to handle seeing a body. He did help, but after seeing those remains, he told me he would be ending his employment at the funeral home. A few days later, he was back working at the nursing home.

Wally

Wally had recently sold his shoe store and retired. He was active in the community and knew a lot of people in town. He asked if he could have a job as a greeter so he would have something to do other than sitting around at home. I explained to him that greeters don't just stand at the door, but also help clean the funeral home after visitations and funerals are over; we always need to be ready for the next day. He said he would enjoy working with us.

The funeral home visiting hours end at 9:00 p.m., but we do not tell families they have to leave at that time; sometimes they are still visiting with friends or it is difficult for them to leave the deceased. Usually, they do not stay past 9:30 or 10:00 p.m.

The first night Wally worked, the family stayed until about 9:20. After they left, we started cleaning the funeral home, getting ready for the next day. About 10:00 p.m. the phone rang. I answered it and Wally's wife said in a stern voice, "Where is my husband?!" When I told her he was still working, she asked me what time the funeral home closed. I told her 9:00 p.m. and then explained that people sometimes stayed a bit longer and after they left, we cleaned and got ready for the next day. She told me that since we are supposed to close at nine, she expected her husband home no later than 9:05; anything later would be unacceptable

Wally never returned.

Vern

I called Vern, who seven months previously had turned in an application to be a greeter, and he came right over for the interview. He was glad to finally get the job. A friend of his was already working for us and had told him what a great job it was.

Vern completed his orientation and was put on the schedule to start work in two days. The very next day, Vern came in and said his wife could not stand the thought of him working in a funeral home, so he would have to quit — though he never really started.

I Am Applying for an Apprentice Job to Become a Funeral Director

A young man called and asked if he could make an appointment to come in to discuss the possibility of serving his apprenticeship with us. He showed up on time, but when I started to tell him what his job responsibilities would be, he interrupted me. He said he wanted to get something straight right away: he would not work weekends, holidays, or nights and would not work over forty hours a week unless he got overtime pay. He told me his dad was a union man and if I had any questions, his dad was out in the car and would speak to me. I leaned toward the young man and told him, "First of all, this interview is over." Then I added, "My friend, go get a union job, if they will hire you."

***

A man arrived for an interview saying he wanted to become a funeral director and asked me to sponsor his apprenticeship. He showed up wearing a sweatshirt with the arms cut off and jeans with the legs cut off almost to his crotch, I told him right off that he should be looking for another profession. He stood up and said, "What! You don't like how I look?! You are narrow-minded!", and walked out.

***

When another young man called for an interview, I asked him to please send in his resume before coming in. He informed me he did not do resumes.

I did receive a resume from a young woman, however. Unfortunately, the many grammatical errors detracted from what she had to say.

Women in Funeral Service

For years, the funeral business was dominated by men. That has changed. Many women have entered the industry and have made wonderful careers for themselves. I have hired several women funeral directors and have enjoyed working with them as much as I have with male funeral directors.

Lindsay

I was having coffee with the "coffee group" at the local watering hole, Duffy's. This group was made up of retirees, local businessmen, city workers, and, of course, the local funeral director. The men, and sometimes women, met toward the back part of the bar and solved all of the world's problems, like coffee groups do the world over. There were always a few men having a drink at the bar. Some of them were coming off from working third shift in the factory and wanted a drink before heading home, and some of them were just always there.

One day, a big man came up to me and said in a gruff voice, "You need to hire my daughter! Since she was fourteen years old, she has wanted to be a funeral director. She has completed her schooling and apprenticeship and wants to work in Flushing." I looked at this formidable man and told him I didn't have any openings at the present but, if she would like to send me her resume, I would look at it and keep her in mind if something should come up. He said, "Okay", and went back to the bar and his beer. His daughter dropped off her resume that day.

A few months later, one of my directors, who was newly divorced and had a young child, decided to move to Florida to be near her family. I had a whole stack of resumes from people seeking a funeral director job and would never have looked at Lindsay's resume twice, but I remembered her father at Duffy's. When I looked at her resume, I decided to phone her. She was already working at a funeral home on the other side of Flint, but I told her I had an opening and asked if she would like an interview. She came over the next day, and I hired her. She has been with me for over nine years.

Sadly, her father has since died, but I did get to know and like him, and I will never forget the love he had for his daughter.

Dana

A woman came to the funeral home looking for a job as a funeral director. When I learned that her dog's name was Rigor Mortis, I hired her.

LAWSUITS

Accidents and mistakes can and do happen. I try to make the funeral home as safe and comfortable as possible. I also adhere to the laws governing my profession.

Some people are clumsy or are simply not careful. Some people are dishonest. Some people are looking for easy money.

A Slip Up

It was a beautiful summer day. Few people were at the visitation for the woman who was lying in state. A man came in from the parking lot and told us someone had left the lights on in their car, so I went in and announced this to the six or so people in the visitation room. A middle-aged woman jumped up and ran through the building, out the door, and into the parking lot. On her way to her car, she tripped, fell on the asphalt, and broke her kneecap. We heard the scream and immediately called an ambulance. She was taken to the hospital. I came back into the funeral home, went to the visitation room, and asked the family who the woman was. They said they had never seen her before.

I knew that when someone was injured on an individual's property, no matter whose fault, the property owner was liable for medical expenses. We have insurance to cover those types of liabilities. A few days after the incident, an attorney called and informed me that we were being sued for one million dollars in damages for negligence. He said that if we had not told the woman about her car lights, the accident would not have happened.

A few days after that call, a private detective came to the funeral home and asked me to show him where the woman had tripped. I took him to the parking lot and showed him the place where she had fallen. Then he asked me what she had tripped on. When I told him there had been nothing there but the asphalt, he looked at me and said, "No lawsuit here."

I found out the woman was a member of the same church where the deceased woman was a member. That explained why she had come for the visitation. About two weeks later, I ran into the minister of that particular church and told him about the lawsuit. He assured me the woman was not the type of person to sue someone unless she really thought the party was negligent.

A few months later, I ran into the woman's minister again. Before I could tell him how the lawsuit had ended, he told me, "You will not believe what happened!" His church had been having an old-fashioned tent revival in the back lot of their church. The woman who had sued the funeral home had fallen on a chair she had been sitting on and had said she'd hurt herself. She had sued the church for negligence. He said the church had found out that she had also sued Hurley Hospital, where she worked in the laundry room, and had slipped and fallen on the floor.

Based on this experience, I put a policy in place at the funeral home that if anyone is injured for any reason, whether staff or member of the public, whoever is on duty is to document everything that happened: time of day, the weather outside, who was there, who saw what happened, what was done, whether an ambulance was called, and what assistance was provided. As the next story demonstrates, it is a good thing I did.

The Aunt

It was a dreary, rainy fall day. The brick walkway coming into the funeral home was wet and had a few leaves that had blown onto it, not more than six or eight leaves. A woman who weighed, my staff guessed, about four hundred pounds came in the door and told our greeter that she had slipped on one of the leaves and was shaken up and needed to sit down. The greeter had her sit in a chair in the foyer and asked if she should call an ambulance. The woman said, "No, all I need to do is to rest a bit and I will be okay."

The greeter took meticulous notes about the event. She even alerted the family we were serving. They said later that evening that the woman who had fallen had told them she was fine.

About three months later, a niece of the woman who had fallen called and told me the family was suing us because, due to our negligence, her aunt was experiencing chronic pain. She said we should have raked the leaves and called for medical assistance. I put the niece on hold, went to my office, pulled out the injury report, and read it to her, even mentioning the names of the people who said the woman had told them she was fine. The niece hung up on me. I did not hear from her again.

Used to Be People Were Honest

The funeral home was recently sued again. Without going into the finer details of the events leading to the lawsuit, I will say that we were sued because the daughter of a deceased woman lied to me about her mother's marital status and legal next of kin.

Throughout my career in funeral service, I have endeavored to be honest with people and to treat them fairly, and I have expected the same from them. Times have changed. I believed this woman when I should have made her prove every statement she made. All the while, she and her husband had been setting me up. My attorney told me I did not have my "bullshit alert" turned on.

We were found innocent of any wrongdoing, but the insurance company paid the suing party $2500 to sign a paper saying this would be the end of it, and it cost the insurance company $26,000 to defend the funeral home. As soon as the case was settled, the insurance company stopped insuring the funeral home. The funeral bill for the woman's mother was $2500. The daughter is being sued by the legal next of kin for fraud.

UNPAID

I'm sure many people think the funeral director gets paid for his merchandise and services as soon as they are provided—not so!

Few people would want their loved one's legacy to be that of never having had their funeral paid and forever being in debt, but that is the legacy of many deceased persons.

I learned a long time ago that when you sue people for payment, what you often get from the court is a piece of paper saying someone owes you money. I have paid attorneys to go after money that I'm owed for funerals, but I have seldom recouped anything; in fact, the amount of money I am owed is in six figures.

These are only a few of the stories of families who have never paid for funerals or who paid for them years later.

Stilson

The family's name — at least the name they gave me — was Stilson. The deceased young man had been working on his car: he had jacked it up, let it down on cement blocks, and crawled under the engine; then the cement blocks had given way and the car had come down and crushed him to death. He had parents and several siblings. It was a fairly large funeral, and family came from all parts of the country. After the funeral, the father told me he would be in within the week to pay the expenses. He had already written checks to the cemetery for their charges, a check to the florist, and a check to the minister for an honorarium.

The next day, the family disappeared. All the checks they had written to hotels, restaurants, the florist, the cemetery, the minister, and others were bogus.

The funeral home could never find any of them. We were never paid for our services, casket, burial vault, obituaries, memorial folders, register book, or anything else.

Later on, I heard from a funeral director in Holland, Michigan, that when the father died, the family used his funeral home. The day after the funeral, the family had again disappeared, leaving bills all over town.

The family had seemed nice and the father's brother had been an officer in the military, but we could not find him, either. I wondered if he really was in the military or if it was a costume uniform. Different people in the community, who had known the Stilson family, said how nice they were and could not believe what they had done. The family's son is interred in an unpaid-for, unmarked grave in Flushing Cemetery.

Wanted

This family seemed really nice. The mother of the husband had died. The funeral service went well, and, as expected, the man and his wife thanked me. He told me they would be getting his mother's affairs in order and would pay for the funeral in a couple of weeks.

The mother had lived with her son and daughter-in-law in a nice subdivision in Flushing. After a month had passed and I had not heard from them, I decided to pay them a visit, thinking maybe they were waiting for insurance proceeds. When I arrived at the house, it was obvious nobody was living there; the lawn had not been mowed and there was trash alongside the house that had not been taken to the road. A neighbor saw me, came over, and gave me the bad news: about two days after the funeral, the son and his wife had packed up their car and disappeared. He said they were in debt and did not own anything, including the car and house. He also said there were suspected drug dealers looking for them, and he thought they had probably lit out for the west coast where they would not be found. They never were.

The Loving Husband?

Mr. Nullandvoid came to the funeral home to make arrangements for his wife, who had died from cancer. He and his wife had two young teenage boys. As in the previous tales, the funeral went well, but, after a month, I had not heard from him. He lived in a nice house in town and drove a new truck, but he would not respond to phone calls or billings. Finally, I paid him a visit.

When I arrived, he was in his backyard with his boys and was talking to a neighbor woman. He did not recognize me right away, and when he asked who I was, I told him I was the funeral director whom he had not paid for his wife's funeral. He yelled at me, saying this was no time to talk about it. He came with me to the car and told me that he had been out of work, had no money, and did not feel any responsibility to pay for his wife's funeral. He never did pay for it, either.

The Faithful Father

The brother of a high school classmate of mine died an untimely death. The man's father and my former classmate came to make the arrangements. My classmate told me that he would take care of the bill for the funeral. I had known the family for years and had no reason to believe he would not keep his word. I was wrong.

My former classmate, who lived out of state, did not respond to my billings. When I was finally able to contact him by phone, he told me he would look into it, which I knew meant he had no plans to pay.

I found out that his dad lived in a travel trailer in Florida, and I was able to contact him by phone. When I told him that I had not been paid for his son's funeral, he responded by telling me he thought his other son was taking care of it. I explained that his son had told me he would be taking care of the bill, but now did not seem interested in paying me. My classmate's dad did not have money to pay, but he had a whole-life insurance policy. He cashed in the policy and paid for his son's funeral with the proceeds.

A few years later, the father died, and when my classmate found out what had happened and that there would be no insurance proceeds, he was livid. He wanted that insurance money, even though he did not need it. He and his wife both had good jobs, lived in a big home, and drove Cadillacs. He knew I would not serve him again, so he called another funeral home to handle funeral arrangements. I thought about calling the other home to warn them, but I didn't.

Try and Get Me!

The mother of a former classmate of mine died. All the family (husband, children, brothers, and sisters) came to make the funeral arrangements. When I told them when the bill had to be paid, the husband said he would be taking care of it, and my classmate assured me there would be no problem.

When I had not heard from them by the due date of the bill, I discovered they had all left town. A friend of theirs had heard one of the family members mention the name of a town in Kentucky, so I used that information to find a phone number for the husband. I called to ask him about the bill. First, he asked me how I had found him and who had told me where he was. Then he said, "Try and get me!"

My former classmate lived in Burton, a town adjacent to Flint, about twenty miles from Flushing. I found his telephone number, but when I called, his wife kept telling me her husband was not at home. He would not return my calls. Finally, I called on the weekend. Again, his wife answered. I could hear her husband in the background, but, again, she said he was not home and that if I did not stop calling them, they were going to sue me for harassment. She told me they did not feel any responsibility to pay for her mother-in-law's funeral. I was never paid.

Deadbeats

A young boy and his girlfriend decided to commit a double suicide. I do not know all the story, but the two were in a motel room when the boy put the barrel of a rifle to his head, and fired. It scared the girl so much that she called the police.

The boy's family was fairly well known in the area—for being deadbeats. I told the family I would handle the arrangements but I needed cash up front. They said they did not have the money, but they begged me to serve them and said they would pay me.

I did, they didn't, and all I got was my piece of paper from the court. Years later—something like ten or fifteen years later—the family came in and paid me. I did not charge interest.

It turns out that they wanted to buy a hot tub and a credit check revealed the family owed for a funeral. The store refused to extend credit and so the family decided to finally pay me so they could buy the hot tub on credit. I knew the people who owned the store where they wanted to purchase the hot tub, so I called and gave them a warning.

The family did not get their hot tub, at least not from that store.

Vietnam War Soldier

A Vietnam veteran died penniless. He had received disability money from the government for his war wounds, but just enough to barely subsist. His mother lived in town and told us that he was a drunk and she did not want a funeral, only direct cremation. When I asked if he had any other next of kin, she said he had a son but she doubted it was really his son. Legally, the son is the next of kin and he would have to be the one to sign the permission form for cremation.

The son was in the military and stationed in Texas. He flew right out when we contacted him. When he arrived, he told me that he did not want his father cremated and he wanted a funeral. He told me he would try to raise the funds to pay for it. When his grandmother heard about this, she said she would have nothing to do with the funeral — but she did come.

I felt sorry for the son, and because his father was a wounded war veteran, I told him there would be no charges for the funeral. I asked only that he pay for the obituary, which was $150. That was the only bill he received.

He thanked me and said he would send the $150 in the mail. He never did.

One Last Fling

Sometimes, as with the family who wanted a hot tub, I get paid years later. In one such case, a woman's husband died. He had a substantial life insurance policy that was to pay for the funeral, but they had no other savings. As soon as the widow received the insurance check, she disappeared for several months. Later, she stopped in to say she had spent all the insurance money for a trip to Hawaii that her husband had always promised her, but she assured me that she would get a job and would pay me a little each month. She did. She paid $20.00 every month for years until the funeral bill was paid. I did not charge interest.

THIEVES

You would think that people coming into the funeral home or church to pay their respects would also respect the premises, but that is not always the case. Over the years, several items have somehow disappeared.

When smoking was popular, we had a smoking lounge and the ashtrays invariably disappeared. We then purchased some very large crystal ashtrays, the largest ones we could find, and they, too, disappeared.

There is a wheelchair lift just inside the main door of the funeral home. There was once an emergency release key that we needed in case the lift got stuck during a power outage. I wanted to be sure the key would be handy in case we ever needed it, so I purchased a decorative ginger jar, put the key inside, and displayed the jar on a table near the lift. The very first night, the ginger jar and the key took a walk, never to return.

My mother had a collection of fine figurines, and she displayed some of them on tables in the funeral home. One evening, just as the mourning family was leaving the funeral home, I noticed that one of the larger figurines was missing. I had just seen it, so I knew one of the family members had taken it. When I confronted them about the figurine, they hit the roof and called me every bad name out there. How dared I accuse them of stealing! They said they would never use our funeral home again. I did not apologize, because I knew one of them had taken it. Twenty years later, the family came back to use our services. The widow asked if I remembered the missing figurine, and I said I could not forget it. She then proceeded to tell me that her sister had been unable to resist taking it that night and everybody in the family knew it. They did not return the figurine.

Something that has happened more than once is that a special floral arrangement will be on display and when the family is ready to go home, the arrangement is gone. Often, we are accused of not keeping an eye on things. Usually, a family member wants the arrangement and doesn't think the rest of the family would want them to have it, so they just take it.

Once, the widow of a friend of mine asked us to take the funeral flowers to the church for her husband's funeral. After the committal service at the cemetery, we returned to the church, got the flowers, and then delivered them to the family. Upon receiving the flowers, they told me that one arrangement was missing, and they accused me of losing it. I told them that someone had to have taken it as we were walking out of the church. They assured me that could not be the case and expected me to call the florist and have a new one delivered. It cost around a hundred dollars for me to replace the arrangement. About two years later, the widow told me that her sister had taken the arrangement; this way, they both got one. She never offered to pay for the second arrangement that I had had delivered.

When I was working in Detroit, one problem came up every now and then: A person would come into the funeral home, express his sympathy to the family, saying he was a friend, walk up to the casket, carefully remove jewelry from the deceased, and quietly walk out.

In another case involving jewelry, a widower brought in a ring. He told me that he had paid twenty thousand dollars for it and wanted it placed on his deceased wife's finger. Remembering what happened at the funeral home in Detroit, I told him I would do that but we would not be responsible if something happened to the ring. He was most upset but took the ring home after the visitation. The next day, he put the ring back on his wife and she was buried with it.

He didn't really accuse us of stealing, but he wanted us to pay for his mistake. I was sitting in my office when a widower walked into my brother's office, which was adjacent to mine. The widower's wife had been buried for two days. He asked my brother, "Where is my wife's watch? That is an expensive watch that her family bought her, and they want it back." My brother told him that the watch had been left on her wrist, according to his instructions. He hit the roof, saying he had never said such a thing, and he demanded we pay to have his wife's remains disinterred to remove the watch *and* that we purchase a new burial vault and have her reinterred. That was when I stepped into the hallway outside my brother's office and told the man that I had been sitting in the next room the night he had told my brother not to remove anything from the casket, including the watch. He turned pale and said, "Okay, her family wants the watch. I'll pay for it."

In another case, a woman's funeral was held in a church. Just before we closed the casket, her son approached me and said the family had changed their minds and wanted to remove the personal items they had placed in the casket. There were pictures, crosses, flowers, a necklace, and her glasses. After we arrived back to the church for the funeral luncheon, I handed the man the items I had removed. About two hours later, he called the funeral home and told me there had been two rings that were going to be given to the children. When I told him I had not seen any rings, he insisted that I pay to have his mother disinterred to retrieve those rings. I did. It cost about $1,500 for the disinterment and reinterment. The burial vault was not damaged and so, fortunately, I did not have to replace it. We arrived at the cemetery as they were lifting the lid off the burial vault. I opened the casket and I could not see any rings. The lady was very big—no, fat, very fat. The folds of skin on her hands hid the rings. I told her son there was no way I could remove those rings unless they were cut off. He said, "Just bend them off. They came out of Cracker Jack boxes."

There was a time when just about everyone who worked in the funeral home smoked. My brother and I both smoked pipes, but we only smoked when we were in the office. My brother had been visiting with the family in the chapel and returned to his office to see that his pipe was missing from his desk. He thought I was playing a joke, but I wasn't. He had a feeling that one of the grandchildren of the deceased had taken it, so he went to the parking lot and found his pipe in the ashtray of a car. He called the local police. When the culprit came out, the policeman not only read him the riot act, but also yelled in his ear, "Who on God's green earth would steal another man's pipe?!"

PEOPLE in a SMALL TOWN

Here are a few stories about people who have impacted my life growing up as well as after I became a funeral director. I hope they give the reader a sense of what it feels like to grow up in a small community.

Mabel Shotwell

Each time we made a removal of a deceased person from the local nursing home, one of the caregivers there was adamant that we be discreet so no one would know we had come and gone. She did not want any of the patients to realize that someone had died, and she told us to be "invisible". I wondered what she thought the residents surmised when the deceased person did not show up for mealtime or the daily card game, not to mention once the resident's room had been cleaned out.

One time, a resident died and we were called to make the removal of the remains. This nurse met us at the door and told us that the residents were just starting dinner, and because the deceased's room was on the other side of the dining room, we would have to wait until dinner was over, because there was no door to close as we passed the dining room. When I told her we could not wait, she said we would have to run by the door with her on the side facing the dining room so no one would notice. The first time through, no one paid much attention to us, and we arrived at the deceased's room undetected.

After we put the deceased on the stretcher and started back down the hall, the nurse was there to plan our exit. She said that, in case someone saw us, we should keep the deceased's head exposed so the residents would think we were headed for the hospital. We were to quickly go by the door with her, again, facing the entrance to the dining room.

On the far side of the dining room sat ninety-year-old Mable Shotwell. Mabel's son-in-law worked at the funeral home and always referred to her as Mother Shotwell, so everyone else did, too. She was a feisty lady and had a high, shrill voice. She spotted me as we were making our quick exit by the dining room and yelled, so I would hear her, "HEY, RALPH! WHO DIED NOW?!" The nurse almost fainted.

Mrs. Hardy

After my brother abruptly left the business in 1988, it was a trying time for me because there was a big transition going from a partnership to being the sole owner. A letter I received helped me, however. Geraldine Hardy and her husband had been friends of my aunt and uncle, so I knew who they were but did not know them well. When Mrs. Hardy's husband died, she called on me to serve her family. That was when I became better acquainted with her.

Shortly after taking over the funeral home, a letter arrived at work addressed to me personally. Mrs. Hardy wrote some of the most encouraging words I have ever read, and they came at the perfect time. She and I became good friends after that; I called her my secret girlfriend and she called me her secret boyfriend. We exchanged birthday cards, only signing "your boyfriend" or "your girlfriend."

Years later, when this grand lady died, I stepped up to the podium at her funeral to express my gratitude to her family for the encouragement their mother had given me, but I was silent. I could not say a word because the lump in my throat was too big. I just stood there with tears streaming down my face. I could only step back and sit down. After the funeral, a man came up to me and said, "Don't feel bad. Your emotions said it all." I still have the letter she sent me in 1988.

My Paper-Boy Family

When I was in grade school, I peddled the *Flint Journal* to all the people living on the west side of the river. The main two blocks of downtown are on the east side of the river, and the papers were dropped off at the Farrar's house on the corner of Main and Terrace. They let me come onto their enclosed porch to fold the papers before I delivered them. I really appreciated having that porch in the winter.

I had about a hundred customers and got to know most of them very well. My parents used to wonder what I was doing when I left the house Saturday morning to collect the money for the papers and didn't arrive home until dark. We had a parakeet, Skippy, that recited, "Where's Ralph? Where's Ralph?" before every meal because they asked the question so often.

I liked to talk to all of my customers while they were finding the half dollar to pay for a week worth of papers. My take was two cents per customer. I became lifelong friends with most of my customers. This is how it usually went: After folding the papers at the Farrar's house, I stuffed them into my newspaper pouch, slung it over my shoulder, and headed out. While collecting, I spent a little more time with some customers than with others. I worked my way up Main St. to Frank Bailey's fuel-oil business (presently Roaring Twenty's Ice Cream Parlour) and talked to him. He had a candy counter in the station and we always flipped a coin for a candy bar. It was uncanny, but I won every time. There was no way to cheat. Frank thought I was cheating, but I wasn't. Then I would make my way up to Mr. and Mrs. Hoy's house. They lived next to the lumberyard. Mrs. Hoy always made cookies every Saturday morning and invited me in for some warm cookies and milk. Then I would cross over Main St. and head up Lynn St. I always hoped that Mrs. Way would be making fudge. Sometimes I had to wait until it cooled. Then, a little way up the street, old Mrs. Neuman would be making cinnamon rolls. Nothing like cinnamon rolls right out of the oven!

Finally, I made my way down Oak St. and then headed up Terrace St. to River Rd. When I reached my last customer on the south side of River Rd., I started back on the river side. If I timed it just right, Mr. and Mrs. Scutt would be having their lunch and would invite me in. In the summer, they ate outside at their picnic table. Then, next door, I stopped in and talked to the Murrays. One year, Mrs. Murray wrote a poem about me and gave it to me for Christmas. I still have it tucked away somewhere. By the time I had finished collecting, it was just getting dark when I crossed back over the river.

One time, after I finished delivering papers, I started getting calls from customers who said they had not received their paper that day. They were all calling from Lynn St., so I had an idea of what had happened. Old Mr. Rosencrantz had trained his cocker spaniel puppy to meet me at the end of the block to fetch his paper every day, so as soon as I turned the corner onto Lynn St., the dog came running. That night, I rode my bike to Mr. Rosencrantz's house and found that there, on the front porch, was a stack of papers sitting next to a cocker spaniel who was wagging his tail and looking very proud of all the papers he had collected.

The only customer I had on the east side of the river was the local bar, LaBarge's. My friends were jealous because inside, over the bar, was a large life-size print or painting of two scantily clad nymphs frolicking in the forest. I opened the door, dropped the paper on the bar, paused to take a look at the picture, and walked out. One Saturday morning when I was coming out of the bar, one of the members of the Baptist church (my church) was walking by. He stared at me and said, "What are you doing in that den of iniquity?" I do not know what possessed me, but I looked up at him and said, "Mr. Murray, I can't get through the day without a nip." His face became a crimson red, he turned, and all I heard was, "Hmmmmgh!" I wondered if he would be calling my father.

A few years ago, while I was shopping for groceries in Bueche's Food World, one of my old paper route customers came up to me and gave me a big hug. He had tears in his eyes, which made me believe something terrible had happened, so I asked him what was wrong. He told me that nothing was wrong; he had known me since I peddled papers and was glad that I would be there for his family when they would need my services and, at a time like that, his family would be so glad to know someone whom they could trust. I have served many of my former paper-route customers, and I still think of them as family. That is the joy of living in a small town.

Chester

Chester always seemed to be happy, but he was also cautious and very tight with his money. One day, he had a lawn tractor for sale in his yard for $450. A man stopped and wanted to bargain, so he asked Chester if he would change the price. Chester said, "Sure!", and made it $500; Chester would not be bargained down. The man bought the mower for $500. Chester laughed and laughed when he told the coffee group.

Another time, Chester came to the coffee group with a big grin on his face. He told everyone that he had just sold an old locked trunk in his garage sale for fifty bucks, even though it wasn't worth five. He told people the trunk had been locked up for years and he had lost the key. Of course, people thought there could be a treasure in there, but Chester laughed and said all that was in the trunk were letters that he no longer wanted, that had been passed down in his family for generations. One of the people at the table said, "Chester, were there stamps on those old letters?" Chester left with a big frown on his face.

Vern

Vern and Ralph met on the street one day.

"How you doing, Vern?", Ralph asked.

"Not so good. Not so good.", Vern replied.

"Why? what's going on?"

"We got ants.", Vern explained.

Ralph suggested helpfully, "You will probably have to clean out your cupboards and get some ant poison."

"No, we got lots and lots of ants."

"Yeah?", Ralph asked curiously.

"My wife and her girlfriend wallpapered our entire house. They had the idea that if they mixed Karo syrup with the wallpaper paste, the wallpaper would stick to the wall better.", Vern explained with a sigh. "It did, and ants love Karo syrup!"

Elwood

My brother and I were down at the local pub, sitting with the morning coffee group. Elwood came in the front door, saw my brother sitting there, came over, and asked him, "Raymond, what is the difference between a regular funeral and cremation?"

My brother looked up and replied, "Elwood, about two thousand degrees."

"I knew I shouldn't've asked!", Elwood said, then turned around, went to the bar, and ordered a beer.

Herman Wheeler

Herman Wheeler owned the funeral home before my family did. He always told everyone that he had not gotten his high school diploma from Flushing High School because he had refused to give a speech at the graduation ceremony.

Herman was somehow related to John Bulger, who owned Flushing Hardware and Lumber, and after hearing that story, John thought it would be a good idea to contact the school board and see if they would present a diploma to Herman. In addition to John, a group of people petitioned the school board to prepare a diploma for Herman.

For Herman's ninetieth or hundredth birthday—I don't remember which—there was a big party, and Herman received his diploma. There was even a write-up in the local paper.

About a month later, as I was cleaning out the attic of the funeral home, I found, in a large ornate frame, Herman's original diploma! I showed it to John, and he was upset, saying, "Well, that ole ...!" He told me to never mention it to anyone. The original diploma, dated "27th day of May A.D. 1899", hangs in the museum that is in the funeral home.

Herman lived to be 103; at the age of 100, he was upset when his doctor told him to stop dancing.

Elmer

There were several morning coffee groups in town and one of them met at the Park Restaurant. One day when I was there, Walt Parkhurst, who worked at the funeral home, told about seeing Mrs. Piper, a well-known lady in Flushing, at Fostrian Manor Nursing Home while he was visiting his mother-in-law, Mrs. Shotwell. He said Mrs. Piper was doing well.

Elmer, who was sitting at the table with us, could not hear too well. What he did hear was Walt mentioning Mrs. Piper and the nursing home, so he assumed that because Walt worked at the funeral home, the lady must have died. He went right home and told his wife, Clinnie, and she immediately got on the phone to tell everyone she knew about the death.

The next morning, the florist arrived at the funeral home with several funeral arrangements for Mrs. Piper and the funeral home started getting phone calls from people inquiring when the visitation and funeral would be scheduled. I realized what had happened, so I called Clinnie and asked if her husband had told her that Mrs. Piper had died. She said, "Yes, and I felt so bad. I phoned all my friends about it."

Another time, Elmer, a not very big man, was leaving the funeral home after visitation and I wondered if he had lost a lot of weight, because his coat looked three times too big for him and was dragging on the floor. A little while later, Cecil Angus, a big man, was trying to put on his coat, but he could not get his arm into the sleeve because it was so small. I told Cecil I thought I knew where his coat was. I called Elmer's house, and when his wife answered the phone, I asked her to check Elmer's coat. It was Cecil's.

The Ring

Albert came to see my uncle Norman, who had arranged for the funeral and burial of Albert's wife several years earlier. My uncle inquired what he could do for him, and Albert said he wanted to take a look at his wife. That was an unusual request, but the man paid for the gravediggers to dig up the grave, lift the burial vault out of the ground, open the vault, and expose the casket. Not knowing what the man might see, my uncle told Albert that he (my uncle) had better take a look first.

Albert agreed, so my uncle opened the casket. The embalming process had done a good job of preservation and her remains were presentable, so my uncle motioned for the widower to step up. Albert looked down into the casket, reached into the casket, removed his wife's wedding ring, turned around, and threw the ring as far as he could. Then he told my uncle, "You can close it now. I am going to get married." He had told his wife that as long as she had that ring on, he would never look at another woman.

Surprise! There Might Be Some Skeletons in the Closet ... along with a Few Relatives

Sometimes when someone dies, unwelcomed family secrets are revealed.

Extended Family

I knew the Charles family very well because they were also members of the local Baptist church, where I had been raised. Mr. Charles worked in the community, and he and his wife were active in numerous organizations. They had two children, both boys. When Mr. Charles died, a young man who looked just like son number one, came into the funeral home. He introduced himself as the son their father had had while still in high school, but by another woman. This is how Mrs. Charles met her stepson and her boys met their half-brother.

Another family learned that they had more, unknown family when a man named Bart died in the hospital with his family surrounding him. While Bart's only son, along with the son's wife and two children, were in the room, three young people came in. One of the grandchildren asked who the three were, and the three newcomers replied they were Grandpa Bart's grandchildren.

Ernie and the Second Spouse

Sometimes the true nature of a second spouse is revealed upon the death of their husband or wife.

Ernie was a heck of a nice guy. Everybody liked him. He, his wife, and their three boys were beloved by everyone. The boys were all grown and had their own families, but they still spent a lot of time at their parents' home. There was a barn near the old farmhouse, and they all met in that barn to work on cars, motorcycles, snowmobiles, and other equipment. They also used the barn to store things they did not have room for at their own homes.

It was sad when Ernie's wife died. He and his wife had been very close and, after her death, he was very lonely. The boys hoped he might find a mate. Their wish came true not too long after the death of their mother.

Ernie met a woman he liked a lot, and they were married three months later. Sadly, five months later, Ernie died. Everyone was sad and felt sorry for his widow. About a week after Ernie's death, one of Ernie's sons showed up at his father's house to retrieve some of his tools from the barn, only to discover that the barn had a shiny new lock on it. He went to the house and found that had a new lock on it, also. After he knocked on the door, Ernie's widow answered and told him to get off her property. He was taken aback but explained that he was just there to retrieve some of his tools. She told him that everything on her property was hers and that he should tell the rest of his brothers to stay away, too.

One of the sons came to me and asked me what they could do to retrieve their property, plus some of the photos and keepsakes that had been in the family for years. When I asked if his father had left a will or had a prenuptial agreement, he said, "No". I told him that his father had either trusted his wife would do the right thing or wanted her to have everything. In any case, she had it all.

I could write a whole book about how many times second spouses refuse to accommodate stepchildren. I have even seen them contest the existing will. My advice is this: If you have children and plan to remarry and want your children to have any of your property, either give it to them before you remarry or have a comprehensive will drawn up by an attorney—and also be aware that some things may disappear before the will is read.

Jerry

Jerry's aunt had died, but Jerry was not at the funeral. He had been hunting in the north woods and no one knew how to get in touch with him. A week after the funeral, he came to my office and told me he needed a bereavement letter stating that he had attended the funeral so he could get credit for his time off from work in the factory. I said I could not do that because he had not been at the visitation or funeral. He said that if he had not been hunting, he would have been there, so he should get paid the bereavement time anyway.

I did not give him the letter, and he expressed to me that he would never use my services in the future.

Mr. Camille

Mr. Camille delivered fuel oil to one of the rural schools. One day, there was about a foot of newly fallen snow when he arrived at the school. Because the building was not yet open, the kids were outside, frolicking in the snow at the playground next to the school.

As Mr. Camille was backing his truck up, trying to stay within the tire tracks that were already there, all of the children started running toward him, yelling and screaming. His heart sank as he realized he must have hit a child!

What actually happened was that the children had put all of their lunch pails in the tire tracks so they would be easy to retrieve, and Mr.

Camille had backed over all of the lunches. He told me he was relieved because he realized that Rossell Funeral Home would not be needed after all.

Admirer

I was home with my wife and small children when the phone rang. A woman was on the line and told me she was the person who had flirted with me at the cemetery. I told her I did not recall anybody flirting with me and that I was a happily married man. She said, yes, she was the one who had been sitting in the back of the limousine.

I sensed that she was starting to cry; her voice was trembling when she told me she had thought I had an interest in her, and her therapist had told her to call me in order to confront the situation.

Barney

The Flushing police department was happy to get a new police car. The assistant chief proudly drove the new car downtown and parked it in front of the post office, which was in the middle of the block. He was standing on the sidewalk, admiring the cruiser, when a pedestrian came up and asked if he could sit in it. The officer responded, "Sure." The man got in and took off. They found the police car in a farmer's field the next day.

Edgar L. Cornwell

Mr. Cornwell lived from October 17, 1886, to May 15, 1961. He was a wealthy man and was prominent in town. I also understand that he was tight with his money. He went in the local pharmacy and soda fountain store every day at noon and ordered a bowl of soup for lunch. For an extra nickel, he would sometimes buy a package of two saltine crackers. He would eat one of the crackers and hand the second cracker to the girl behind the counter and tell her to keep it for the following day because he didn't want to spend an extra nickel.

When Mr. Cornwell died at the age of ninety-four, the only survivors and heirs were nieces and nephews, none of whom lived in the area. They called my uncle and told him that money was not an object and they wanted the most expensive casket he could find, so my uncle called around and found a full-couch bronze sarcophagus with a thistle velvet interior. The money he made on that funeral was used to put aluminum siding on the funeral home.

Apparently, Mr. Cornwell had thought Flushing needed a park, so he left money to build a small park at Main and Cherry Streets, where the old beautiful bank building had stood.

Dr. and Mrs. N. A. C. Andrews

Dr. and Mrs. Andrews lived in a large house across the street from the funeral home and his office was located there, as well. The doctor was also a medical examiner, meaning he pronounced people dead and determined the cause of death.

It was a real advantage to have Dr. Andrews live across the street. When I was born, I was very sickly. In fact, for the first few weeks after I was born, I was not expected to live. I suffered from asthma and always had a hard time breathing. I could not run half a block without being out of breath.

When I was seven years old, I keeled over on the living room floor in the apartment above the funeral home. My father picked me up because I was turning purple and he ran to Dr. Andrews's office. Dr. Andrews put a shot of adrenaline directly into my heart. From that time on, I never suffered from asthma again. He truly saved my life!

Dr. Andrews was an interesting doctor. He made house calls for sick people and in his black bag he kept bottles of pills in different colors. He once confided to me that all these pills were sugar pills. He told me if a sick person's room was blue, he would give him blue pills, if red, red pills, etc. He said it was mind over matter.

One day I asked Dr. Andrews why he had not replaced the dilapidated sign in front of his office. He told me that a new sign would give people the impression that he was just starting out; the old sign would indicate his experience.

Though she had a heart of gold, Mrs. Andrews—everyone called her Melba—was a busybody. She knew everyone's business.

Melba's bedroom was in the front of the house. She sat in her bedroom, knitting, while watching everything going on outside. When I was a teenager, she called my parents and told them what time I arrived home from dates. After I had been married for nine months, she told me, "Well, I see you did not have to get married."

One day, Melba was in her front yard, directing her son, Del, who was standing on a two-story ladder while painting the house. A little girl who lived around the corner approached Melba and asked, "Mrs. Andrews, are you a witch?!" Del started laughing so hard that he dropped the paint bucket and nearly fell off the ladder!

Augie

Augie Staley was one of the few plumbers in town, and I think he knew the infrastructure of not only the city, but also every building in it. Sadly, a lot of that knowledge died with him. When I was young and living in the funeral home, which was a very old building, Augie often came to work on plumbing. I watched and learned. I always thought it was so neat that when he needed a hard-to-get part, he would go home to his barn to see if he had it. He usually did; it might have been a used part, but it always worked. Now I have a barn, too.

Temporary Harry

One of the electricians in town, who also came frequently to take care of the funeral home, was Temporary Harry. Everyone called him that because after every job he did, he would say, "That will fix it temporarily."

Harry had his own way of doing things. He had been in a car accident that caused some brain damage that affected his motor skills. His hands shook violently. It was a wonder he could put two wires together, but he did it for many years. I told him it was good he could turn the power off when working on electricity. I was surprised when he told me he always left the power on because then he would not have to guess whether it was on or not. Years later, when another electrician worked in the funeral home, he said, "Yep, that's Harry's work."

The Barber

As a boy in the 1950s, going to the barbershop on a regular basis was almost a requirement, especially since I grew up in a funeral home. Getting a haircut was also a social event where you would hear all the gossip that was going around in town. There were a few barbershops, but I always went to Rupe's Barbershop on Main Street. It was first come, first served, and everyone hoped they would get Rupe, the owner, rather than Sam, his employee. You see, Sam was a talker; the more he talked, the more he cut. If, after Sam cut your hair, you walked into the local drugstore where the soda fountain was, people would look up at you and exclaim, "So, Sam cut your hair today!"

Middle-earth

Every so often during a visitation, someone would approach my brother or me to strike up a conversation. Sometimes, the conversation would last a long time, keeping us from greeting other people coming into the funeral home, so we had a solution. When one of us saw this happening to the other one, he would go to the office and ring the second phone line, then come to the one being held up and say, "Excuse me, you are wanted on the phone." That would break off the discussion.

One night, a man kept walking in and out of the foyer, looking at his watch each time and saying, "Two o'clock. Two o'clock." This happened several times before, finally, he stopped and started talking to my brother. He told my brother all about Middle-earth and the people who lived there, and that many people did not know that the portal to Middle-earth was in the Arctic Circle. My brother kept glancing at me, wanting me to go ring the second line, but I didn't want him to miss out on anything!

Flushing Optimist Club

It is good for business people to be involved in local service organizations. The one I was most active in was the Flushing Optimist Club, which organized fundraisers and programs for the youth of the community. It was a great group of men who met once a week for breakfast, followed by a speaker. I worked my way up in the club and became president. After being president, I was elected to be lieutenant governor of zone 7 of the Michigan District Optimists. One of the duties of this position was to organize a yearly meeting to bring the clubs in my zone together for a dinner, give awards, and have a pep rally for the following year's activities. The attendance for one yearly meeting was not very high because, although the regular membership was invited, it was mainly attended by the club officers. I thought maybe the meeting was too dull, so I called my friend John Antos, lieutenant governor of zone 8, and asked if we could combine our meetings and maybe, along with the regular program, have some lively entertainment. He agreed, and we booked Italia Gardens in downtown Flint to provide the space and food. John asked a woman who taught at a belly dancing school and was a professional belly dancer if she would be our entertainment, and she agreed. We did not advertise that she was going to be there. Her act was artistic and erotic, but definitely not lewd. The men enjoyed her dancing so much that we paid her to perform for an extra hour! A few days after the meeting, we started to get some feedback. Most of the men had enjoyed the entertainment, but some were upset because they thought the dancing was inappropriate for the annual meeting. One of the members of my club said, "I will not tell you I did not enjoy the entertainment, but this is certainly not what the Optimist Club is all about." We received a letter from the higher-ups of the organization that we were not to have such programming in the future. The next year, John and I again hosted the two district meetings together. We did not tell anybody that we were not providing entertainment. The attendance was triple that of the previous year because the members were expecting a repeat performance of belly dancing. Many were disappointed!

PREMONITION

I definitely believe in premonition, so I have included these stories.

Mr. Spaulding

One evening, a prominent citizen came into the funeral home to pay his respects to a friend who had died. I had known Mr. Spaulding only as a businessman; we were acquainted but had never spent time together. There was a large group of people in the foyer as Mr. Spaulding was leaving. By chance, he caught my eye, smiled, turned back, and made his way toward me. I did not put my hand out to shake it because he did not offer his. I had the feeling he wanted to communicate something to me but was trying to figure out how to start. I stood there, and after a few seconds, he said that he was glad to see me and that he thought we might have some things in common, and maybe we should get together in the near future. I told him that would be nice. He said, "Thank you. I really appreciate you are here." Then he left.

He died two weeks later. He was in his mid-fifties.

Dave

Dave was a high school classmate. I saw him around town and, once in a while, at the local restaurant or pub. We were not especially close friends.

I was in my office one day when my secretary paged me and said there was a man who had come for a visitation and had asked if I happened to be in the funeral home. When I told her I would come down, she said, "No, he would like to see you privately in your office."

I met Dave at the top of the stairs and led him into my office; I sat down at my desk while he sat on the opposite side. I thought maybe this was just a social visit, but I asked if there was anything I could do for him. He said he just wanted to stop and say hi and to ask me how things were going. We chatted a bit about our families, the weather, and some of our former classmates, and then, after a while, he stood up and said, "Thanks. I am glad you were here when I came in."

A few weeks later, he was out with some friends when he collapsed and died. He was sixty.

A Nice Family

An elderly woman died, not unexpectedly, and was survived by six children, who were all married and had families. Because the family was large and they were well known in town, many people came for the visitation. The visitation was not as somber as some because the woman had lived a long, fulfilling life and had died peacefully in her sleep.

During visitation, I was sitting in the lounge with some of the woman's sons and a few of their friends when the eldest son said rather bluntly, "Well, I guess I will be the next one to go."

Everyone looked at him, wondering what had brought that on. I asked, "Why would you think you will be the next to die?"

"It stands to reason; I am the oldest.", he replied. I think I made some kind of comment about only God knows, and then everyone went on with their own conversations.

The eldest son left the funeral home, went home, and put a gun to his head. He was buried the same day as his mother, whose funeral was delayed by a day.

New Friends

My wife and I became acquainted with a couple and started to spend time with them. One evening, we were at a local pub when the wife started asking my wife about funerals and cemetery lots because the topic had been on her mind a lot.

The next time we went out with them, the woman again started talking about funerals and where she wanted to be buried. When we returned home, my wife told me how disturbed she had been by this conversation because no one else had ever spoken to her in this way.

Our friend also spoke at length about how much she loved her husband and daughters. She hesitantly revealed to my wife that she had "the gift" and that others in her family had "the gift", as well: they could foresee the future. Her first grandchild was a girl, and my wife suggested that maybe her next grandchild would be a boy, but she said no, her *fourth* grandchild would be a boy.

About two weeks after having had dinner with them, the husband called to say that his wife was dead. She was fifty-eight and had died from the flu. While talking about funerals, the woman had told my wife that she wanted to be buried near water, with trees and flowers nearby. She was buried in a large cemetery and the grave had not been purchased prior to her death.

The following summer, my wife went to the cemetery to visit the grave. She had never been there before, and no one was in the cemetery office to show her where the grave was. She started driving around and, remembering the friend's detailed description of where she wanted to be buried, my wife drove directly to the grave.

Recently, our friend's daughter gave birth to the next grandchildren—twin girls.

Stock Market

Shortly after my wife and I started a family, we began saving for our children's education. I invested all of that money in the stock market. On a Wednesday night, I woke up with a start around two a.m. I woke my wife and told her we had to sell all of our stock. She thought I was crazy and told me to go back to sleep.

The next morning, I called the stockbroker and cashed in everything we had invested. The following day was later called "Black Friday" because the stock market plummeted. When my accountant saw that I had sold our stock, he called and asked me how in the world I had known to do that. I replied that it came to me in a dream.

My wife and I used the money received from the stock sale to purchase an old building located next to the funeral home. In renovating, we created space for a business on the first floor and an apartment on the second. The rent we received provided a good return on our investment and went toward our children's education.

Camping

My wife, our two small children, and I were on our way to go camping in the Canadian Rockies. After driving a long way, we came to a beautiful campground somewhere in the province of Alberta. We found a nice private campsite surrounded by trees. After setting up the tent and getting the kids settled, we enjoyed sitting at the picnic table to relax. Suddenly, I turned to my wife and said, "We have to leave."

She responded, "I know."

That was it. We packed up everything and drove two hundred miles to another campground. The next day, we heard that a tornado had hit the campground we had been in.

A couple of years later, we were camping on our way to the province of Quebec, Canada. It was getting late, and we were a few miles outside of Kingston, Ontario, when we started thinking about where to camp. The first choice available was a field where a farmer let people camp; the second choice was to go on into Kingston, where there was a nice campground. We drove past the farmer's field; after traveling several miles beyond the field, I told my wife, "We have to turn back and camp in the field."

She replied, "I know."

During the night a tornado hit Kingston, including the campground there.

PARANORMAL HAPPENINGS

Some things I have encountered have been inexplicable.

The Long Trip

I was still living in the back apartment of the funeral home with my parents, and my brother and his wife were living in the front apartment. My father and brother had left early in the morning to take human remains to a funeral home in Kentucky. They were driving straight down and back without stopping, and we did not expect them to arrive back home until early the next morning. About one a.m., my mother came to my bedroom and woke me. She said she had awakened with a dreadful feeling that something had happened to my father and brother. I told her that because we had not heard anything, everything was probably okay and that she should go back to bed.

Not fifteen minutes later, my brother's wife came to my bedroom and woke me to tell me she had awakened with a bad feeling that something had happened to my brother and father. I thought that was weird but told her the same thing: no news is good news.

My brother and father arrived several hours later and then got a few hours of sleep. We were all at the breakfast table when my brother told us that he had thought he and my father were goners. Around one a.m., a man had apparently fallen asleep at the wheel and his car had veered into the opposite lane, heading straight for my father and brother. My dad had slammed on the brakes, spun 180 degrees, and missed a bridge abutment by inches.

Apparently, the other guy was okay, because he turned his car around and took off down the highway. After they had gathered their wits about them, my father and brother had continued driving home.

Who's There?

While making funeral arrangements for her father, the daughter of the deceased related to me the circumstances of his death.

The elderly patient had lived a good life, but during his last year, cancer had taken over his body. He was on the ninth floor, "the cancer floor", at Hurley Hospital in Flint. One wall of his private room had two large windows overlooking the city. There was no balcony or ledge outside the windows, just a straight drop to the ground. Because the man's health was deteriorating, his daughter stayed next to his bedside. She was seated in a chair, facing away from the window, next to her father's bed.

She was having a normal conversation with him when, suddenly, he looked beyond her toward the window and exclaimed, "Who are all those people out there?" It was already dark outside, so the man's daughter was surprised by his comment. She turned around to look out the window but, not having seen anything, she turned back to her father. He was dead.

In the Ambulance

My father and uncle were taking an elderly woman to the hospital in the ambulance. My uncle was driving, and my father was in the back of the ambulance with the patient, watching her as she lay there. Suddenly, she raised herself halfway out of the stretcher, pointed her finger skyward, and with a surprised expression, said, "OH, LOOK!" She then fell back, dead.

Mom, Mom

The young man, about seventeen years old, had been coming home from a night job. He lived out in the country, and there was a long stretch of dark, desolate highway he had to drive. The best anyone could surmise was that he had fallen asleep at the wheel, veered off the road, and slammed into a tree. The accident was not discovered until the next morning. The medical examiner determined that the time of death was around 1:00 a.m.

The young man had been an only child, and the parents were, of course, devastated. It was a sad time.

About a month after the funeral, the boy's mother came to the funeral home and asked if she could talk with me in private. I said yes, then took her into my office and closed the door.

I did not say anything, and, at first, she did not, either; we just sat in silence for a few minutes. Finally, she began to speak in a shaky voice. She said she had not told what she was about to tell me to anyone else, even her husband. She was afraid everyone would think she was crazy, but if she did not tell someone, she *would* go crazy. There was silence for a moment, and then she looked up at me and realized it was okay for her to continue her story. She told me that on the night of her son's death, she and her husband had gone to bed early. While they were sleeping, she heard the phone ringing, and because her husband had not heard it, she got up and answered it. She told me that the voice she heard was a soft, raspy whisper that she recognized as that of her son. Her son said, "Mom … mom", and then the phone went dead.

When I asked her what time this had happened, she said she remembered because she had looked at the clock by her bed before answering the phone. It was 1:00 a.m. This was in the days before cell phones.

Wagon Wheel

One of my employees, Walt, once related to me something that had happened when he was nine years old. At the time, doctors in Flushing often operated in offices connected to their homes. "Ole" Doc Miller performed tonsillectomies in his home office. During one of these operations, the doctor had been unable to control the bleeding, and one of Walt's friends had died. Walt was asked to be a pallbearer for the boy.

Back then, a common floral arrangement, to place at the head of the casket, was a large wagon wheel with one spoke missing; the wheel represented the family, and the missing spoke represented the family member who had died.

The funeral started with the child's friends, serving as pallbearers, lined up at the foot of the casket. During the funeral, the wagon wheel, for unknown reasons, came loose from its stand, rolled across the front of the casket, and hit one of the young pallbearers. A week later, that boy drowned. Walt said three things happened after the drowning: (1) It scared the hell out of the remaining pallbearers; (2) none of the boys wanted to have their tonsils taken out; and (3) none of the boys ever wanted to serve as a pallbearer again.

Twenty Times

The man knew a lot of townspeople in Flushing and came to many of the visitations at the funeral home. In the evenings, my brother and I usually greeted people coming into the funeral home. This particular man always came up to us and said, "Good evening", followed by our names. For whatever reason, though, we could never remember this man's name. We could only reply, "Good evening."

One particular evening, the man came in and greeted both my brother and me using our names, and, once again, we could not remember his name. My brother decided that it would not happen again, so he waited until the man had signed the register book and stepped away from it. My brother went over to see what the man's name was, then went back to the office where he wrote the man's name on a pad of paper twenty times, satisfied that the next time he saw the man, he would be able to call the man by his name.

By the time my brother came back to the foyer, the man had already left the funeral home. About two hours later, the funeral home phone rang. The hospital called to notify us that a man, who had had a heart attack, was brought to the emergency room where he died, and the family wanted us to handle the funeral arrangements.

My brother recognized the man's name.

Haunted?

I suppose there is at least one ghost house in every small town. Flushing is no exception. I became friends with a couple who moved into a house one block away from the funeral home. They told me some strange things were happening in their house and wondered if I knew the history of the house. My friends had already asked people in the neighborhood for information, but no one could recall anyone who had lived in the house. Strangely, I could not remember any families who had lived there, either; I knew we had buried people who had lived there, but I could find no records of the funerals. I contacted one of my classmates who had lived directly across the street from the house. She also remembered the house but could not remember the people who had lived there.

I asked my friends what the strange occurrences were. They told me these stories.

Their dog freely roamed the house but refused to go into the kitchen, which was right off the living room. The dog would sit at the doorway, staring into the kitchen, moving his head all around as if seeing something floating about, though they could see nothing. Because of this, the wife had set up a remote camera in the kitchen door and left it overnight. When they viewed the results, they had seen orbs of light floating about the room. She showed me the video. Another time, the wife had been putting her grandson to bed when he looked beyond her and asked who was the person standing in the corner. When she turned around, she saw no one else in the room.

Strange House on the Hill

There is an old large, two-story house within the city limits of Flushing that has been in bad repair for years even though people have been living in it. The window draperies and shades are always closed, the hedges in the yard are overgrown, and it has a dirt driveway. I have never seen anybody in the yard or lights on in the house at night.

Three apparent suicides by hanging have occurred in this house, all three in unrelated families, and none of the families knew each other.

THE DAILY LIFE of a FUNERAL DIRECTOR

The typical day in the life of a funeral director is not boring. These are some of the stories that have kept my life interesting.

Still Not Satisfied

My father always told me to treat the families we served like I would want to be treated. He said if I did, the business would succeed. I took his advice to heart, but it took a while for me to understand that some people, no matter how hard you try, cannot be pleased. I always take it personally when someone is not satisfied and I try to placate them, but some people will not be appeased and are plain nasty.

One older man came into the funeral home without an appointment and said he wanted to prearrange his mother's funeral right then. I happened to be free and spent the next two hours going over all the details of the funeral for his mother. Then he used the restroom. He came back and told me that our toilet paper scratched his ass and he would not be using our funeral home.

***

My father had many cousins all over the state of Michigan and beyond. The relatives who were nearby would call on us to serve them when a loved one died. We always gave the family a discount. There was one cousin whose family we had previously served: we had buried her father, mother, some of her siblings, and also her husband. When she died, her uncle called us to make the removal and take care of the funeral arrangements, however, her two daughters came in and told me I would not be serving them this time because their mother had not wanted me to see her naked. Even though I could have arranged for someone else to prepare their mother's remains, they would not be satisfied using my funeral home.

***

There was a man who lived in Flushing for a long time and sold cars at a local dealership. We bought our funeral cars and our personal cars locally and never dickered on price. When this man's mother died, he came in and made all the arrangements. After the appointment, before he left, he told me to hold off on everything. Two hours later, he came back and told me a funeral home in the next town would do all the service for five dollars less. I told him I charged a fair price for service rendered, and he said, "You mean you won't come down for five dollars?" I told him it would not be fair to my other clients. He used the other funeral home.

***

In another instance, a distant relative of my wife's family had the misfortune of delivering a stillborn baby. The husband called and said he wanted me to handle the arrangements. He also told me he wanted a simple funeral because they had very little money. He was worried his two sisters-in-law would urge them to have an elaborate funeral. I assured him that I would be able to accommodate his wishes. He said his wife was still in the hospital and they would come in as soon as she was released. I told him to call for an appointment before they came in.

I was very busy serving other families when the husband, his wife, and her two sisters came in, without an appointment. The sisters told my greeter that they were there to make arrangements for the infant. On the way to the office, the husband whispered to me a reminder of his request to keep the cost down. Because we deal with infant funerals, we understand that finances can be tough, so we have a package deal that includes our service and a casket-vault combination. When I offered this package deal to them, one of the sisters stood up and yelled at me that they wanted the best there was.

I looked at the husband, but he said nothing, only shrugged. I told the sister that what she wanted might be more than her sister and brother-in-law could afford. She yelled at me again, saying that her sister and brother-in-law had their whole lives to pay for this funeral. I asked her if she was going to help with the bill. In response, she said, "That's it! We are going to another funeral home!"

I looked at the wife and husband. She said nothing, and he, again, just shrugged. They all walked out. A few days later, after the funeral was handled by a funeral home in Flint, a friend of the mother came in and told me that the family had purchased an expensive funeral, casket, and vault they could not afford, and she apologized to me for her friends; she knew I did what I had been told by the husband to do. She added that the two sisters were bitches.

City Hall and the Fence

The building right to the east of the funeral home, now called Parrish Community Center, was originally the Flushing Community Center. It is a large building that, over the years, was used for many functions, including parties, dances, town meetings, and meetings for service organizations. It even provided classrooms for the Flushing School System. The Flushing Library was housed in the west portion of the building and had its own front entrance. As Flushing grew and became a city, the auditorium of the community center was partitioned into city offices and the police department was housed in the basement. In back of the funeral home and the community center are parking lots that were shared for many years. The driveway between both buildings was also shared. The only time the lot became congested was when the funeral home was conducting a large funeral. Cars would be blocked in, but for no more than an hour. Nobody ever complained until Flushing hired a new city manager.

After the library moved to a different location, the 67th District Court moved into the former library area; this resulted in a greater need for parking than had originally been expected. By the time the city, police, and court workers were parked, there was little parking left in the shared lot. On the first day of court, the funeral home parking lot was full of cars of the people going to court, and we had to put a sign out explaining that the parking lot behind the funeral home was for funeral home parking only. Some of the city workers had to park in a lot a few blocks away.

This arrangement worked fairly well until the new city manager's car was blocked in during a large funeral. After the funeral was over, my father and his helpers were busy cleaning the funeral home to get ready for the next funeral. The city manager stormed in through the door of the funeral home and demanded that his car never be blocked in again. If it was, he said, he would put up a fence and block the city parking lot from the funeral home. My father did not argue with him. He reached in his pocket, pulled out a nickel, and said, "Here, I will help pay for it." The city manager stormed out, not knowing that the driveway between the two buildings was owned by the funeral home. My father then called a fence company and arranged to have a fence put up; he also moved the large garage (the previous horse barn) into a corner of what the city thought was part of their parking lot. The city was left with only one in-and-out driveway. I am certain my father would not have done what he did if the city manager had been polite; after all, the city needed our drive as much as we needed their parking. The judge of the court came over and complained that we had put the garage on his parking space. Eventually, due to the lack of parking, the court soon found a larger facility and moved out of the building.

Years later, a new city administration building was built, along with a new police department. The community center sat empty and in disrepair for several years. Fortunately, a foundation was formed, donations were made, and the old community center was restored to its former beauty. It is now called the Parrish Community Center and it houses Goggins Hall, which is rented and used for private and community events. The fence remains. Good fences make good neighbors.

Disinfectant and OSHA

For years, the standard disinfectant used in the preparation room was bleach. A few years ago, trade magazines published that bleach mixed with formaldehyde formed a chemical that was a dangerous carcinogen (cancer-causing agent), so we started using alternative disinfectants that were available from our chemical suppliers.

We are required to take education courses regarding OSHA (Occupational Health and Safety Administration) laws and regulations. I attended a course that was sponsored by the Michigan Funeral Directors Association, and a representative from OSHA was the speaker. During his presentation, he stated that the most effective disinfectant to use in the preparation room was bleach. I raised my hand, and, after a few seconds, he acknowledged me. I told him that I had thought bleach mixed with formaldehyde produced a carcinogen. In a low voice, he told the class, "That would be minimal," and then continued where he had left off. Unbelievably, no one else brought up the subject.

Allergy

The skin of one of the embalmers I worked with started breaking out. First it looked like alligator skin and then it oozed. His doctor gave him some ointment and told him to take a few days off from work. The embalmer went home, and the problem cleared up. When he came back to work, the problem seemed to be worse than before. Again, he took some time off and the problem cleared up. Although tests said otherwise, the doctor thought maybe the embalmer had an allergic reaction to the fumes from formaldehyde in the embalming fluid.

When the embalmer went back to work again, the problem became so bad that his doctor admitted him to the hospital. While there, his condition worsened. When another doctor heard about the case, he thought he knew what was happening; The embalmer was allergic to fluorescent lighting. At work, he was under fluorescent lighting all day. When he went home, there was no fluorescent lighting and the problem would go away. When he went to the hospital, the problem became worse because there was even more fluorescent lighting. From then on, in the preparation room, the embalmer wore a light-weight ski mask, sunglasses, a wide-brimmed hat, and latex gloves that would not allow any light through. We kiddingly asked him if he was going to rob a bank on the way home.

Inspections

When I started working as a funeral director, the funeral home was inspected on a yearly basis by the state board of examiners of mortuary science. I always felt good because the inspectors told us our preparation (embalming room) was one of the cleanest in the state. I thought all of them should be squeaky clean.

The state board of mortuary science no longer inspects funeral homes, and I have been told, by embalmers and removal personnel, how filthy some of the preparation rooms are. Some, they said, they would never work in.

Boiler

We have a steam boiler in the old part of the funeral home. We maintain it and it has always worked properly. An insurance company representative inspects the boiler yearly and so does an inspector from the State of Michigan. Although the state hires an inspector, the state also requires that an independent journeyman be hired by the funeral home to inspect the boiler. This journeyman fills out a form that is later shown to the state inspector as proof that he was hired by the funeral home. I pay $200 to the journeyman, $300 for the state inspector to see that the boiler has been inspected by the journeyman, and another $300 for a boiler permit.

Elevators and Lifts

In the funeral home, we have two elevator lifts. Nobody rides on them: they are used to carry caskets, human remains, and flowers from one floor to another. According to regulations of the State of Michigan, they have to be inspected yearly, as does our wheelchair lift. Of course, we maintain the lifts and our insurance company also inspects them. We pay $300 for each lift to be inspected and another $300 per lift for permits to operate them. For $300 per lift, the state inspector watches each one go up and down, then signs the paper so we can receive the permits.

One time, one of our lifts was leaking a bit of hydraulic fluid, and I asked the inspector how I could fix it. He replied that he did not know — he was a displaced real estate person and his brother-in-law had gotten him this cushy job. Another inspector told me I had to hire an elevator expert to come in and make sure each unit was able to carry its weight limit. We have probably never had more than 10 percent of the weight limits put on any of the lifts. It cost me $800 to have a man come in and put weights on the elevators and say, "Yep, they lift properly." That inspector told me that yearly weight inspections were required, but he never returned, and no other inspector has ever mentioned that legal requirement.

Insurance Company

Usually, the funeral home insurance company is very thorough in its inspections, which I am glad about, because, if there were ever a lawsuit, I would know that we were always up to date on all safety regulations. One time, however, when I was escorting an insurance inspector around the funeral home and asking him questions about safety regulations, he did not seem to know what I was talking about. When I asked him why he did not know the answers to my questions, he told me that his mother was the actual inspector and he was filling in for her.

I called the insurance company and complained. I think that was the last day of work for the mother and her son.

Printing

Before computers and copy machines were available, we had to take blank folders and prayer cards to the *Flushing Observer*, the newspaper owned by Don and Bob Beebe, to be printed. When the Beebes retired, I bought a printing press and learned to typeset, a very time-consuming process. After the funeral home was closed, with all the main lights turned off, I sat at my work table in the basement of the funeral home with a bare bulb over my head, setting one letter at a time. After the typeset, I had to ink the press and print one card at a time. With hundreds of cards to do, I often finished in the middle of the night. The printing press is now housed in the Manwaring Building-Print Shop of Crossroads Village in Genesee County, Michigan. Computers and copiers make printing so much easier and quicker!

The first copy machine I used was at the public library located next door to the funeral home. I prepared all our financial spreadsheets by hand and, before sending them off to our accountant, copied them because I did not want them lost in the mail. It cost ten cents a copy.

The first computer I bought for the funeral home was a 386 MB computer that required you to type in the commands you wanted it to perform. The salesperson told me 386 MB would be all the memory I would ever need and that I would not need a modem because there would never be a use for it. The first program I wrote was to print memorial folders, and the second program was a spreadsheet.

Jewelry

Often, people bring in jewelry that they want their deceased loved ones to be buried with, especially wedding bands.

While making funeral arrangements, when a family handed me a ring, I used to have the habit of looping it onto the paper clip that was attached to the funeral folder. After the arrangements were made, I would give the folder to my secretary, and she would keep the ring in a safe place until we put it on the deceased. On one occasion, after the family had left, I walked into my secretary's office and put the folder on her desk, only to discover that the ring was not there. I went back to the arrangement office, but the ring was not there, either. I panicked. My secretary and I looked all over, from office to office, but still no ring. I even called my wife at home, and she came down and looked. It took a while, but she found the ring. It was on the far side of the casket showroom, resting on its edge, right next to a wheel of one of the casket carts. The ring must have slipped off of the folder as I was escorting the family to the exit, then rolled through the doorway of the casket showroom, and ended up approximately twenty feet across the room. It was barely visible. Now I put jewelry in a plastic container with a tight-fitting top.

***

Al, one of my employees, once went to the hospital to bring a deceased woman to the funeral home. The family was in the room when he arrived, and, before he left, they gave him their mother's diamond wedding ring to take to the funeral home because they were afraid they would misplace it. Al called me at home at three a.m. to tell me he had lost the diamond ring. He told me he had put it in his jacket pocket and, when he arrived at the funeral home with the deceased, he had removed his jacket and placed it on the front seat of his car before entering the funeral home. After he brought the woman into the funeral home, he returned to his car to get the ring from his jacket but it was not there. He thought maybe the ring had fallen out when he took off his jacket. The problem was that there was about two inches of newly fallen snow in the drive and a three-foot snowbank nearby. I helped him look for the ring and, after searching for what seemed like an eternity, I finally went home and got my metal detector. I found the ring buried under about two feet of snow in the snowbank at 5:30 a.m. Whew!

Guard Dog

I had never had a dog and did not want a dog, but my wife, who grew up with dogs, did, and she told me she was going to the Humane Society to get one. I did not think she meant it.

She came home with a dog named Gina. I wondered how we were going to keep a dog in the funeral home, but it took less than a day for me to fall in love with her. It was not long before Gina would come down to my office and sit under the desk. She was always quiet and content — until a salesman came in. I do not know how she distinguished salesmen from other people, but all the while a salesman sat across the desk from me, she would let out a steady soft growl. I am sure it gave me an advantage when negotiating deals.

OTHER FUNERAL DIRECTORS

I share the same business principles with many funeral directors I've encountered throughout the years. These stories are about some of the other ones.

Wrong Place

When I answered the door, there were about six people standing there telling me they had an appointment to make funeral arrangements for their father who had died. He had told them that he had a prearranged funeral with us. I told them I had not been notified of the death, and they said their brother had called to check to make sure the prearrangement was in place and had made the appointment.

I invited them in, looked in our files, and, sure enough, their father did have funeral prearrangements with our funeral home. Then I called the hospital where their father had died. The person at the hospital told me they had released the remains to another funeral home, one in Flint. I called the other funeral home and discovered that the brother was waiting there for the rest of the family.

The family had previously used the other funeral home, and the brother, not knowing where the prearrangements had been made, had called that funeral home in Flint. He asked the funeral director there, Otto, if there was a prearrangement there for his father. Otto not only told him there was one, but added that he had often talked to the father. The brother then made an appointment with Otto. Of course, there had been no prearrangement with that funeral home, so we had the remains transferred to our funeral home. When one of Otto's two partners found out what Otto had done, he was most upset; in fact, he was screaming at him when I went to pick up the remains.

No Choice

In northern Michigan, when there is a death in the winter, burial often does not occur until spring, when the snow melts. It is not that the ground is frozen (there are heaters to put on the grave to thaw the ground) but because the snow can be several feet deep. It is difficult to plow a cemetery around headstones to get to a grave.

When remains cannot be buried right away, the body is either stored at a funeral home or, if available, in a cemetery storage facility. I was once delivering casketed remains to be stored in the cemetery storage facility of a small northern Michigan town. I did not know how to get to the small country cemetery, so I called the only local funeral home. The funeral director told me to come to the funeral home and he would take me to the storage facility because he had a key. When I arrived at the small funeral home, which was located on the main street just blocks from the downtown, I went in and saw that there was a visitation going on. There was no funeral home staff there, so I looked for and found the office: it was a mess, with papers stacked all over and everything in disarray. There was no one there. I went back out to the foyer, hoping to find someone connected to the funeral home.

One of the mourners asked me who I was and I explained that I was looking for the funeral director. He said that I could probably find

Jack down at the local bakery/coffee shop. I walked down to the bakery, where several men were having coffee. One of them noticed I had a suit on and, figuring out I was the director with the body to be put in storage, introduced himself. Jack was dressed in work clothes like the other men at the table. When I asked him who was taking care of the funeral home, he gave me quite a detailed explanation. Although Jack never wanted to become a funeral director, he went to mortuary school to please his father who wanted him to take over the family business. After his father died, Jack started his own construction company, and, because the nearest funeral home to the town was miles and miles away, he decided, for the good of the community, to keep the funeral home open. He did not want to be there on a regular basis, so the townspeople would, for the most part, run their own funerals. It worked for this town.

When we arrived at the storage facility, I saw that caskets were placed on large storage racks. I noticed right away that there were only two kinds of caskets: a medium-priced blue one and an inexpensive cloth-covered wood one. When I asked why there were only two kinds of caskets, he told me he carried only the two styles; if people were going to use his funeral home, they only had two choices.

More Money

There used to be an active Genesee County Funeral Directors Association and I was a member. When people had no money to pay for a funeral, there was State of Michigan money that families could apply for to help with expenses, and this money would be paid directly to the funeral home.

One time, a group from the association asked for a meeting with state representatives to ask if they could get more money to help with funeral expenses. I was in agreement with this request because the money available to funeral directors did not even cover the cost of the funeral. I was shocked, however, when most of the members of the association showed up to the meeting driving Cadillacs, wearing fur coats with expensive clothing and jewelry. I thought, *if you are going to ask for money, maybe you should dress down a bit.* They did not get the requested funding.

Taking Advantage

One funeral director in Flint always bragged that he sold more solid copper and bronze caskets than anyone else. He said it was simple: he would show families only copper and bronze caskets, and he showed less-expensive caskets only if he was asked if there were less-expensive caskets available. If the family kept wanting less-expensive caskets, less expensive than those he had shown them already, he would take them to the basement, where he kept cheap-looking caskets.

This funeral director also told me that he sold expensive burial suits and dresses to families who could not have open-casket funerals because of the condition of the remains. When I asked him how he dressed the deceased who was mangled or burned, he told me he just put the box of clothes in the casket on top of the deceased. By using this method, he told the family he had put the clothing on the deceased.

***

Another funeral director told me the technique he used to become one of the top casket salesmen for his funeral home: While melancholy music played in the casket showroom, he reminded families that, because they loved the deceased so much, they could demonstrate this love by having a really nice funeral. He added that bronze and copper caskets were the best and asked, "Isn't that what your loved one deserves?"

***

Another funeral director, who was employed by a conglomerate funeral home, told me that the owners were interested only in sales. He said they did not care about what met the needs of a family; they were interested only in the bottom line so they could show their investors favorable spreadsheets. He told me each funeral director had a quota to fill, so there was a lot of pressure to convince people to spend more.

A Great Scheme

Hubert was the manager of the funeral home I worked for in Detroit. He always had a scheme—often unbelievable—to make money. Around the time when air conditioners were first being introduced in automobiles, Hubert came in with a surefire get-rich-quick device. He said people did not have to buy expensive air conditioners when they could buy his device: a box that would hold a gallon of ice, with a fan attached that would blow through the ice, thus cooling the interior of the car. It would sit between the driver and passenger seat and be connected to the cigarette lighter.

Hubert spent a lot of money for this device and he stored boxes of the them in the back office of the funeral home. When I left the firm months later, all the boxes were still there.

Cheater

My wife and I once sat by a funeral director at a district funeral director meeting who, during dinner, told my wife how he cheated the government on taxes. He said he told families that if they paid him cash, he would discount the funeral. Then he did not report the transaction to the IRS and saved a lot of money in taxes. My wife was stunned when he told her that I should consider the practice because it was so lucrative.

III.

PLANNING, HELP NEEDED, LOOKING AHEAD,

and PERSONAL LOSS

PRENEED

*M*any people want to know what is going to happen to their remains when they die. They also want to have a say in the last of the four main liturgies of their life: baptism, confirmation, marriage, and death (which is the celebration of a life — their life).

When I started working as a funeral director for my father in 1971, all of the funeral pre-arrangements were kept in a plastic bank-money pouch. There were twenty or so bank accounts with money set aside for clients' future funerals. The people who had these accounts mainly wanted to know there would be money put aside to pay for their funerals; each bank account was in both the client's name and the funeral home's name, so when the client died, the money would be put toward funeral expenses.

A few unethical funeral directors have spent clients' money instead of securing it for future funerals. These directors apparently hoped to have enough cash on hand to cover the funeral expenses when a client died. Some of these disreputable funeral directors would even disappear with the money. Although the law has changed now so funds are deposited with a third-party escrow agent, there are still some dishonest funeral directors going to jail for not depositing funds properly.

***

Once, when my father and I were in the local grocery store, a woman approached him and told him that when she died, she wanted a certain shade of lipstick used. My father simply said, "Okay." I asked him how he was going to remember her wishes or who would know if he were not around, but he didn't answer.

When I got back to the funeral home from the grocery store, I started a file for each person who had made prearrangements. Hers was the first, followed by the people whose accounts were in the bank pouch. I found out later, when the woman died, that she had seen my father and all her arrangements had been made before she died. Of course, the only thing important to her had been the shade of lipstick.

On other occasions, I have had people tell me that when they die, they want me to handle their funeral arrangements. Then they go home and tell their families they have spoken to me and their funeral arrangements have all been taken care of. This becomes a problem because some families think their loved ones have paid for the funeral and that we have the money when we do not. The folders I started help a great deal because now we know exactly what has been planned and paid for and what has not. We now have hundreds of folders of people with specific information about their wishes upon their death and whether or not the services have been prepaid.

The following stories are about a few of the people who have told me their wishes.

Sarah

After I got to know her a bit, I called Sarah my girlfriend, but she always called me her funeral director. The first time Sarah called me, she asked if I could come out to her place because she wanted to talk about her funeral arrangements. She was in her eighties and lived in a small farmhouse off a dirt road in the country, where she and her husband had farmed no more than a hundred or so acres. That had been their livelihood. Since Sarah's husband had died years before, her daughter and son-in-law would come till the land, but they did little else for her.

When I arrived, I saw that the grass was tall and weeds had taken over the garden. The house was old and in need of painting. A path led out to an old, tired-looking outhouse some twenty-five yards from the house. A few hundred feet from the house, a barn was leaning like it was trying to find a place to steady itself. The barn door was hanging on only one hinge. Rusted farm implements were scattered about the yard. There was no path to the front door, and the wooden front porch was sagging precariously; it was apparent that it had not been used in a long time.

I stepped up onto the side porch and went to the door where Sarah met me with a big smile, opening the wood-framed screen door and inviting me in. The door led into a warm, clean, and tidy kitchen, where a vintage green-and-white porcelain stove sat against one wall. The only running water came from a hand pump located next to a porcelain sink; the pump brought water directly out of the ground.

Sarah invited me to sit at the old oak kitchen table and served me a steaming cup of tea with some cookies. After some small talk, she went to a bureau, opened the drawer, and pulled out a worn folder that had yellowed with age. From the folder, Sarah pulled out an old photograph of a young girl with long velvety hair and a beautiful smile.

She was wearing a flowing pink silk negligee. Sarah told me the girl was her twin sister and that her sister had died the year the photo was taken. She had been sixteen years old when she had died. Sarah said that her sister had been buried in the same negligee she was wearing in the picture. What she told me next was unexpected: "When I die and am in the casket, I want to look just like my sister, and I want to wear the same type of negligee." All I could think to say was, "Sarah, I will do the best I can."

I stayed for several more cups of tea, and we chatted about a lot of different things. Then I took the yellowed envelope with the picture and left. When I arrived back at my office, I put the envelope in a folder, labeled it, and wrote inside, *"Wants to look like picture. Wants to wear the same type of negligee."*

It was months later when I heard from Sarah again. She called me and told me she was now living in Marion Hall, an assisted living facility located in downtown Flint. She told me her doctor wanted her to eat a certain type of cracker and she could not get out much, especially to get a ride to Flushing. Because her daughter rarely visited her, Sarah asked if I would go to Bueche's, a grocery store in Flushing, because, she said, that was the only store that sold that kind of cracker. She asked politely if I could pick her up a box and drop it off the next time I was in Flint. I did so.

Marion Hall was an old building, still in good shape, that had had several other uses before becoming a facility for the elderly. It had an elevator and Sarah lived on the fourth floor. I checked in with the receptionist and made my way to Sarah's room with the crackers in hand. Sarah greeted me with her great smile and a hug, and then I gave her the crackers; she thanked me, went to a large bureau, and put them in the bottom drawer. Then she pulled me by my arm and said, "Follow me, I have something to show you." She took me down the hall to a bathroom. She led me in, walked up to a toilet, and reached over and flushed it. She turned to me and said, "Isn't that the most wonderful thing? And I don't even have to go outside!" Then she took me down the hall and knocked on everybody's door to tell the occupants that I was her funeral director. That got some looks!

After that first visit, I made several more trips to bring crackers and to see Sarah. Whenever the receptionist saw me, she would say, "Here comes Sarah's funeral director!" Sarah would always take the crackers from me, put them in the bureau, and then we would chat. She always wanted to know about my wife and children and often gave me little trinkets for my children that she had purchased at a local drugstore. We had great talks together.

One time when I went to see her, Sarah was not in her room. She had stepped out, so I went to the bureau to put the crackers in there for her. What I found in the drawers was a big surprise! In every drawer, there were crackers, all unopened! It was then I realized this was Sarah's only way, she thought, to get her funeral director to come and visit with her!

I saw Sarah several times after that, always bringing her crackers, and then one day I got the call that she had died. We brought her remains to the funeral home, and I prepared her for her funeral and burial. When I finished, she did not look much like her twin sister, but she had the same wonderful smile and she wore a negligee very much like her sister's.

Imminent Death

I was having coffee with one of the morning coffee group of men that met daily at the Park Restaurant, the local diner. One of the men was in distress. He explained to me that his ninety-year-old mother was in Fostrian Manor Nursing Home and was not expected to live. The nursing home had called each of the five children every night for the past five nights to tell them to come there right away if they wanted to be there when their mother died. Their mother had continued to hold on, and the children were exhausted. To compound the situation, their mother owned a house in Florida and the real estate person had called every day to tell the children they needed to come right away to sign the papers to sell it and that, if they did not arrive soon, they would never get as much money as has been offered.

I had a solution. I told the son that he and his siblings might not be with their mother when she died but they could come in and make all the funeral arrangements: We could write her obituary; they could pick out a casket and burial vault; they could bring in her picture so our hairdresser would know how she wore her hair; and they could bring in the clothing that she would be wearing. If she died while they were away, the arrangements would be in place and we would have everything ready when they returned from Florida. Then, all that would have to be done would be to set the date and time of the funeral.

He thought it was a good plan and he conferred with his siblings. They all agreed, and they made the arrangements.

Ten years later, I called the man and told him his mother's dress had been hanging in the closet for some time and perhaps it should be cleaned. His mother lived to be 103.

The Ultimate in Preplanning

A longtime married couple made an appointment to purchase a cemetery monument because they wanted their headstone to be in place at the time of their deaths. They had one daughter, who had died. At the time of their daughter's death, they had purchased four grave spaces. Their daughter already had a cemetery headstone, so they wanted one headstone that had a space for three names. I thought this was an odd request, and when I asked about it, they gave me an unusual answer—one that is the ultimate in preplanning.

Their daughter was buried on the end of the four-grave lot. They wanted the marker to be placed in the middle of the three remaining burial spaces. The father's name would be closest to his daughter's headstone; next to his name would be the mother's name followed by a blank space for a third name, as yet unknown. They said whichever one of them died first would be buried next to their daughter. When I told them that putting their names on ahead of time might mean one of them could be buried with the other's name over their grave, they said that did not matter. They told me that after the first of the two died, the next space would be for the surviving spouse. That left one empty grave space. They told me that when one of them died, the other one would surely remarry, and whoever it was would want to be buried next to their spouse.

They were in their eighties. They are now both deceased, and the second one to die never remarried. They are buried under the correct names.

Sometimes, preplanning does not go so well, however.

The Haunting

Often, we talk about funerals when we see one or attend one. A man and his wife were driving by Flushing Cemetery and saw a group of mourners at a graveside service. He told his wife that he did not want anybody grieving over his dead body. He said he wanted no casket, no viewing, no flowers, no period of mourning, and no memorial service. He told her he did not want anybody spending money because of his death. He looked at her and said, "If you do anything different, I will haunt you for the rest of your life!" (I call this "dictating from the grave.")

The next day, before the man's children came home from school, he was cremated. He was forty-five years old and had died suddenly of a heart attack. His wife followed through with his wishes. He had three children, eight brothers and sisters, and parents who never saw him again. The man's parents and siblings completely excommunicated his widow. They never saw or talked to her again, not even her children, because they thought the way she had handled his funeral had been all her idea. *Their* son would not do that to them! The man's children were in counseling for years, unsure if their father had died, run away, or just disappeared.

Dear reader, be careful what you say to your loved ones. This is your last request and they will follow through. Before you tell your loved ones what your needs might be, think about what their needs might be. After you die, you cannot help them. Survivors need to mourn and share their grief. They need to celebrate that a life has been lived. Do not take that away from them.

Hospice Man: Dictation from the Grave

A woman called and asked if I could come to her home. She told me that her husband was home in a hospital bed, under hospice care. The two of them had talked it over, she said, and thought it would be a good idea if I came out so her husband could tell me his wishes for the final disposition of his remains.

I arrived at a small ranch house just out of town. When I entered, I saw that the hospital bed was in the living room, presumably so the man could look out the front window. He seemed to be feeling fairly well. We chatted for a while, and then I asked them what I could do for them. The husband told me he wanted it to be clear that he wanted his remains cremated. He wanted no embalming, funeral, or visitation. He did not want a memorial service.

Up until then, I never told people that they should alert all of their friends and relatives about their final wishes. I now tell everyone because of what took place in this family.

The man lived several more months. When he died, as per his wishes and with his widow's approval, we made the removal, completed the necessary paperwork, and had his remains cremated. The following morning, I could very well have been dead if the father of the deceased had been armed. The man's father and his brother, both standing well over six feet tall and looking like centers on a football team, stormed into the funeral home and demanded to see me immediately. They said there was no way under heaven their son and brother would not have wanted a viewing, visitation, and funeral and that no way would *he* have chosen direct cremation. The father told me they wanted me to change the paperwork and they were going to take over the arrangements of his son's funeral.

I had to tell them that legally they could not do that. Only the legal next of kin has that right, and that person, in this case, was the man's wife. When I told them that their son and brother had already been cremated, I thought they were going to attack me. I was glad the desk separated me from them. They called the poor widow every profane name they could think of. They said the wife knew in her heart that these arrangements were not what her husband or his side of the family would have wanted.

I tried to explain to them the arrangements the man and his wife had made with me and that I had talked to him personally and knew those had been his wishes. I told the father that his family could, on their own, arrange for a visitation and a memorial service at the funeral home, even though that was not their loved one's wishes.

They got up and yelled all the way out of the funeral home that I was a @#*% liar and their son's wife was a *&%#*. They eventually arranged a memorial service at the Presbyterian church in Flushing. They never talked to the widow again.

Up until the time of their loved one's death, they had been a loving family and had always gotten along with the man's wife.

Cold Ground

A man and his wife were driving by a cemetery. They had sold their home and were heading to their retirement home in northern Michigan. While looking at the cemetery, the wife commented, "The ground is so cold." On their way north, they were struck by a car and the wife died. Because she had made the comment about the ground being so cold, the man wanted his wife placed in a mausoleum rather than putting her remains in the ground. A place in a mausoleum is very expensive, but he went ahead, mortgaged their new home, and bought two spaces in the mausoleum. It was not practical, but it met what he believed were his wife's wishes.

One man told me he wanted to be buried facedown so he could see where he was going.

A woman told me she wanted to be buried naked because she had come into this world naked and wanted to go out naked. I asked her if I could put her in swaddling clothes.

Additional Comment

I tell my wife, "When I die, do what meets your needs." That might be a caisson with six white horses or a plain pine box. After all, the funeral is for the survivors.

THE WIDOWS NOT-SO-MERRY

The task of the funeral director is to facilitate the grieving process. This is done, of course, by attending to all the details of the funeral. Being a funeral director in a small town, my work goes well beyond the funeral arrangements and the funeral itself. My staff and I assist families with a variety of matters that arise after a death, including filing for insurance claims, helping with Social Security death benefits and surviving spouse benefits, assisting with veteran benefit claims, and some grief counseling. If we see a need, we recommend grief support groups or licensed grief counselors.

There are also times when our services go above and beyond what might be expected.

The Bankers

A prominent community leader and influential Flint banker died. He and his wife had led a very active social life, often appearing in the paper after attending various fundraisers and social events. They lived in a large home, both drove new Cadillacs, belonged to several service organizations and were active in their church.

The trouble started for the widow after the lavish funeral was over. Her husband had not wanted his wife to ever have to deal with anything except being a housewife. She had never seen a bill and had never written a check. She knew nothing of her husband's business affairs or their own personal financial affairs. She had no idea about utility bills, taxes, or even what a budget was.

Sadly, all of the wealth she and her husband appeared to have had didn't exist. They did not own anything and had substantial debt. Her husband had no life insurance.

Later, after the funeral, she came to see me and asked if I could show her how to write a check because she wanted to pay for our services. The first time she became aware that things were not right was when I had to call her back in because her check had not cleared. She did not understand the concept of insufficient funds.

She had to sell the house, the cars, and whatever else she had, find a job, and start her life over. She was in her sixties.

***

The widow of another prominent banker called me and asked if I could come out to her house because she wanted to talk to me privately. I had known the family for a long time and knew her grown children from school. When I arrived at the spacious house on a large beautiful lot in the country, she greeted me at the door and invited me in. I stepped into the living room and saw that it was full of various sizes of boxes scattered around, all crammed with papers. The widow had me sit in the dining room adjacent to the living room and brought me a cup of coffee. Then she told me her story.

As long as she had been married, her husband would not let her have anything to do with finances because he believed the role of the woman was to keep the house, cook meals, wash clothing, and raise the children. Now she was at a complete loss as to how to proceed. She added that her husband had told her that if he should die, all of their papers were in these boxes.

The first thing I asked her was if her children could help her. She told me she was too embarrassed to tell them that she knew nothing about her affairs. I thought maybe the boxes were in some kind of order, so I started looking through them. I saw a box entitled "Lion's Club" and found that it contained material from years before, when he had been a member of the club. I was ready to put the box aside, when I noticed a folder sticking up that said, "John Hancock". It contained his life insurance policy. There were boxes of high school papers and papers from previous jobs, and in those boxes, there were also current papers that needed attention. In other words, every box had to be gone through—a monumental task!

Luckily, this widow was in very good shape financially. She had some learning to do, but she got along well.

The Light Went Out

I was home around nine p.m. when I got a call from a widow who was distressed. She was crying and told me she needed my help, and she asked if I could come right over, because she did not want to bother her son, who lived a few blocks away. I got dressed and drove to her house.

She was in tears as she took me to the hallway leading to the bedrooms. She pointed at the ceiling in the hall and said the light bulb was burned out. Her husband had always changed it and she did not know how to do it. Would I please change it for her?

The Four-Poster

Mr. and Mrs. Thurber, an average middle-class couple, lived in a small ranch house in one of the subdivisions in town. They had a daughter they were very proud of, and she had become a missionary who went to far-off lands to minister to people. Mr. Thurber was nearing retirement when he died as a result of a heart attack. It was not surprising to Mrs. Thurber that their daughter could not be reached in a timely manner, so she went ahead and arranged the funeral service.

After a few weeks had passed, Mrs. Thurber started to downsize and had a garage sale. When her neighbor commented about the large four-poster bed sitting in her yard and how she was asking only $200 for it, Mrs. Thurber explained that it was the bed she and her husband had shared. Because she could not bear to sleep in it alone, she just wanted to get rid of it.

The bed was one of the first things sold in the yard sale.

About a month later, her daughter was able to fly home to be with her mother. She was anxious to tell her mother a secret that she had kept. Her father had told her that he had been stuffing money down the hollow posts of the large four-poster bed for years and was planning to surprise her mother by using the money to go on a cruise upon his retirement.

"Oh dear!", Mrs. Thurber said.

Mrs. Newberg

It was snowing and blowing when I woke up. Because we had a funeral scheduled for later that morning, I hurried to get dressed so I could get to the funeral home to shovel about six inches of snow off the sidewalks.

I had just finished clearing the snow at the funeral home, when my wife called and said that the widow who lived across the street from our house, Mrs. Newberg, needed me to call her right away. When I called, Mrs. Newberg was upset and did not know what to do. Her driveway was full of snow and she wanted to know if I could please come over and clean her driveway and sidewalk as soon as possible.

Several years ago, when Mrs. Newberg's husband had been living, we always knew when it was snowing because, no matter the hour, we would hear *scrape, scrape, scrape*—she had her husband out shoveling as soon as the first snowflake hit the driveway.

I took my suit off, put on my jeans and sweatshirt, and drove to her house. I shoveled her driveway and sidewalk and made it back to the funeral home in time to conduct the funeral. It was late that night when I finally cleared the snow from my own driveway and sidewalk. Mrs. Newberg did not go out for several days!

Another night, I came home from work about ten p.m. It was dark, misty, rainy, and slightly foggy. I happened to glance over to Mrs. Newberg's house and saw what looked like a ghost in her backyard. It gave me the creeps! The apparition was in a flowing white gown with what looked like a sword in its hand, and it was just standing there, looking in my direction. I didn't want to pass up the opportunity to see a real ghost up close, so I ventured into Mrs. Newberg's yard. As I approached the eerie sight, I heard a loud, "Shh! Shh!" I hadn't said a word up 'til then.

I appealed to it, "Who are you?"

When I heard the answer, I knew it was Mrs. Newberg. She had a long stick in her hand with a spike on the end of it. She yelled out, "You've ruined it! I have been standing here for the last two hours, waiting for that dang mole to move so I could stab it. It will never move now with all of this commotion!"

Mrs. Jones

I was in a good mood. Things were going well at home and at the funeral home. It was a beautiful day, and I had just picked up the new Chevy station wagon that my wife and I had ordered. It was early morning, so I drove the car to work and parked it in the middle of the parking lot. There were no other cars. I was standing on the back step of the funeral home admiring the new car when Mrs. Jones drove into the parking lot.

She was coming to pay for her husband's funeral. She had not driven a car in years but decided it would be a good time to learn again. She was heading straight toward our new car. I watched as panic overcame her and she forgot how to stop.

She drove into the rear quarter panel of our new car.

I called my wife and told her that we did not have to worry about our new car getting wrecked. It had six miles on the odometer.

Insurance

A couple married right out of high school. The man went to work for General Motors in the factory on the production line. There were a lot of benefits for a union man working the line, including full health benefits, a pension, and a sizable life insurance policy.

The marriage did not last long. Years went by, and the man remarried. No one knew what had happened to the first wife. After being happily married to his second wife for many years, the man died. When the widow came in to the funeral home, she was sad, of course, but was grateful that her husband had an insurance policy to pay for the funeral and a pension that she could survive on.

We often assist families in processing insurance and pension claims, so we helped this widow. When we contacted General Motors, it was discovered that the lady's husband had never contacted the personnel office to change the beneficiary of his insurance and pension to his second wife. The first wife was entitled to it—and because no one could find the first wife, no one would get the benefits. Our client had not only lost her husband but now also had to find a job. It took her years to finally pay for her husband's funeral. I did not charge her interest.

A Word of Advice

Many of our clients worked for General Motors and had sufficient health and death benefits, and the families knew money was there to pay for after-death expenses. Since the economy has changed and many people have become responsible for their own insurance, I have found that some people never think about insurance. Many of my clients come in with little savings and no insurance.

I often see advertisements on television about insurance for seniors. I advise people to listen to those ads. Do not leave your relatives with the only option being inexpensive direct cremation. For younger people, term insurance is inexpensive; look for policies that can be converted to whole life policies.

Pension

Years ago, when people were hired by General Motors, they had to specify who their beneficiaries were for life and pension benefits. One year, there was a man who protested about a certain amount that was taken out of his paycheck to go to the pension fund. In that one year, the man convinced nearly every worker at the Fisher Body plant to forgo the benefit and that they were better off keeping and investing their own money.

After that one year of hiring, the issue did not come up again; all the new employees signed up to have part of their paychecks deposited in a pension fund. Years later, when I learned that a deceased husband had worked for Fisher Body, I asked what year he had been hired. Many times, if it was the year no one had signed up, I had to tell the widow that her husband had chosen not to sign up for the pension. This would be hard for her because, while many of her widowed friends were living comfortably on the pension and Social Security benefits of their husbands, she would have to survive solely on Social Security. Not one of the widows who heard the bad news from me had any idea that her husband had refused a pension. Many of them were not only devastated but furious that their husbands would do that to them.

***

An elderly woman came in to make funeral arrangements for her husband who had basically died of old age. She told me she had plenty of insurance to pay for the funeral and handed me about ten policies.

When I saw them, I thought, *Oh, my!* All of the policies had been purchased from flyers that had been inserted in the newspaper. They were
inexpensive and they were all accidental death policies. The couple,
who were in their late eighties, had been paying on the policies for
years. They were in ill health and were not likely to be doing much
traveling. To top it off, the policies were quite specific as to what claims
they would pay. Her husband would have had to die in an accident
involving an airplane, a train, a bus, or a commercial ship.

***

Dear reader, if you have not done so lately, it is time to check with
your insurance company and pension department to make sure things
regarding your beneficiaries are in writing. Also read your policies to
see if they are term policies, which decrease death benefits the older
you are, or whole life policies that are "in force." Some widows have
brought policies to me, not knowing that their husbands had borrowed
from the cash value or had stopped paying on them and let them lapse;
when the men died, there was, unfortunately, very little or no money
left.

Often, people keep their important papers in a lockbox at the
bank. Years ago, when someone died, the box would be locked until it
could be audited by the IRS. As soon as someone died, and before the
bank was notified of the death, families ran to the bank and cleaned out
all their cash and valuables. Thieves knew this, and, as soon as the family left for the funeral home, they would break into their home. The
banks no longer put seals on lockboxes. Keep your valuables safe; leave
them in the lockbox.

Mrs. Bancroft

A well-known lady in town who had been widowed for a long
time called from the assisted-living home. She said she was in a fix, was
embarrassed, didn't know who to call, so she called the funeral home

because we had helped her when her husband died. She had thought that if she subscribed to a lot of magazines, she would have a good chance of winning the Publishers Clearing House Sweepstakes. She was getting close to fifty magazines and each month they were taking a chunk out of her Social Security. It took a while, but we managed to have all of the unwanted subscriptions cancelled.

Trying to Help

We always tell survivors that our service does not stop after the funeral and if they have any questions regarding the death of a loved one, they can feel free to call us. Most of the time, insurance claims can be handled with a simple phone call, sometimes it takes more work. Usually, there is a lot we can do to help. We do advise families when we think they should consult an attorney.

Sometimes, people have brought in whole boxes of papers for us to look through to see if there is anything needing attention. One time, a family brought in an old insurance policy. This policy was an industrial policy, which many insurance companies sold. The agent called on his client once a month, collected fifty cents or a dollar for the insurance, and answered any questions the family had. Many times, these insurance policies were for a fixed death benefit, but some increased with age. This family's policy had been taken out in the early 1920s from a company in Texas. The family was fairly certain the company was long gone and there would be no proceeds. The face value of the policy was $500.00. I told them if they did not want to try to get the money, I would dispose of the policy; otherwise, I would try to claim the benefits for them. It took some time (this was before computers), but I discovered that the company had been sold and the policy had been passed down from one insurance company to another. Several insurance companies were involved, but I was finally able to find out which company carried the policy. The family received about $700.

***

We used to take survivors to the personnel department of the factories where their spouses had worked if the deceased had life insurance and a surviving spouse pension. I knew personally all of the factory agents from Buick, Chevrolet, and Fisher Body. I particularly liked one agent because he was so personable and kind to the widows and widowers. I thought his job would be really cool to have because he was helping so many people. As a side note, years later after he retired, I ran into him, and he told me that he always thought my job would be really cool to have because I was helping so many people.

***

One time I was taking a very large lady to the Buick benefits office. When we were finished, I escorted her to my car and opened the door for her. She plopped into the seat, and, just as she was reaching out to grab the frame of the door to shift her weight, I slammed the door shut. The door was shut and her fingers were sticking outside. My heart sank as I hurriedly opened the door. She said, "Golly gee, that hurt!" That was it. There were no broken bones, much to my relief.

***

Another thing we did was to always take our clients to file for Social Security benefits. One time, one of the Social Security workers kept asking the widow if her husband was currently working. I told the Social Security worker that her husband was deceased. Then he asked her if her husband was currently living with her! I replied for her and said, "Why don't you just let me fill out the form."

After that incident at the Social Security office, we obtained some claim forms, which we filled out and sent in for our clients. This sped up the process so our clients could start collecting benefits as soon as possible. About eight months after we started doing this, we received a call from the Social Security Department saying that we were doing someone else's job and had to stop, so we resumed taking people to the

Social Security Department and helping their agents fill out the forms. All I could do was sigh.

***

Thankfully, factories and insurance companies are usually more than happy that we assist our clients with claims because it saves them a lot of time and resources. As with Social Security, however, this is not always the case. For example, members of certain credit unions were automatically covered by life insurance provided by the credit union. When there was a death, the credit union required the survivor to call and make an appointment with one of the credit union representatives. Then the representative contacted the insurance company and requested a claim form, and the insurance company then sent the claim form to the credit union agent. When the claim form arrived at the credit union, the agent called the beneficiary and made another appointment for the beneficiary to come meet with the credit union representative again to sign the claim form. The beneficiary was also told to bring in a certified copy of the death certificate, which had to be sent to the insurance company. Once signed, the claim form and death certificate were sent back to the insurance company. I thought this was a cumbersome process because it would take weeks to process a claim, so I called the insurance company and asked them to send me a bunch of claim forms. When I knew one of our clients had been a member of the credit union, I completed the claim form and had the beneficiary sign it, and as soon as we obtained the certified copies of the death certificate, I sent the claim by certified mail directly to the insurance company and my client received the proceeds within a week. About a year later, we got a call from the credit union, saying we were doing the job of their representatives and we could no longer assist our clients with the insurance claim through their company. Again, all I could do was sigh.

A CHAPTER for STACE

Stace Smithson was a true friend to me. He and I stood up in each other's weddings; we helped each other get settled into our homes; and we called each other when there were major events in our lives. Sometimes we met up for breakfast; this was when we caught up on all the events going on in the family. He was always excited to tell me what his wife and children were up to, and I would tell him all about what mine were doing.

I did not hear about his cancer from him, however. I heard it from his brother-in-law, Ed. When I heard, I called Stace and said, "What the heck! Why didn't you tell me about this?" He told me it was no big thing and they were dealing with it. Then he asked me how I was. Stace always seemed to be more concerned about other people than he was for himself.

He had not been in the chemo program very long, when I went to Ann Arbor with him for one of his treatments. As I was watching him get ready to get in the chair for the chemotherapy, he looked up at me and said, "What?" I told him that this was a beautiful facility and it was great that it was available, but I was wondering who would have thought we would end up here. He asked, "Are you feeling sorry for me?" They were just getting ready to hook him up for the treatment when he jumped out of the chair and told me to follow him. He took me down a hall and through a corridor, then pointed at a door. He said he would be fine but that if I wanted to feel sorry for someone, I should go in there and come back when he was done. It was the Children's Cancer Treatment Center.

I was also with Stace when he was in rehab at McLaren Hospital. The nurses were desperately trying to get him to concentrate on his balance, but Stace, instead, waved at everybody and asked how they were doing and why they were there. He kept saying, "I'll be fine. I'll be fine."—this at a time when it was clear he would not be.

Stace taught me a few lifetime lessons. I was a way more serious person than he was. He taught me to lighten up and that it was okay to have fun, no matter what anybody else thought. He taught me not to take myself too seriously. If he thought I, or anybody else, was bragging too much, he would say, "That is pure, unadulterated bull shit!"

There were some people Stace did not like, but he never harped on them. He would just put them out of his life and not think about them again. Otherwise, he treated everybody the same and always talked fondly about his friends, always wanting to know how everybody was doing.

When he was too sick to attend our forty-fifth high school class reunion, I took get-well cards to the reunion and asked everybody to sign them. I took them to him and handed them to him, thinking that he would be touched. He was, but as we sat there, he asked me about each person who had signed the cards.

One of the last times Stace went to the University of Michigan Hospital in Ann Arbor, he told me that if he went home again, he would not come back for any more chemo. He said he thought he was cooked. After he was taken to his room, I went to see him and asked how he was doing. He told me that wasn't important; he wanted to know how I was doing and how my family was doing.

For the nine years that Stace struggled with cancer, he was mostly upbeat, at least around me. There was only one time that he had a cross word with me, and I was really taken aback. It was the last time that he was in Ann Arbor, and things were getting worse. His wife, Suzanne, was staying in the hospital hotel, but she was very sick with the flu and had asked if I could come down and sit with Stace, so I did. When I arrived at the hospital, the nurses were trying to get him to eat the food they had brought him, and he told them he would do so. The nurse came back a little while later and asked if he had eaten very much, and he said he had, but I spoke up and said he had not. Stace looked at me with fury in his eyes and said, "Rossell, you can go home right now!" After he said it, a few seconds went by, and then he was no longer angry with me. It wasn't until later that I realized that Stace, in his own way, was telling me that he was dying and that I should let him go. At times, he was short with Suzanne, and it was hard on her, but, again, I believe that was his way of separating himself from the ones he loved.

Stace was kept comfortable at Avalon Hospice. He could not eat, and he could barely move, but he could look at you when you talked to him. The last time I saw him move was when I put my hand on his and he slowly lifted my hand to his mouth and kissed it. This was his way of saying, "Farewell my friend, farewell."

WHERE DO WE GO FROM HERE?

Funerals as a Part of Life

There are three very important events that happen during the funeral process. The first is when the family chooses a casket. Nobody wants to buy a casket, but, by doing so, they are not only doing one of the last things for the deceased, but also experiencing the first step toward accepting the death.

The next important event is when the family first views their loved one in a casket. It is a very hard and emotional thing to do, but that is the next step in accepting the death. This is an important time for the family to have friends standing by their side.

The third most important event is the funeral dinner. This gives the family time to share the good memories and sets the stage for the future. It is much easier for them to return to life the best way they can, knowing they can still share the life of the deceased with their friends.

When someone dies, people grieve — not just the family, but all the people whose lives the person touched. All those people need to take part in the grieving process. They feel the need to do something for the family: bring in food, help greet visitors, act as chauffeurs, or send flowers. Believe me when I say, as I stated before, flowers are appreciated by bereaved families; even if a single rose is given, it says everything without having to say anything.

The funeral liturgy is just as important in a person's life as a confirmation ceremony, a baptism, or a wedding. The body is the temple of God, even though the spirit is not present. We need to respect it as such.

Times Have Changed (not necessarily for the better!)

Early on, growing up in the funeral home, I saw that people came to the funeral home dressed in mourning clothing, black dresses and dark suits, and conducted themselves with respect to the family and deceased.

Now I have seen people come to the funeral home in cut-off jeans, sweatshirts with the arms cut off, and even halter tops and shorts. One teenybopper came in with a scant halter top and short shorts cut so low that the beginning of her pubic hair was visible. Flip-flops completed the outfit. I have seen pajama bottoms, some with slippers, and shop shoes that left grease marks on the carpet. I have also seen shorts worn with Hawaiian shirts. Many men wear their baseball caps, not only for visitation but also at the funeral; some wear them backwards. One man walked into the funeral home with a cigarette in his mouth, walked up to the casket, then dropped the cigarette and smashed it into the carpet with his foot. Rarely do people take their hats off at the cemetery during the committal service.

When I was young, it was the norm for people (on both sides of the road) to pull off to the side of the road when a funeral procession went by. Some people got out of their cars and took their hats off. Now if a procession gets in the way of a car, it is not uncommon for the procession to get the finger.

Educating the Public

Dorothy French was once the home economics teacher at the junior high school in Flushing. She wanted her students to understand the importance of funerals and wanted to help alleviate any fears they might have about going to the funeral home. She called me and asked if I would be willing to give tours of the funeral home for her students.

I said I would be glad to and scheduled a time that was convenient for both of us.

It was amazing how interested the students were in the funeral home and the funeral process. All too often, their perceptions were based on horror movies they had seen. A question I often received was what was at the closed end of the casket. One student thought we somehow had to cut the body in half in order to get it in. I opened different caskets to show them what was inside and even under the pillows and mattresses. One young man asked me if he could have a radio put in his casket.

I know that a lot of the questions the children asked were not asked by their parents because they were afraid they would appear stupid. I explained some of the myths concerning dead bodies. It seems like everyone has heard about a deceased person who has sat up in a casket. I am here to say that this story is designed to frighten people, especially young children. Sometimes an unembalmed body may move slightly, but that is caused by rigor mortis that dissipates in a short time. Another myth I often hear is that hair and fingernails continue to grow after death. Many people claim to have heard about a casket being disinterred and inside there's a body, usually of a woman, with hair that never stopped growing. It is true that sometimes stubble may appear on a man's face, but that is caused by dehydration. The skin shrinks just enough for the stubble to protrude ever so slightly. Also, I have not heard of any casket that, once opened, had claw marks from a person trying to get out of it. I will add that bodies seem to be cold, but are only room temperature.

While going through the funeral home, I showed the students the visitation rooms, the lounge, the offices, and the rooms where caskets and supplies are stored, as well as the room where we do the embalming and preparation (There were no bodies present). They were surprised to see that the preparation room looked much like an operating room.

When the brother of one of these students died in a horrific automobile accident, I realized just how important these tours were. Of course, the family was in shock and grief, but when the young man came in, he explained to his family where everything was, and where the preparation room was and what we did there. He also told them that he knew all about caskets. He was well prepared for what had to be done and knew the process.

We conducted these tours for many years until Mrs. French retired. Sadly, the new teacher did not continue with the program.

***

Some people want to know what they should say to a family when their loved one dies. It is sufficient to say, "I'm sorry for your loss." What's most important is being there to provide support. Do not say, "This is God's will." (How do you know?) Do not say, "He's better off." (How do you know?) Do not say, "I know how you feel." (No, you don't.) Simply be there for the bereaved.

When you see the survivors at a later date, it is okay to talk about the loss of their loved one. You will be surprised how people need to talk. Their grief will subside but will never go away completely. Don't be impatient with people because you think they should be getting over their loss. Bringing up memories with them is okay and helps the grieving process. The visitation and funeral are the starting points of the grief in a family, and having friends and relatives next to them to share their grief is helpful, because, as Rabbi Earl Grollman has said, "Grief shared is grief diminished."

***

Children can sense something has happened. If grandma died, tell them, "Grandma died and we are all very sad." Answer their questions sincerely. If you believe grandma went to heaven, tell them so. If you do not know the answer, tell them you do not know the answer. Do not tell them that grandma went on a trip (they will want to know where). Do not tell them grandma is sleeping (they may not want to go to sleep).

Children are very concerned about how a death is going to affect them; "Who is going to take care of me?" "Am I going to see grandma again?" "Are we going to have to move?" "Am I going to die?" Assure children that they will be taken care of and answer their questions even if the questions seem trivial.

CONCLUSION

$\mathcal{G}$rowing up in the funeral business has certainly been different from what most people experience. The hardest thing for my wife to understand was that the funeral business is open twenty-four hours a day, seven days a week, and there are no holidays off. It has always been hard to make plans because families cannot wait when they are in need of us. The people of Flushing have always known that we stand ready to serve no matter the time of day or night, and they have, for the most part, been supportive and appreciative of the service that Rossell Funeral Home has provided. For this, I am very grateful.

Years ago, when I first started out, my wife and I were at a party when a successful Flint attorney came up to me and asked if being a funeral director was easy. I told him, "Most of the time, my clients are a pleasure to serve." He told me the same thing about his practice, and then he told me the 90/10 rule: 90 percent of the people he serves are a pleasure to serve, but 10 percent make his job difficult. What makes one businessperson better than another is knowing how to deal with that 10 percent, he said.

People sometimes shudder when they hear what my profession is, and they ask how anyone can do something so morbid and see the awful things that I see. The same people, however, will pay to go to a movie and see blood and gore, often worse than I have ever seen. When people need my services, they are glad they know someone they can trust, and they often come back after I have served them and thank me for undertaking this important job of caring for their loved one.

One thing has not changed as Flushing has transformed from a small rural community to a thriving city: Flushing is still a great place to live with many good people working together to keep the small-town atmosphere that it has always had.

And remember, I am the last one to let you down.

Acknowledgments

*T*hank you to my best friend, my wife, for the enormous amount of help with revisions, editing, and putting this book together. Thank you to my daughter for editing and for encouraging me to publish the book. Being in the funeral business is a struggle for the funeral director's family. It has been hard on them, but they have always been there for me: my wife, Elizabeth, an educator; my daughter, Lisa Rossell Riccobono, also an educator; and my son, Nicholas Rossell, an attorney.

Thank you to all of the families the funeral home has served, and especially to those who have taken the time to send me a thank-you note. It means a lot!

Thank you to the many people who have served on our staff; some have been with the funeral home for many years. You all have contributed to making the Rossell Funeral Home the success it is.

Thank you to the people of Flushing who make our city the great place it is.

Thank you to the people at Dog Ear Publishing for all their assistance. They always picked up the phone when I had a question and treated me like I was their only concern.

And a final thank-you to my Facebook friends in "You know you grew up in Flushing if" for suggesting that I write the book and for encouraging me along the way.